janapar

Published by Janapar Media Ltd.

Printed and bound by CPI Group (UK) Ltd,
Croydon, CR0 4YY

Edited by Tara Gladden
Jacket design by John Summerton
Jacket photography by Tom Allen
Illustrations by Tenny Adamian
Produced by James Newton

ISBN 978-0-9574956-0-9
A CIP catalogue record for this book is available
from the British Library

Janapar Media Ltd.
15 Gordon Road,
Sevenoaks,
Kent TN13 1HE,
United Kingdom

janapar.com

First paperback edition, 2013

The author has tried to recreate events, locales and conversations from memory.
In order to maintain their anonymity in some instances, the names of individuals
and places have been changed, as have some identifying characteristics and
details such as physical properties, occupations and places of residence.

*For saying 'yes' when the chance comes to
divert into unknown waters*

ABOUT THE AUTHOR

Tom Allen left home on a bicycle in 2007 at the age of twenty-three, and has since travelled on four continents by bicycle. He lost count of miles pedalled when his cycle computer was stolen, and is absolutely fine with that. Travel and adventure now occupy a central role in his life. He has no fixed abode, has bases of sorts in the UK and Armenia, and runs a popular adventure cycle-touring website at **tomsbiketrip.com**.

Janapar, written alongside a documentary film of the same name, is his first published work.

Janapar

By Tom Allen

CHAPTER 1

The Sahara doesn't really look like I'd pictured it. But then nowhere ever quite did.

My bicycle rests against the milestone. A slope of crushed red rock drops from the roadside and slips into the sand. I pull a bottle of water from the rear pocket of one of my bags; take a swig. It's hot enough for a bath.

I replace the bottle. These dusty bags contain everything I need to survive the world's largest desert. A thin sleeping-bag, a handful of tools, a change of clothes. I'll soon run out of water and food. But just because this is the Sahara doesn't mean there's nobody here. There's a road, after all. A brand new road, unadvertised, running down through the Sahara. Sooner or later, roads mean people. And people mean water and food. Right?

The sun has barely set, but I'm cooling down now, my senses recalibrating to a motionless world. When life is scrolling past you, it's difficult to register all the detail and intrigue – especially in a place as otherworldly as this. And there's a stillness and silence here of a kind I've never felt before; beautiful, yet at the same time deeply frightening.

My breathing gradually slows, and as it does, the last remaining sound dies away. I take off my boots, and with bare feet I pad around in the sand. It feels cool and soft between my toes. I look about. Broken mounds of black and crimson rock stand out against the sand, all painted in twilight pastels.

There is nothing here. I shouldn't be here, a young man from rural England, at home with green and pleasant. This is a place to run from, not to explore.

And I don't know how far I'll have to ride before I find supplies. I bought a reassuring amount of food and water and then pedalled south before I could change my mind. A day of riding later and I still have no more idea of what lies ahead. I am banking on little more than a roll of the dice. And my number had better come up, because a bad roll in a place like this could have the worst consequences of all.

I unstrap my belongings from the bike, telling myself that this is probably just another dip. The world has been merciless with my emotions. A free meal can have me beaming with joy, but this joy can be turned to rage by a single thoughtless driver. Too often I feel like I'm hanging onto my mood for dear life as it thrashes and squirms. It was never such a rollercoaster when I had someone next to me.

My tent sits upon the sand, constructed. I don't remember putting it up. I must have done it out of habit, I think, and I rummage for my video camera. This thing has had the questionable privilege of seeing me at my worst and my best. I'm not quite sure where tonight is going to fit into the spectrum, but for almost two years the camera has been my closest confidant, so I find a rock on which to sit. Adjusting the tripod legs, I position myself in front of the lens, the interaction as familiar as picking up the phone and calling a friend.

Flipping open the tiny screen so that I can see myself, I recoil with surprise. Matted greasy hair of about three months' growth is plastered against my scalp. My beard has reached a length at which it adds a decade to my age. The bridge of my nose is burnt deep red, and my skin and clothes are coated in a beige film of dust, sweat and grease. I look worn out by thought and worry. My face, it seems, could tell my story on its own.

I adjust the camera to produce the best possible picture. The well-practised calibrations happen in an instant. I have lost count of the hours of footage I've shot. I usually capture plenty of the scenery behind me, but something suggests that the important thing tonight will be written across my face, so, pressing the red button, I zoom in slightly and my mirror image fills the frame: some guy, talking to a camera in the middle of a desert. I fold the screen back out of sight, fix my gaze on the dark circle of glass, and open my mouth to begin to speak.

' . . . '

I try, desperately, to force a word – just one word – to come forth. But it's as if words have lost all meaning. I am entirely unable to speak. Because there is no utterance on Earth that comes close to expressing how I feel.

I shake my head and stare into the distance, looking around at the desert, as if answers will come springing from behind the dunes. I look back. There it is. Right before my eyes. How stupid. How stupid to think that I could pour it all out into this thing, this little black box of cables and microchips. It is nothing but a placeholder for what I *really* want, which is to take her in my arms and to tell her I love her and that I'm a poor stupid fool for having done this; to beg her forgiveness and to lie down on the ground and tell her how scared I am right now.

I try again.

I must continue telling this story.

Well . . .

This is it. This is where it gets tough.

This is the . . . um.

This is the . . . er . . .

This is the furthest I've ever been from civilisation. In my life. In the Sahara Desert. Of Sudan.

Yeah, I just . . . I just cycled out of this little port town, and into just these vast, empty wastes. Of nothing. Of nothingness.

There's not . . . I . . . I can't hear a thing. It's completely and utterly silent. There's no slight background noise from a road. There's no dogs barking in the distance. There's no birds singing. It's just completely and utterly silent. And that makes me feel even more . . . even more exposed than I do anyway.

I really don't know . . . what I'm doing. I've got off this boat, and I've put about twelve litres of water on my bike, stocked up with enough food to last me for about two days – and just left! And now I'm just hoping for the best. I have no previous experience of dealing with vast distances in the desert. I've no experience with cycling in sand. I've no experience of cycling in this kind of weather. Just pure . . . un- . . . un- . . . pure . . . ugh, my god. I can't even string a sentence together.

I need to get my head round all of this.

Yes. Just pure unbroken sunlight from sunrise to sunset. Not a single cloud – no, nothing. Completely empty sky. Completely empty dead landscape. Just me. On my own.

And I just feel . . . I just feel confused. Really. Just confused. What am I doing? Where am I going? I don't know what direction I'm going in, because every direction looks the same. There's no traffic to stop and ask. There's a river – the longest river in the world – around here somewhere, though I've no idea where! How ridiculous is that?!

My god, it's just . . .

And this is just Day One.

Tomorrow morning I'm going to ride my bike. And however I feel, it doesn't matter – I've just got to keep going. That's all. Nothing else. Going, from one little pocket of existence to the next.

And I really – I miss Tenny so much. So much. And right now I'm here, talking to a camera, and she's in Armenia, on her own. Waiting for me to come back.

And I know she's there, and I can't be with her. Because I've decided to do this instead.

A grey pallor seeps into the sky. Ripples of fabric brush up against each other, nudged by a hint of breeze, but there is little else greeting my groggy awakening. With a practised contortion I unzip the tent door by my head, roll over in the thin sleeping-bag and look out again at the world, all painted in bone and soot, without sound or sensation, as if time itself has ceased to flow. The murmur of pink in the east will soon become a roaring angry whiteness, a heat of such ferocity that it could actually kill me. I drag my bike and trailer back up the slope to where the new road still glistens absurdly, like a liquorice lace flopped across an orange tablecloth. Last night I stood here, more afraid than I had ever been. But the time for self-pity and doubt is over.

So I swing a leg over the top-tube, feel the teeth of the pedal connect with the sole of my boot, lift myself into the saddle, and suddenly the wind is untangling my hair and the sticky tarmac is crackling and the world is scrolling past like a computer game. I have returned to my natural state: pedalling until the action is unconscious, dealing with whatever pops over the horizon, forgetting what falls away behind – until the end of the day, when a moment to digest may present itself. Until then, momentum is all I need to sustain this life – this life of glorious simplicity.

I peer out through my mangled sunglasses. I dropped them long ago – in the Alps, I think it was – and ran over them before I noticed. Still, they do their job. As mile after indistinguishable mile goes past, palpable waves of heat pass through me. The brown tint of the glasses makes the place feel even hotter.

A distant whir invades the trance. I pull over to watch the passing of my first vehicle in Sudan, when it's still just a shape in the north. The shape grows quickly, and then in a spectacular explosion of dust and violence the first of many trucks thunders past me in the greatest sensory assault I've had for twenty-four hours. Of course – it's the day after the weekly ship comes into port from Aswan. Skipping the paperwork has put me a day ahead of the slow train of trucks and buses that begins to rumble past, drivers honking elaborate symphonies in greeting. Then I come across a little lizard perched upon the roadside, and it's as if between the tiny animal and the enormous vehicles I've somehow found my place within this family of desert travellers.

As if to confirm the notion, an encampment comes into view, figures and machines moving slowly through the dust. The tarmac comes to an abrupt end, and I rattle along a tyre track, emerging into a wide circle of shelters and shipping containers. Stinking tar-stained barrels sit beneath the sun among mounds of sand and gravel, like heaps of dye powder waiting to be mixed on an artist's workbench. Under one of the shelters is a group of men. I instinctively send a wave in their direction. The act of smiling seems to change my mood, and I suddenly want nothing more than to join them in the shade for a nice little glass of tea. Luckily – judging by the way they're waving me over – it seems that they're of a similar mind. I flop down in the shade, feeling immediately at home, and all the trepidation of the previous day evaporates into the heat of the desert noon: I know now that everything in Sudan is going to be OK.

The labourers are not surprised to see a white man on a bicycle. I know nothing about them, the Nubian culture here in the north, or the circumstances of their employment out in the desert. But it's clear that they've been camped here, blasting rock and moving earth, for long enough to have seen my kind before.

'How often do you see a cyclist?' I ask the most forthcoming tea-drinker. He regards me from between a moustache and a furrowed brow, his front teeth missing. I put him at around forty. He's wearing a tidy cotton shirt and trousers with socks and smartly polished shoes. It's an interesting outfit for a road-builder in a stifling desert camp. Roughly once a month, a cyclist – or usually a pair – is seen passing through these parts, he says. That's more than I'm expecting to hear, but I'm not altogether surprised. Because it seems that the renaissance of the long-distance bicycle journey is about to begin.

A few months ago, Scotsman Mark Beaumont had set a

new world record for a bicycle-powered circumnavigation of the globe. A few gruelling months of unsupported cycling, linked up with flights between the continents, had secured him a place in the record books and a television career. Several retaliatory attempts on the record were announced, and soon Mark's record had been broken, then broken again, until almost halved in duration. It's funny, because – aside from our mode of transport – I feel little in common with Mark and his peers. My reasons for being here have nothing to do with a circumnavigation, even less to do with breaking a record. I've learnt the hard way that the essential beauty of the bicycle journey lies with the freedom that it gifts the rider: bound by no route, beholden to no timetable. My ride wasn't always so unstructured. But a lot has changed in the last couple of years.

'You see?' asks the chief tea-drinker, walking me out into the sun and pointing up. Squinting, I scan the skyline from our spot deep in the stony hills. Ridges sit starkly in all directions against the burning sky. Following his outstretched arm I notice the telltale lines and angles of a man-made structure. The size and purpose, from this distance and with my less-than-perfect eyesight, are indistinct. Given its hilltop perch, however, I guess at an old military watchtower.

He lowers his arm and looks me square in the eye.

'British!'

With a grin whose meaning I can't fathom, he catches me out with my own ignorance. I smile sheepishly, not knowing what to say. Nobody has taught me about my home nation's imperial past except for these people, the descendants of its subjects. Given the scale of its influence in the world, though, the British Empire seems quite an omission from my history lessons.

But the look turns to laughter and he claps me on the back: there's far too much tea-drinking and lying around to do to bother teasing a *khawayya* – a white guy – over a historical triviality. He sits down, and I glance back up at the watchtower. Up on the hilltop I imagine tiny figures: bored, feverish redcoats, wondering what whim had torn them from their families to travel thousands of miles and sit sweating in the sun, looking out over the parched, diabolical landscape of Nubia, days away from even a modestly sized town. And I laugh, because right now I am doing exactly that.

Refreshed and rejuvenated as much by the pleasant company as by the tea and the shade, it's time to continue. I say my thanks, heave my dusty mountain bike up from the ground, and set a course for the least treacherous-looking path on which to disappear over the horizon – forever out of sight and mind of another collection of souls who briefly became the closest thing I have out here to friends. I didn't even learn their names.

The camp sinks away beneath a ridge of rock. Ahead of me and in every other direction lies the desert; the same sand-blasted landscape that has existed here for millennia. And my road – my final thread of attachment to the world of man – has vanished. Only a faint set of tyre tracks disappearing into the nothingness indicates that anyone has passed here before.

Well, I came here for a challenge, didn't I? For something I wouldn't be sure I could pull off unless I tried. It was the only way I could justify the decisions I'd made. And now I've found it.

CHAPTER 2

I never planned to be cycling alone through Sudan. But now that I am, I have plenty of time – too much, perhaps – to dwell on the complicated tale of adventure and romance that led me here.

In fact, I'd never planned on being anywhere *near* Sudan, alone or otherwise.

'I would rather not bike in Africa at the moment,' I'd replied in a typically hard-headed email to my good friends Mark and Andy. 'There's a lot of screwed-up stuff happening there, and there are places in the world that I'd rather see.'

No – the dream that brought us to my parents' house in Northamptonshire one summer's day, bikes packed and ready to leave on the ride of a lifetime, was not of cycling to Africa.

'Speech! Speech!' someone shouted, and the chatter died down in anticipation. Mark was the first to respond, with his typical understated humour:

'Right – see you all in a bit!'

Everyone laughed.

Mark was standing outside the front door on the patio of my family home, me and Andy next to him, our heads all

roughly shaved the previous night by someone who'd had
a drink too many before picking up the clippers. In front of
us was a garden table, and upon it was the huge rectangular
cake which my mother had baked in preparation for the big
send-off. The white icing was studded with little paper flags
on cocktail sticks, each one wishing us a safe journey. And
around the table were friends and acquaintances whose
chatter dimmed as they sensed the ceremony about to begin.
I looked down at the massive cake. It seemed misplaced, as
if delivered to the wrong house that morning, leaving some
birthday boy or girl in tears.

The crowd watched solemnly as together we grasped the
knife handle and cut firmly into the cake. Then, tentatively,
we each raised a slice of cake to our mouths. The crowd
cheered.

'Right at Rockingham!' shouted my dad from the back of
the hubbub. He loved to create a scene when there were
enough people within earshot to make it worth the effort.

'Straight on, isn't it?' I mumbled half-heartedly through
my cake, being just the opposite and hating the fact that I'd
been put at the centre of attention.

'Which way is it at the end of the drive?' asked Mark.

'Er . . . right,' I replied, not sure whether he was being
funny.

'Right? OK – cheers.'

'You will send us a postcard, won't you?'

'Do you know which way you're going, Tom?'

'Do you have a plan?'

'Is it Gretton?'

'And then Harringworth?'

'Amsterdam's the first stop, isn't it?'

'You know it's not signposted from here?'

I remember it so clearly – pottering down to the corner of the high street with the chattering entourage, the way my bicycle nosed its way along as I nursed it down the road on foot, the surprising weight I found myself heaving upright when the unfamiliar machine began to overbalance. And I remember the eruption of cheering and the waving of banners as I transferred my weight onto the right-hand pedal, gripped the handlebars, and stepped away from the ground and into motion.

Every component gleamed with that special sheen that only something freshly pulled from its packaging can exhibit. I shifted my weight back onto the handmade leather saddle. Simultaneously, the left-hand pedal rose upwards and, as I engaged the pedal clip with a metallic snap and looked up towards the road ahead, the crane operator swept the big camera up in a smooth arc, panning to capture Mark and Andy rolling forward ahead of me. We rode round the bend at the bottom of the hill and out onto the main street of the village, amid cheering and clapping, beginning to gather speed.

It felt so unnaturally cumbersome, the steering so heavy – but then it was, after all, the first time I had ridden a fully loaded bicycle. As we passed beneath a string of white balloons, I suddenly wobbled – before nervously correcting my balance. I grinned, imagining the ribbing we'd receive if we collapsed in convoy on the way past my front door. The small crowd passed behind me; rows of familiar faces brought together by us and our journey. I was moved by how many had turned out to see us off – people coming from all over the country. It had given me a real sense of just how important it was, this thing that we had decided to do. I looked ahead at the brightly coloured luggage of my two friends with whom I was going to live out the next chapter of my life – a chapter that I knew without doubt was the beginning of a monumental tale.

I stole a glance in the rear-view mirror by my right hand, where the send-off party was drifting out of sight. Looking ahead again, I was struck by how smooth the bicycle's motion was. It was a sensation of unstoppable grace, unlike any bike I'd ridden before. The quality of the machine was tangible, the intricate choice of parts coming together beautifully. Given our very specialised requirements, no off-the-peg touring bike had really fitted the bill. Those bikes were invariably designed for road touring, and I couldn't think of anything more tedious than following paved highways for years on end. Nor could Andy, who was riding just ahead of me; tall, lean and broad-shouldered, trusty old blue-and-silver helmet strapped to his freshly shaved head, cargo trailer close to bursting with sacks of equipment, shiny cardboard label still swinging from his handlebar bag. Together we had spent almost a year working towards this moment.

Andy had been a close friend since our secondary school days. We'd grown up on a healthy diet of English, maths, science and football at a small-town comprehensive in the East Midlands; a diet inevitably supplemented in later years with girls, loud music, experimental hairstyles and underage drinking.

But Andy and I differed from our peers in one fundamental

way. We lived in tiny villages and travelled each day to the big town school by bus. In the afternoons I returned home to the ancient little cottage where my family lived in peace and quiet, and this, for me, was home. Mum and Dad taught at local primary schools, we went on our annual holiday to warm and sunny places, and life moved slowly, one year indistinguishable from the next. Kettering was little more than the place where I happened to be dumped for a few hours each day, its politics and dramas as strange and foreign as the upbringings of the town kids around me. I'd travelled ten thousand miles on that school bus before my eighteenth birthday, ears plugged with headphones, peering out through the grubby glass at the unchanging farmland of rural Northamptonshire.

During the holidays, Kettering vanished from existence and the land surrounding the villages of the Welland Valley became mine to explore. It was little more than some unremarkable fields, rivers, woods and railway cuttings. But there was always the hope of discovering something that everyone else had overlooked. These escapades would always be carried out with my younger brother, because our parents had sent us to a different secondary school from the other village kids, and my early childhood friends all vanished when we went our separate ways. As I grew older, Andy's village became an achievable destination for a bike ride, and in that way we became each other's local riding partners.

Then university swallowed everything. Life in Exeter brought brand new friends, unmentionable kinds of fun, socialising and studying in a self-contained bubble. I found people who shared my taste in music, and presented a campus radio show to which they would sometimes even listen. This bubble lasted for three years before silently bursting, leaving me equipped with a large box of records and the theories of Computer Science but absolutely no idea what to do with them. And there was the growing feeling that I'd chosen the degree out of the necessity of choosing one, rather than out of any real passion for the subject.

One autumn day I was interviewed for an appropriate-sounding job as a software engineer in Barnstaple. I sailed through the interview and took a handful of tests to prove my skills in the fields of programming and database design. But when I was offered the job on the spot, I realised with a shock that this could actually be my future. Did my destiny really lie in an office in a small Devonshire town? It was a recipe for a stable, comfortable existence – of that, there was no doubt – and there was much to like about Devon, with her coastlines and moors and custard and her ever-so-quaint traditions. But at the age of twenty-two, what was the value of a stable, comfortable existence? Where was the risk? The excitement? The adventure?

I told my potential employer that I'd think about it, drove home in my mum's Vauxhall Astra, gave my Dad back his tie, and tapped out a short email to the company.

'I'm writing to let you know that I will not be able to accept your position at this time,' I wrote. 'I have decided to spend some time exploring my options before I commit to a career.'

The young and enthusiastic director with whom I'd spent the morning talking wrote back within minutes.

'Sorry to hear that, Tom. You were first on my list. But probably good to get it out of your system. Good luck!'

So I was going to explore my options, duty-bound to 'get it out of my system'. I just wasn't sure what these options were, or how I was supposed to find them. And I soon found myself back in the musty old bedroom of my adolescence, ten thousand pounds into the red, with my graduation-day portrait hanging in the downstairs loo and a depressing-looking question mark above the last three years of my life.

If anyone else had suggested it, I'd have thought twice. But when a text message arrived from Andy a few months later, the last piece of the jigsaw fell into place.

'Mate. I have decided to cycle round the world.'

I read Andy's message from my spot beneath a tree. In my lap was the copy of *The Adventure Cycle-Touring Handbook* that I'd just put down – a book which explained, in detail, the practicalities of cycling round the world.

I'd bought the book whilst browsing in a store that morning, not knowing it would become one of those twists of poetry that sometimes emerge from everyday life. As I sat under the tree, the future came into focus. Job applications had long been shelved. Shunning the temp-job circuit in favour of eking out a living as a freelance programmer in my bedroom, I had no ties that couldn't easily be cut. I'd been stashing every penny I could in a savings account, and with nothing else to lose, the idea could not have made more sense. Yes! My best mate and I were going to cycle round the world!

The idea thrilled the heck out of me. *Cycling round the world!* It was such a delightful little combination of words. It undermined the status quo so wonderfully. A bicycle was for short journeys, and for eccentrics, fitness freaks and the financially challenged. What better way to blow people's expectations out of the water and cement my maverick reputation?

Since graduation, my university friends had developed a habit of donning backpacks full of expensive apparel and credit cards and Lonely Planet guidebooks and setting forth into the unknown. They'd go for months at a time, wandering the Planet's well-worn paths in – I scoffed – a Lonely kind of way. But they inevitably came back with curiously similar photos, stories, bank balances and signs of premature ageing brought on by heavy drinking and sunburn. Then they would leap back into the rat race as if the mind-expanding experiences they'd yarned about in the pub had turned out to be nothing but a long holiday, a temporary escape from reality and responsibility; an obligatory part of being Western and middle class and in one's early twenties and having money to spend and an easy passport to travel on. And all too often their stories seemed to involve starting out poor and itinerant and hard done by, becoming enlightened as to the folly of Western materialism, and then putting those new Eastern philosophies into practice by getting a high-powered career in a multinational corporation.

I could certainly see the appeal of full-moon parties on South-East Asian beaches, of performing improbable yogic stretches at sunrise in Goa with the aroma of fish curry still lingering in my dreadlocks, of pretending that sleeping in a hostel was poverty redefined. But I was always held back by a feeling that there must be more to it than those recycled clichés; than bus journeys, bedbugs, touts, temples and the company of other rich young white people on unique journeys of self-discovery. And so I never bought a seventy-litre backpack or a pair of ultra-light zip-off trekking trousers, and I never danced the night away in Thailand or pulled a muscle one morning in India.

No. I wanted adventure and authenticity, bewilderment instead of beauty, challenge rather than charm. I wanted my preconceptions dashed against the rocks of reality. I wanted to discover how little I knew.

With a similarly deep distaste for conformity, Andy had also avoided the backpackers' trail. The difference was that he'd found an alternative, rather than sitting on his backside like me. While I was moping about in my East Midlands village and my mates were elephant-trekking in Thailand, he'd been working as a mountain-bike guide on the small Croatian island of Korcula. Through his experience and passion for riding, Andy had taught me everything I knew about bicycles. There was no way I would be able to get my act together without him. I thought his idea a stroke of genius, taking mountain biking to its natural conclusion.

The ball was soon rolling. Both being far more interested in off-road than on-road cycling, we quickly hit upon the idea to attempt the round-the-world journey on dirt roads alone. It would be done for the thrill of adventure, of course, rather than to break records, though in all likelihood it would be the first journey to be carried out in such a way. What could be more worthwhile than doing what we loved, mountain biking across a vast range of landscapes for the next few years? And we would learn so much about life outdoors. Given the terrain we were likely to cover and the laughably small budget on which we would need to do so, bushcraft skills would be needed simply for day-to-day survival. I mail-ordered a set of brass rabbit snares and a pocket-sized copy of the *SAS Survival Guide* in preparation.

A route plan was soon under way, and I dropped an email to my old university mountain-biking buddy and housemate Mark, who had recently lost his job at the owl sanctuary in Dorset and was labouring away unhappily as a mortgage analyst for a building society.

'I was going to email you to see if you were interested in the first bit of next year's bike trip,' I wrote. Though it would still be more than six months until we departed, I was excited and I wanted to share it. I'd been scouring maps and books detailing long-distance walking routes, pilgrimage trails and cycling paths across Western Europe, and my efforts had strung together a fascinating-looking tour of France and Spain, heading as far south as Gibraltar before looping back up via the Alps to Geneva, where some friends had offered to put us up. Between bouts of heroic biking, the plan featured a healthy menu of medieval and religious history, cutting-edge continental culture, gastronomic wonders, and spared time for the beautiful women we would meet along the way. About two and a half thousand miles in length, it had been designed to gobble up maximum distance and variety before we left Western Europe, and I guessed that it would take us two or three action-packed months to complete it. From Geneva, Andy and I would head east towards Turkey, offering Mark an easy route back to England via Belgium. Having a girlfriend to think about, Mark only wanted to spend a couple of months with us, rather than choosing freedom, ditching the relationship and becoming a fully signed-up member of our team.

Mark had been a good friend throughout our days as a student; a bookworm, sceptic, passionate eco-warrior and Bob Dylan enthusiast, tall and skinny, with a floppy blond mop and a thoughtful-looking goatee. The fact that, like me, he was not particularly athletic was comforting, although I noted that he had become a dab hand on a unicycle. Studying for a degree in English meant that he'd spent a lot of time reading, usually without getting out of bed. And, when he wasn't devouring literature, the house that Mark and I had shared with five other students had become the venue for debates of great philosophical significance, as well as Mark's occasional fire-juggling performances. After graduation, he'd spent a week with me and Andy on a spur-of-the-moment bike trip through the Scottish Highlands. The two had hit it off and a great deal of hilarity had ensued. Despite the trip itself being ridiculously ill-planned and thus the coldest, wettest and most miserable week of our lives, we returned home with the strange conviction that it had been the most fun we'd ever had. The trip had sown the early seeds, and so Mark was the obvious third rider. Our combined intellects would surely be able to find novel answers to many of life's great questions as we undertook our unprecedented mountain-biking odyssey.

I liked Mark because he would never back down from a debate. He held strong opinions and extolled them with passion, particularly when they involved science, religion, or – heaven forbid – both. He was quick to point out flaws in others' arguments, and I considered him the kind of ultra-rationalist who'd be able to defuse disagreements between me and Andy, helping us to work logically through the challenges we'd face. As well as this, Mark managed to be laid-back to an almost fatalistic degree, and his relaxed and candid demeanour would help me avoid taking myself too seriously. The trip, after all, was supposed to be enjoyable. Mark's company would make it all the more so.

'Ever thought about just heading south from Spain to cycle down through Africa?' he wrote in response to my email.

I didn't want to go to Africa. It was too dangerous. There were far too many problems in Africa – it was all I ever seemed to hear about in the news. A terrible place for a bike ride. In any case, Mark was treading on my toes: I'd spent ages coming up with these route plans, investing weeks of my time in the creation of intricate off-road routes. Mark wasn't even coming with us all the way – he was just going to tag along for a few pleasant weeks in Western Europe, at my invitation!

Eventually I suggested that we cycle to Gibraltar and hop on the ferry to Africa for a day or two before continuing on our way, and returned to my route-planning for Eastern Europe and Turkey. It'd be easier to find off-road routes from that point on, because paved roads would obviously become rare once the developed world was behind us. Mark's enjoyable and provocative company would be welcome during those first months in Europe; the months that would be the testing ground for our equipment, and where we'd toughen up for the hard riding ahead. We would depart as a group of three, and setting off from my front door seemed the natural way to begin.

There were no more emails to send. No more questions to answer. The stack of to-do lists remained to-be-done. And it no longer mattered, because we were finally on our way. Norwegians, I'd heard, called this moment 'the doorstep mile' – the first step of a long journey, and the most difficult to make.

Resting on a roadside verge a few miles east of my village, I tried to suppress what I supposed was the ache of separation, pretending to Mark and Andy that everything was fine. They were in high spirits on what was turning into a pleasant English summer's day, adrift with the fragrance of flowering broad bean and rapeseed. I didn't want to disturb this by complaining about homesickness while still a stone's throw from my own bed, so I kept my thoughts to myself. Mark and I sat in the sun while Andy rooted through his bags to find the tools to adjust his saddle position. Then we stopped again so that I could tweak the angle of my pedal clips, and again for Mark to dig out his sun cream. But the pace was unhurried, and we chatted together about this and that – the music at the party, the sensation of wind on our freshly shorn bonces, the crawling slowness of climbing hills with all this weight on our bikes. We trundled through limestone villages of receding familiarity, and in the mid-afternoon I checked our progress on the newly installed odometer.

'You've got to be kidding.'

'What?'

'What's the mileage, Tom?'

'Well, according to this, we've done *seven and a half miles.*'

'Jesus . . .'

'Is that all?'

'Maybe there's something wrong with the connections . . .'

'My thighs are already killing me.'

23

'Perhaps we should have done some kind of training?'

Then Ben and James, the filmmakers, turned up in their car, talking enthusiastically about setting up a big cinematic shot with Harringworth viaduct in the background. I put on a fake smile and did a lot of nodding.

Our route out of England had been designed as a quick getaway. The nearest port being Harwich, on the East Coast in Essex, I'd photocopied the relevant maps and planned a fairly direct three-day route on cycleways, bridleways and public footpaths to the port. Resuming our ride, it wasn't long before we reached the first unpaved section of the route, which had been marked as a footpath on the map. This represented the beginning of the off-road ambitions we'd spent so long fostering. Off the road we finally turned, and along the edge of a freshly ploughed field. By the time we'd arrived at the far end of the field, our tyres were caked in mud, and we'd had a rough time trying to haul our heavily loaded bikes along the rutted trail. Why was dashing down these tracks so much more difficult than on a normal mountain bike?

Reaching the stile that led to the following field, we realised that to cross it would involve taking all the luggage off the bikes, detaching the three trailers, and repeating the process in reverse in the next field. And the same would need to be done for every gate, fence and stile thereafter. For the entire circumference of the planet.

This hadn't seemed a particularly big deal while I'd been studying maps and guidebooks in my bedroom, but it was clear that doing so would demand an enormous amount of time and energy. It would take us *weeks* to even leave *England*, let alone reach the south of Spain.

'I'll go and have a look at the next field,' volunteered Mark, 'and report back. And then we can decide what's best.'

As he climbed the stile and disappeared through the undergrowth, I looked down at what had begun life as a mountain bike. It was now a cumbersome machine with an extra wheel, fat tyres and beefy suspension forks, piled high with all the equipment I thought I'd need for an off-road expedition round the world. It was about as nimble as an elephant. It weighed almost as much as *me*.

'It's even worse over there,' said Mark, coming back into view.

'Right, let me have a look,' I replied, striding over. Andy remained quiet. I climbed the stile and pushed through the mass of thorns and saplings blocking what was supposed to be a public right of way, and emerged into the daylight to find that the next field was precisely that. A field. There was absolutely nothing about it that screamed: 'Ride across me!' It was just a boring, empty field. To drag our bikes and kit through it would be completely pointless.

We hung around dejectedly for a couple of minutes before picking up our bikes, yanking them round, and starting the long push back towards the road, in silence. And we set off once more down the tarmac lane. We would reach Harwich much more quickly by road, anyway. And once we left the familiar confines of England, we'd press ahead with our carefully laid plans. After all, it would be within those unknown lands that things would start getting interesting.

Searching the countryside for a place to hide three tents and three very conspicuous bicycles, we finally found the perfect spot: Deenethorpe Village Green. As well as being surrounded on all sides by the mansions and meticulously tended gardens of the local gentry, we were also clearly visible to anyone passing through the tiny village. Despite Andy's complaints, Mark and I decided that the green was absolutely ideal. A fantastic find – I'd been looking forward to wild camping for so long.

'We'd be looking for two tents,' I'd said. 'We basically need to be independent, because we're thinking we might ride separately for some of the time. And obviously we'd each like a bit of privacy from time to time!'

With a few months to go before departure, Andy and I had found ourselves selling our grand idea to an outdoor equipment retailer. We'd got as far as their meeting room by cold calling every outdoor equipment manufacturer and retailer in the United Kingdom of Great Britain and Northern Ireland. After weeks of rejections or non-responses, I'd become frustrated by how little interest these companies seemed to take in our project. I couldn't understand why any marketing manager would pass up on the publicity our journey would generate for the sake of a few quid's worth of gear.

Then one day, Andy – who had been emailing sponsorship proposals to companies for weeks – received a reply from an outfit who asked us over for a chat. We designed a logo, ironed it onto a couple of cheap T-shirts, printed out some important-looking lists and rolled up to their office in Coventry.

'Well, lads, I have to be honest,' said Jeremy Burgess, leaning back in his chair with a squeak of leather, 'when I first heard about this from Martin, I thought you guys must be complete idiots.'

The two of us smiled nervously.

'But I think you've convinced me that you might actually do this.'

Finally somebody was listening to us – the managing director of an on-line outdoor gear retailer, no less! A simple contract was drawn up: we'd wear their T-shirts, put their logo on our website, sticker the heck out of our bikes, and plug their brand whenever we could. We'd also send them a monthly report by email, which they would send out to their subscribers to demonstrate how generous they were with support for noble expeditions like ours. And, in return, we'd be given essential items of equipment – tents, camping mats, sleeping-bags and various small accessories – free of charge, which of course was what we wanted to get out of the whole thing.

At this point we still didn't have any actual bicycles to ride. But we'd finally got our sponsorship drive out of the starting blocks, and we felt sure that other companies would follow in this supplier's footsteps. We set a departure date for the early summer, put a bundle of leaving party invitations in the post, and I set to work on publicity for the project, which by now we'd branded Ride Earth after a brainstorming session by Andy. Playing to the circumnavigation, the cycling and the off-road nature of the journey in one catchy slogan, Ride Earth rolled off the tongue far better than Pedalling To Purgatory, Circum Gravitation, and A Wheelie Long Way, which had been some of his other ideas.

Physically extracting the equipment from Jeremy and his merry band of outfitters proved easier said than done. With only a few weeks to go until the big day, I was parking the Astra outside Andy's house, having just returned from

Coventry where I'd had an unexpectedly brief encounter with the company's marketing manager, Dominic. But I had managed to retrieve what I'd gone for, and, dumping a big cardboard box on the lawn in Andy's back garden, I ripped it open and began inspecting our haul.

'Did you see anyone apart from Dominic?' asked Andy, pulling a bundle of tent material from its carry sack and sniffing it curiously.

'No,' I said. 'I didn't actually go into the office at all. No Jeremy, no nothing.'

'You'd think they'd be a bit more enthusiastic.'

'I dunno. I don't understand either.'

'Bloody hell!' exclaimed Andy, wrestling with the elasticated tent-poles as they unravelled. They seemed to have taken on a life of their own and were now in danger of causing serious facial injuries to his dad, who had come to watch from the safety of the kitchen doorstep.

'That's absolutely ridiculous!' I laughed, ducking out of the way of the whirling mess of poles. 'I've never seen anything like it! Is it fibreglass? Or some kind of bizarre metal?'

'Metal, I think. Aluminium or something, with a bit more spring in it. Bit of extra elastic!'

'Now, that's good, isn't it?' remarked Andy's dad as the poles clicked together and began to behave. He was a mechanical engineer and loved all things functional and cleverly designed. The family's little garage had not contained a car in several decades; instead it was filled to the brim with arcane machinery and projects in stages of semi-completion, stinking of rust and oil, every surface littered with drill bits and bolts and jars of important-looking coloured fluid.

'My god – I feel rough,' I muttered, coughing. I'd caught a cold and was trying my best to ignore it and continue ploughing through our ever-growing stack of to-do lists.

'Yeah, I noticed that on your Facebook,' said Andy. 'Oh yeah – I started a group for Market Harborough Swimming Club . . .'

'Yeah, I saw that.'

'. . . and loads of people I used to know started joining it!'

Andy had always been a natural athlete. I had not, and this was slightly concerning. I worried that as a dismally below-average sportsman I'd be unable to keep up; that I'd drag the ride down by being slow and unfit. But these were small hurdles. We'd find a way round them, just as we'd find a way round anything else that got in our way. Once we set off, we'd have no choice.

Returning to the task at hand, we inspected the semi-constructed tent, smooth and humpbacked like a fat green slug. It was my first encounter with this stratum of outdoor equipment, the type that gets displayed prominently in shops like Millets' and Blacks' with price tags that make you feel guilty for even *looking* at them.

'You have to bend these quite a lot, don't you?' said Andy, having consulted the instructions, now clipping the tent's body onto the naked pole structure. 'I mean, it's quite spring-loaded. But it is very straightforward. Hopefully.'

'Andrew, did you want this ice cream and peaches?' called his dad from the doorway.

'Yeah, in a minute,' he replied, not looking up. He draped the waterproof flysheet across the tent and it finally began to resemble the illustration on the front of the booklet. He groped through the fabric for the pole structure and lifted the entire thing off the ground with one hand. It seemed to float weightlessly into the air like a pointy green wind sock: my home for the next few years.

'That's pretty damn light!' he said, putting it back on the grass and stooping to unzip the door. He crawled in on all fours, lay face down with his socks sticking out of the doorway, folded his arms by his sides, and ceased to move altogether.

'That feels good!'

'Nice.' A sudden image came into my head of this exact scene played out at forty degrees below zero, deep in the Siberian tundra.

'Did you want these peaches and ice cream, then?' came his dad's voice.

'Yes, for god's sake!' snapped Andy, irritated at having his crowning moment disturbed by a parent.

'Do you want it in the tent?'

'No . . .' replied Andy, wearily, extracting himself.

'Aerodynamic!' remarked his dad, stepping out onto the lawn. 'If the wind's blowing, which way d'you pitch the tent?'

'Erm . . . well, that way, don't you?' replied Andy, drawing a line in the air from the rear of the tent to the open door.

'Well, yes, I would say so. I mean . . . basically, that's how it's designed,' continued his dad, going into demonstration mode and pacing about on the grass, gesticulating at the construction, 'because you'll be camping in hurricanes sometimes, and obviously – if the wind's blowing *this* way – it'll make it calm *here*, won't it?'

Andy seemed embarrassed at his dad's sudden display of interest. He pulled another plastic wrapper from the box and shook out the contents. 'I guess this is the floor protector,' he said to me. 'Does it go underneath the tent or inside it, d'you think?'

'I'd guess it went underneath,' I replied. 'But then I'm only a novice at this kind of thing.'

'Well, I'm only a novice as well. I don't know any more than you.'

'I love how it comes in its own special "sac".' I pointed at the little bag on the ground.

'Everything comes in a "sac", doesn't it, when it's to do with the outdoors?'

'Yeah.'

'It's never a bag, either. It's always a "sac".'

'Yeah.'

'A "sac" with a drawstring.'

Andy unrolled the groundsheet on the lawn in his parents' back garden. 'This'll be nice for picnics. In the Himalayas.'

Of the many reasons why I was happy with the idea of working with Andy on this epic mission, foremost was his off-the-wall sense of humour – the ideal temper to my hard-headedness and ruthless sense of justice. If anyone could keep spirits up when the going got tough, it would be him, and for that I was thankful.

He'd always been a creative mind – a maligned genius, holed up in his bedroom until the early hours, producing artwork and musical compositions of marvellous complexity that nobody could understand. On one occasion, answering an unexpected knock on the door late in the evening, I'd been confronted by Andy, who'd run several miles across the fields in the dark, taking shortcuts through people's gardens and hiding in their hedgerows to avoid being seen, for no other reason than his own amusement. He had just popped by for a cup of tea and to ask if I wouldn't mind giving him a lift back home.

Andy cared little what anyone else made of his behaviour. He had once turned up for a big night out in his mother's horse-riding jacket, insisting that it was perfectly appropriate attire, yet to this day I'm not sure whether he was being ironic. For Andy, the world was a place in which to experiment and to defy convention, and he was just the sort of lateral thinker you'd want along on a journey round the planet.

As Ride Earth grew in scope and ambition, respectable brands from the cycling and outdoor industries became attached to the project, and we found ourselves attending a series of newspaper, radio and television interviews. Sponsors expected to have their brands promoted in return for the freebies, so we were obliged to seek the kind of attention that would keep them happy. Our crowning achievement was a short feature at the end of the regional news on BBC One, in the slot that would normally be filled by some feel-good tale of local eccentrics and their quaint little projects.

The significance of what we were about to do was confirmed when we were invited to a meeting with one of the owners of Kona Bikes, a long-established manufacturer of bikes for true cycling enthusiasts. The meeting would be in Switzerland, naturally, in a posh chalet overlooking Lake Geneva with a cracking view of Mont Blanc. Andy and I flew out one morning, touched down to find Central Europe bathed in an unseasonal warm spell of weather, and spent an enjoyable day chatting on a sunny balcony over wine and pizza, impressing our prospective sponsors with the detail and subtlety of our research. Finally, we were offered whatever we liked from the company's product catalogue, driven back to the airport, and arrived back home in Northamptonshire in time for tea. Even though Kona didn't actually make off-road expedition bikes, we'd chosen two bicycle frames upon which to build our own, together worth *several hundred pounds!*

The meeting's organiser had asked if Mark was coming too, but – without bothering to mention this to Mark himself – I'd told Kona that he wasn't part of our core mission, so there wasn't really any point. I didn't want someone piggybacking on all of my hard work if they were only coming along for the easy bit of the ride.

Following Kona's involvement, interest in Ride Earth snowballed. Although we thought we knew exactly what we were doing, we decided to attend an expedition-planning weekend within the ornamental halls of the Royal Geographical Society in London. There we sat as part of a small audience in a workshop dedicated to the planning and logistics of long-distance bicycle journeys. A woman and two men sat in a row at the front, looking laid-back and unimposing. They almost looked *normal*. This was not the kind of impression I'd expected from three celebrated expedition cyclists who, having collectively pedalled several times round the planet, were clearly anything but normal. One of the guys had recently wrapped up a five-year epic of more than fifty thousand miles, yet now seemed more interested in doodling on his notepad than impressing the budding adventurers who positioned themselves expectantly before him.

And I wondered just what these three individuals had been through on their adventures, and how their experiences seemed to have humbled them, rather than helping them to grow confident and outgoing. My own return to England, of course, would be far more heroic.

Dumping our bikes on the grass in Deenethorpe, we nervously unpacked our tents and tried to remember how to pitch them. We'd chosen this particular model of tent for its natural shade of green that would blend into the foliage, and I had been looking forward to putting them to the test. I hadn't expected the reality of it to be so fraught with worry. Looking up from the instruction manual with a mouthful of left-over party cake, I saw with horror that a passing middle-aged couple had noticed us.

They slowed their Sunday evening walk; muttered something to each other. Then the wife quickened her pace while the husband crossed the road and marched onto the green with a look of intent.

I gulped down my cake and hissed a warning at the others. *Shit.*

We'd been busted on our first attempt, and were about to be booted out into the night!

The idea of wild camping had been a fantasy for years, but I'd never had the balls to actually *do* it, at least not outside a few TA training weekends as a student. This was not for want of trying. On one memorable occasion, Andy and I had set off across the fields near my home with a backpack containing a knife, some firewood and a six-pound salmon, intent on finding a spinney somewhere, lighting a fire, roasting the smelly fish and sleeping in the shelter that we would build with our bare hands. Having failed to find any trees in the dark and become entirely lost and covered in mud, we'd trudged all the way back to the village before cooking the salmon in the oven at two in the morning and going to sleep in Andy's dad's trailer-tent.

Well! This time, things would be different. Wild camping, after all, would be the ultimate expression of freedom. It would be the exercising of our natural-born right to sleep on land which had once been owned by nobody. We would spend weeks – months – at a time under canvas, living a monk-like existence, sitting round campfires, quoting philosophy, learning constellations, and putting the world to rights as we gradually pedalled round it. Oh yes.

'Just here for the night, are you?'

'Uh. Yes. Hopefully. Or something. We're – uh.'

Ridiculous!

'We're cycling round the world.'

'Right . . .'

A pause.

'So when did you start?'

'Erm . . . this morning . . .'

'Well, I guess you'd better come in!'

It was with more guilt than pleasure that I found myself sitting in the newly renovated kitchen of Mr Look-Of-Intent and his wife. As it turned out, the lady who had hurried away from the malevolent-looking bicycle-gypsies was none other than my primary-school teacher Mrs Chamberlain, who I hadn't seen since I was eleven. She slid another helping of strawberry pavlova under my nose, while a nearby platter of assorted cheeses eyed me in a seductive fashion. Despite being wracked with guilt at yet another wild camping failure, I couldn't quite believe our good fortune.

We *did* manage to salvage some kind of credibility as adventurers by politely refusing an offer of sleeping on the conservatory floor, Deenethorpe Village Green being far more appropriate for our first night in the wild.

'Cycle on the right, cycle on the right, cycle on the right . . . or die!!!' hollered Mark as we rolled off the ferry and onto the European mainland. There was no turning back now: we had escaped the British Isles and set foot and rubber on the soil of the Netherlands, five days after my parents' driveway fell out of sight in my rear-view mirror. It was staggering how little time it had taken to cycle to another country – just five days! How small England suddenly seemed – how silly that I'd never thought to cycle more than a dozen or so miles away from my home until now. It seemed so ridiculously easy to hop on a bike and ride it into the great unknown, and I tried to remember why it had taken me an entire year to work out how to do it.

I knew why, of course: the *real* mission ahead was a true epic, rivalling some of the greatest journeys undertaken by man. The surface of the earth now lay unbroken in front of us, from the Hook of Holland to the tip of Singapore eight time zones to the east. At my best guess, we'd be riding for more than a year before reaching that impossibly distant point, tackling extreme conditions and passing through wildly foreign lands. This winter we'd be battling searing heat in the deserts of the Middle East; as spring broke next year we'd be crawling through the mountains of Central

Asia, or perhaps India; meandering through China and South-East Asia as the following year drew on; and we hoped to reach Australia by the end of the second year. Some time later would come the Americas. There was no way such a mission could be accomplished without careful preparation. And my heart leapt at the image of such a line snaking its way across the surface of a globe. What a thing to do!

CHAPTER 3

Yes – that was the plan, wasn't it? A line, so simple and straightforward. It is impossible to recall how it could have seemed so clear. The miles between then and now have clouded the road to a point where I'm riding into a never-ending dust storm.

The end of each day looks the same as its start, the rubble of the Nubian desert extending endlessly in all directions. Only occasionally do I catch sight of palm branches to the west, rows of green asterisks on the horizon line, reassuring me that the set of tyre trails I've chosen to follow is the right one, or that at least it's heading in the same direction as the Nile. It's not much on which to base my progress. But it's all I've got.

My tyres roll through bulldozed rubble. They sink into patches of sand. They bounce over the furrows that emerge from the passage of trucks, hammering at the corrugated dirt. Gusts of hot air carry grit and dust through the channels of this rugged landscape, sometimes from the side, sometimes behind, but mostly from ahead of me – from the south. Only the wind has the power to make a mockery of my best energies. The going has never been harder than this. Yet, in a way, riding is still easy. Any act of endurance is nothing but one small action, repeated. Press down once upon a pedal and I move forward a few feet. Do it again and

I've travelled a little further. Another million repetitions later and I'll have cycled to Cape Town and the end of the African continent. On a physical level, it really is as simple as that – given enough motivation, which is where things have become more complicated.

Right now, I cannot say what I'm trying to achieve by taking this on. I've been telling myself that searching is not going to produce any answers. I don't need to focus on a goal, navigate with precision, or reach some destination. I need to do exactly the opposite. I need to let go of myself, and get completely and utterly lost. Only by doing so can I hope to find my way. This is easier said than done, given my particular menu of personality defects. I find myself prone to wild flights of introspection, harangued by warring voices in each ear: one telling me how great everyone's going to think I am for cycling across the Sahara desert; the other reminding me that I'm a self-absorbed bastard for doing what I did in order to be here. I need a way to switch these voices off. And so I've developed a technique. It's very simple.

Devote one hundred percent concentration to the simple act of preparing breakfast. By doing so, everything else ceases to exist. Extract, with undivided attention, a bag of bread from the right-hand pannier. Break off the black mould around the edges. Squash a banana into a floury wrap. Devour. Taste the moist, sweet banana; feel the brittle graininess of the bread. Squint briefly at the horizon. Mount bike in a manoeuvre of acrobatic grace. Press down once upon a pedal and move forward a few feet.

I'm hiding behind my bicycle for a couple of hours, because there's nowhere else that I can get any shade in the middle of the day. I don't know how long it's going to go on for. Luckily there's the occasional truck going by now, so if I do run out of water I should be able to get hold of some more.

And I was also just thinking about what we mean when we say that we want to go somewhere hot and sunny. And I was thinking that what we actually mean is that we want to go somewhere hot and sunny, and that we can escape from . . . erm . . .

I'll try that again.

When we say we want to go somewhere hot and sunny – on holiday, for example – what we mean is that we want to go somewhere where we can escape from it being hot and sunny whenever we want. (Oh – a ladybird. Hello.) So, yeah. It's like people who say that they like cold weather. It's not really that, it's the fact that they can enjoy it whilst being protected against it.

And I guess it's the same for any kind of extreme, isn't it? I mean, really – it does get boring, being out in the sun. It does get very unpleasant, if there's no way of getting away from it, as I'm now finding out in the middle of the Sudanese desert at midday.

There's no air-conditioning. There's no water-cooler. There's no shady little hut, or anything like that. No, it's just burning desert, and nothing else! Not a pleasant place to come on holiday – that, I can promise you.

Towards the end of the day I come across a second group of road-workers, blasting their way through rock and pounding reddish foundations. They wave and shout greetings when they see me bouncing past in the distance, and I head towards the huddle of ageing canvas tents pitched in the desert, because given the choice between two options I might as well take the more interesting one.

I drop my bike on the sand and greet the workers in a flurry of handshakes and *as-salaam-alaikum*s. One of them gives me a tour of the camp. It doesn't take long: a circle of tents, each lined with flimsy bed-frames, tatty mosquito nets held together with masking tape, and a few blankets. In the centre of the circle is a rough quadrangle of stones dragged from the desert and a couple of small rugs, grey and indistinct in the dusk, but oriented in a familiar direction: the camp's mosque. A cylindrical water tank squats on a trailer, dropped off by a tow-truck. I refill my plastic bottles with the tepid, rough-tasting water. Then I sit on the ground in the largest tent, and the half-dozen workers and I share the evening staple of bread and stewed beans. Illuminated by a dim light bulb and entertained by the growl of the diesel generator outside, there seems little need for conversation, and the evening passes quietly.

Early the next morning I depart with thanks and continue to pedal south. After a jittery start in Sudan, that all-important momentum is back and I want to make the most of it. I stop mid-morning to watch an earthmoving machine crawling along the trail, reassigned to pave an indistinguishable section of Nubia that I have already passed. This entire stretch of road, from Wadi Halfa to the capital, will be complete in less than a year; the final leg of a paved route running the full length of Africa. Although it's futile to think in such terms, I can't help wondering how long it will take me to reach the end of the road, and what might happen along the way. And I can't help thinking back along that same road to the early days of my journey. How impossible it would be to invent the story that led here!

As the vibrations subside and the dust begins to sink back towards the ground, I feel another rumble. But there are no vehicles to be seen. This rumble is coming from within. And I panic, stupidly, because – despite being in the middle of the very definition of 'nowhere' and probably the only person for miles around – it seems inappropriate to drop my pants there and then. So I dash around in agony, trying to find a human-sized crevice in the landscape, where I discover that there is something green in the desert after all. And this leaping from the saddle settles into a pattern that continues for the rest of the morning. It is a huge relief when, with the sun overhead and the furnace at its hottest, I spot buildings in the distance, and I veer off the track and strike out across the bare earth towards them. Palms rise up behind the little village, reminding me that the Nile is just beyond. I wonder what I'll find in my first Nubian settlement. What does a Nubian home look like? How do its inhabitants make a living? What kind of food do they eat?

After all this time, I love the fact that I still have these simple questions. The answers are not really the point.

It was on Day Six of Ride Earth that we rolled down the metal ramp and onto Dutch concrete, sniffing the air of a brand new place, allowing the unfamiliar to flood our senses – the cute interlocking pavement tiles, the slanted bicycle-friendly kerbs, the low brick dwellings that lay scattered across the flat and featureless plains. But the colourless fog overhead served as a reminder that we weren't yet so far from home.

Before we'd set sail, Mark and Andy had found an Internet terminal and mail-ordered bicycle parts to be sent to

Amsterdam's main post office, from where we would later collect them. Andy had been suffering from back pain and sore wrists, and in his wisdom had diagnosed a case of wrongly sized handlebars. Mark was still struggling to fit all of his kit into the hold-all that he carried on a cargo trailer behind his bike, and had decided that a saddlebag was in order. It made complete sense to have these items posted from England to Amsterdam, the cycling capital of the world, rather than to buy them from a shop there. What if they didn't have saddlebags or handlebars in Amsterdam? It was a risk we couldn't afford to take.

In the meantime, Mark needn't have bothered worrying about which side of the road we cycled on – the Netherlands sported a fantastic crop of cycle routes, winding among coastal dunes, weaving along old railway cuttings and delving through leafy forests. Soon it started spitting with rain. Lightly at first, then with increasing zeal, until by the time we emerged from the tangle of bike paths into the industrial outskirts of Amsterdam it was positively torrential. I donned my serious-looking army poncho. It collected rain in large quantities and channelled it into my boots. Back in the saddle, the poncho acted as a massive parachute, billowing superhero-style behind me and wrapping itself around my torso whenever I tried to gather speed.

We stopped beneath an overpass and I put on my sponsored waterproof socks and neoprene over-boots. Their performance was astonishing: never had a product so effectively stopped the water already inside my boots from escaping! Things continued to go downhill through the grey, drenched flatness of Amsterdam's suburbs. Reaching the centre, we found a youth hostel, marched in swinging our video cameras, claimed we were from the BBC and demanded a generous discount.

I lay on my back in the dormitory, alone and deflated. We'd been defeated by a bit of bloody rain. What had happened to this heroic adventure I'd spent so long imagining? All we'd really done was make a stressful dash out of England and then grind through the rain all the way to Amsterdam (where we didn't really need to go), before handing over precious cash in exchange for one night in a youth hostel (in which we didn't really need to stay). Even the hostel had a torrent of rainwater pouring through the ceiling into a bucket on the floor.

The next day we got up early and set off to find the post office. It was closed. Today was Saturday, and it wouldn't reopen until Monday. We would now have to spend the weekend in the city, putting us several days behind schedule. At this rate, we wouldn't even make it to Gibraltar before winter set in, let alone all the way across Europe!

Bike safely stowed in the hostel's backyard, I wandered into the city to calm down, finding that Amsterdam was just as I remembered it: brick, canals, bicycles, charm; a happy, circular city of trams, pedestrians and pedals, and a welcome change from the traffic-clogged roads and miserable commuter towns of England. I returned to the hostel buoyed up by the novelty of being in a foreign land. I found the others in the laundrette next door, Mark gazing absently into the distance, Andy drooping towards the floor, half-asleep, as the machines clinked and churned around them. They were obviously feeling the same homesickness that I'd experienced during the first couple of days on the road, and they both wanted to remain at the hostel for the whole weekend. I told them exactly what I thought of *that*. What a waste of money! Far better to find a park, crawl beneath a clump of greenery and sleep there, heroically. After some wringing of hands we came to a grumpy compromise and pedalled off to a campsite on the outskirts of the city, passing several good wild-camping spots in the process. We pitched our top-of-the-range tents in a neat row next to a hundred cheap and cheerful vestibules. Then we hung around in the communal kitchen eating instant mashed potato, while happy European families cooked elaborate dinners, sat down to eat on the opposite side of the room, and carefully avoided eye contact with us.

On Monday, after a protracted wild-goose chase, the errant packages were found in an out-of-town parcel depot on the wrong side of the city. And thus it was mid-afternoon on Day Ten by the time we left Amsterdam, where we'd expected to stay no longer than a night. But our collective woes were forgotten, and all was smiles, because we were finally on our way to cycle round the world.

'Tell you what,' said the red-haired girl behind the bar, 'I'll give you these three on the house. And then the rest . . . well, you can decide for yourselves.'

'Wow!'

'Thank you!'

We were perched upon barstools, Andy to my left, Mark to my right. Thick dark liquid began sliding into the second glass, tilted expertly to allow a steady build-up of foam atop the beer. The result looked like a pint of Guinness in an oversize wine glass: we were about to take our first sip of the famous Belgian Trappist ale.

'Mmm . . . that's delicious!' Andy took a sip from the first glass; a golden brew with a warm sweetness and a touch of fizz.

'You like ale, yes?' the lady asked Mark, putting the second glass in front of me.

'Yes!'

'OK – wait.' She paused, raising a finger. 'I have something special for you.' She turned and headed purposefully in the direction of the fridges at the back of the bar.

'She's going to open the vault!' joked Mark as she rummaged amongst clinking bottles and returned with a dusty-looking specimen.

'This,' she announced, parading the label in front of us, 'is really one of the strongest. You see,' – she pointed out the wording – 'this one is a "double". There's a "triple" here, too. It's, like . . . seven percent.' And she reached for the bottle-opener.

I raised my glass victoriously: another long day of riding into stiff winds had been conquered, and country number three had rewarded us with friendly people and a place to sleep, as well as the most welcome free beer ever dispensed! We toasted to the day: to the simple joy of celebrating the end of a hard slog with a couple of good mates.

Andy grinned. 'Why bother eating when you can drink beer?!'

We hadn't even seen a signpost to announce our arrival into Belgium, another small step in our mission to cycle the globe. Lost in the early-evening drizzle and with nowhere to sleep, we'd flagged down a trundling motorist and asked sheepishly if he had any idea where we might spend the night. The elderly man had shrugged off decades in an instant, hopping back into the driver's seat as if finding accommodation for three foreign cyclists were his very *raison d'être*. And so, having desperately chased the born-again boy racer through the suburbs of Maastricht, we'd arrived at a countryside park visitors' centre where the kindly manager, on hearing of our quest, had set us up on a patch of grass outside the kitchen door – and was now treating us to a well-earned drink.

Mark took a small sip, replaced the glass on the bar counter, closed his eyes, clasped his hands on top of his head and leaned back. A smile widened into a laugh. Perhaps it was the hunger and the tiredness of a full day on the road. Or perhaps it was that Belgian monks really did brew the world's finest ale.

'I'm going to order some food,' he said shortly, opening his eyes. 'Anyone care to join me on that?'

I looked at Andy, who was sat to my left in his matching sponsored T-shirt. 'What do you reckon?'

'Erm . . . we could have a look at the menu?' he said.

'Mmm,' I mused. 'Depends on the price, really.'

Mark passed over the menu. It was filled with descriptions of food that made my salivary glands ache. But giving in to temptation would set a precedent – one which could easily leak funds away and sabotage our carefully planned budget, which was to spend as little as physically possible.

'Basically,' I said, unable to look up from the menu, 'I really can't afford to do this while I've got perfectly good food in my panniers.'

'I'm sure we could afford this kind of thing occasionally?' suggested Andy. Mark sat quietly, admiring his glass of beer.

'Well, go for it, then,' I replied, closing the menu and

putting it back on the bar. 'But I reckon I'm going to cook something back at the tents.'

'Right . . . so what about the food budget? I mean, we've all paid for *that* food, too,' said Andy.

'I dunno, mate. But I can't afford to splash out every time Mark wants to eat in a restaurant.'

Andy had brought up a difficult point, which was that we'd pooled our cash to cover our basic costs. This had been averaging just under five euros a day for each of us, which had required dedication and effort to stick to. We'd been sleeping rough since Amsterdam, picnicking daily on supermarket groceries and boiling up variations on the theme of 'pasta with sauce' in the evenings. But if I cooked and ate alone from this shared food store, I'd be eating a meal that the others had subsidised. And if Mark used the shared money to buy a restaurant meal for himself, then we'd be subsidising *that*. Unless we stuck to a regime, attempting to share our cash would cause more problems than it solved. And each of us feeding ourselves alone would take three times as long, and put the group dynamic strangely off-balance.

'Well – what are we supposed to do, then?' I asked, half-rhetorically. The others were silent. This was frustrating. Andy was clearly quite happy to shell out for a home-cooked lasagne. Or a massive burger. Or a juicy steak. Or a delicious pizza. Or a big bowl of soup.

'Look, guys,' sighed Mark. 'I'm going to eat here. I'm not on as much of a budget as you two. So I can happily afford a blow-out meal every now and then. If you want to go back to the tents and eat what's there, that's cool . . . I'm quite happy sitting here. I've got my book . . .'

'Right, well I'll eat with Tom, then,' sighed Andy. 'But I want to finish my beer first.'

'Yeah . . . of course! I honestly don't –'

'Fine, OK,' I interrupted. 'Well, I'm going to start cooking before I get too pissed to walk straight!'

'See you in a minute, then,' said Andy, watching me as I got up.

Since I couldn't remember how to get round to the bikes, I took a shortcut through the kitchen where Mark's dinner was being prepared. Stepping out into the failing dusk and hunting amongst the bags, I discovered that our gas stove was buried at the bottom of Mark's giant cargo sack. Finally, after arranging all of the ingredients and cooking apparatus in a neat little circle, I sat down by the light of my head-torch to open a tin of tuna and realised that we'd brought along one of those multi-purpose penknives with a built-in can-opener, yet I hadn't the foggiest idea how to use it.

We grew stronger as summer matured. It was a tangible, measurable feeling of strength; a growing confidence in the capability of our bodies to handle hours of exercise every day. Our regime, and that of every other cycle tourist on the road, would have had personal trainers the world over up in arms, bemoaning the complete absence of recovery time, of stretching routines, of cross-training, of good nutrition, and all the other things that the exercise industry proclaims to be right and proper. Instead, we were hacking our bodies, bludgeoning them into performing the task at hand, learning the effect of calories eaten upon energy levels, the relationship between hydration and general wellbeing, exertion and rest, clothing and climate; things which could not be taught but which gradually came to be understood through observing the effects of our experiments upon our bodies.

Belgium morphed into France, and a happy routine emerged of long mornings in the saddle, games of 'who's got the biggest baguette' at lunchtime, two-hour siestas in the sun, and relaxed afternoons among the charms of rural Alsace-Lorraine, where the French land still retained hints of its German past, memorials littering the hills and valleys as a reminder of how that particular disagreement had been resolved. Only the frequent appearance of rain threatened to dampen our spirits, and these hours were whiled away in village *lavoirs* – ancient stone bath-houses – where Andy experimented with the camera he'd bought for the journey, I filled jars with jam I'd cooked from scavenged fruit, and Mark practised his juggling routines.

'Basically, I wanted to ride to Spain, and then Gibraltar,' Mark was explaining into the video camera, 'because – er – I'd been to Greece in the past, and I wanted to go somewhere that was also similarly sandy and beautiful, and find lonely mountain retreats, and fish.'

We'd been on the road for three weeks, reaching the alpine foothills of the Jura in eastern France. Spain, it had to be said, still felt a long way off.

'But the last couple of weeks, we've just been meeting loads of really interesting people from different walks of life,' he continued as I thrust the camera in his face. Like all of us, he was still uncomfortable before the lens. Thoughts which would be freely expressed amongst friends flattened out into dry exposition as soon as a camera was introduced. We'd never realised what a challenge this would be: presenting ourselves and our journey as we would like them to appear to an anonymous audience.

'And I think that if we . . . head east,' continued Mark, trying hard to loosen up, 'we're more likely to go to a number of different countries that I know nothing about – I'll know nothing about the people, their way of life, or what they eat. And there'll be more of an opportunity to find out about the world.'

The delivery was stilted, but the idea itself was interesting. Heading east, as Mark had indicated, would be a radical change of tack, and in my mind's eye I saw weeks of route-planning disappearing into thin air. I expected to feel a pang of regret. Instead, it was almost a liberation to watch the hard-line itinerary dissolving away.

We hadn't been able to follow the plan closely, anyway. On several occasions we'd attempted to head off-road through the hills – attempts that had invariably ended in failure. One particular afternoon, the two stronger bikers had bitten into a particularly rough climb with gusto, leaving me to drag my bike up the track on foot. Fuming about having been left behind, I'd found them waiting for me about ten minutes' walk up the trail.

'This is completely and utterly pointless!' I shouted from a distance, feeling a nice big argument coming on.

'We're here now, aren't we?'

'Well, I can't ride. I'm going back.'

'What the hell?'

'If you hadn't buggered off I'd have told you that ten minutes ago!'

'This was your idea, Tom!' shouted Andy.

'What do you mean, *my* idea?'

'Well, *I* never decided to turn off that road and follow these blue triangles!'

'I thought you didn't know the route!'

'I did know the route! It carried on along that road back there!'

'Erm . . . so what do we want to do . . . ?' enquired Mark, trying to bring some diplomacy to the exchange.

'If we're supposed to be on the road,' I continued, ignoring him, 'then why the hell aren't we on the road?'

'Because you said, "Follow the blue triangles!"' shouted Andy.

'No, I said that the *tourist office* said that the mountain-biking routes were marked with blue triangles!'

'Fucking hell! What a dick!' muttered Andy, loud enough for me to hear it, wheeling his bike round to face me. 'So why did we suddenly start following them?!?'

'Because there was no-one telling me that there was any other bloody route to go!' I raged.

'Well, we don't normally just *randomly* turn off the road onto a track, do we? Why put a random route into the equation?'

'Because nobody said we were going any other way!!!'

It was the kind of verbal brawl that felt immediately pointless. Andy and I found ourselves sheepishly apologising to each other on the roadside. It wasn't the first time; nor would it be the last. But through discovering the limits of our off-road abilities, we'd found that it was possible to travel more quickly – and to meet more interesting people – by stitching together a new route on minor roads and cycleways. Given that, maybe a change of tack wasn't such a bad idea.

I wandered over to Andy, who'd been listening to Mark's monologue into the video camera, sitting in the sun on some wooden steps that led up the hillside.

'I've been wanting to head east most of the time anyway!' he said, flashing a wry grin in Mark's direction. He'd been suggesting this since Amsterdam, and now, I grudgingly conceded, it seemed that he might have been right all along. Heading east now would lift all the pressure of having to circumnavigate Spain and be back in Central Europe before autumn. It would mean that we really could relax into the journey instead of feeling constantly in debt to this big detour we'd promised to make.

'I wasn't going to get in anyone's face,' insisted Mark. 'I'm not really like that! I'm a pretty flexible soul . . .'

'I was hoping Mark was going to go to Spain, though, because he's starting to annoy me,' smirked Andy into the camera.

Mark looked on with obvious amusement. 'You two would die without me! You'd be fighting the first night!'

Which was almost definitely true.

The decision had been unexpectedly amicable. It was probably the encounters of the previous weeks that had made notions of route and direction seem less of a concern. The ups and downs had depended far more on attitude than altitude. Gibraltar, then, was off the map, and a new target drifted into view: *Istanbul*. Though always part of the plan, it sounded so foreign, now; so impossibly far away.

Mark hefted his bike upright and began to pedal slowly up

the long incline. Andy was already disappearing out of sight behind the shoulder of the hill. Tomorrow, then, we would pass into Switzerland and begin to pedal east. I would contact my friends near Geneva and let them know that we'd be dropping by rather earlier than originally planned.

Billowing grey clouds were forming intricate landscapes of their own above the valleys of the Jura, hinting at the nearing of the Alps. The ground where we'd rested was cast into shade, the western horizon growing orange and brooding in the late afternoon, a band of pure colour cutting across the sky. Amid darkening lands a few wooded hilltops still glowed, touched by shafts of illuminating sunlight – too far away to make them out in detail, yet carrying some strange hint of promise.

CHAPTER 4

Midday in the Sahara. There's no-one to be seen. I push my bike amongst the outlying buildings. All is silence.

A small boy darts from nowhere and makes a snatch at my trailer's tattered flag. I yell at him, he yells something back into the bright heat and darts away again – gone.

I hear the squeal and clang of a metal door and follow the sound, emerging from between the low houses and courtyards and onto what I guess is the main street; a slightly wider piece of desert between the mud-walled compounds. So this is a Nubian village. It is hot and sunny; eerily quiet. Obviously. Who'd be outside in this weather?

Padding towards a doorway across the street, I almost walk into the young man who steps out as I approach. If he's surprised to bump into a grimy sunburned tramp wandering through his village, he hides it very well. More faces peer out from what I can now see is a little shop; men in purest white, women colourfully wrapped, stepping outside to meet me, all smiling broadly. This smile seems to be something of a permanent feature of the Nubians. With some exaggerated miming I explain that I am ill, desperate, and looking for a place to rest.

Immediate hilarity ensues and the entire village springs into life. Calls to action bounce down the street like squash balls: suddenly there are people everywhere. I'm ushered through a gate into one of the nearby compounds. Enclosed by a thick high wall of Nile mud, robust as concrete in the heat of the desert, the house I find inside is big and spacious. Little distinction is made between indoors and out – windows, doorways and arches have been carved from the dry walls, some areas roofed with palm-branch lattices, and the entire structure is painted in white, yellow and blue, appealingly simple in appearance. The young man introduces his three colleagues: civil engineers from faraway Khartoum, working on the new road. They will be my hosts, he says, for as long as I remain in need of a place to stay.

I'm shown to a spare bed, where I sit quietly and think, left for a moment to my own devices. I have been asked for no money in return for this hospitality. Yet the place is not a wealthy one; whatever my personal budget and notions of frugality, there's little doubt that I have come here bearing the riches of kings. Should I offer something by way of thanks? Or would doing so strip away that human altruism that has brought such joy to my journey? Before I can find an answer to that question, my hosts return, and I am whisked off on a tour of the area.

The village sits beside a stripe of fertile land that reaches down to the banks of the Nile, criss-crossed with irrigation channels, dotted with stands of tall date palms and cultivated with wheat and beans. The little fields are fed by rusty diesel-powered pumps that are occasionally fired up to fill the channels with river water. Next come the house visits; I am a source of curiosity in Wawa, and I'm passed from family to family for the rest of the afternoon.

At the end of the day I find myself sharing a communal hang-out in the village centre with a handful of men. The

TV is on, beaming images of crisis from around the world into this tiny dwelling in the desert. The day after I'd received my visa to enter Sudan from the country's embassy back in Cairo, the international community had issued an arrest warrant for Omar Al-Bashir, the President of Sudan, over the small issue of several hundred thousand deaths and the displacement of two-and-a-half million of his own people. This was merely the latest set of figures to give the illusion that Sudan's eternal conflicts were somehow quantifiable. The following day, all visas were off. I could call myself lucky to have got that green sticker, if it weren't grotesque to mention good fortune at all in the light of the events that led to such a decree.

And I think of none of this, because I'm sitting in the cool shade, drinking tea and laughing with strangers. And the sun sinks below the skyline in the ravaged, war-torn, peaceful and hospitable country of Sudan.

OK.

I wish.

I wish . . . I could be doing this with Tenny. I have to say it.

This is such a fantastic experience. But I really . . . I really wish I could be sharing it with her. It would be so good to be able to do this with, er . . .

Yeah – with the woman who I love.

I know that right now it's not possible. I know that, but it doesn't make any difference: I'm always thinking about it. Always. Always thinking about her, being with her . . . that moment when I see her again.

And every time I have an experience, whether it's good or bad, I'm always thinking: it would be so good – it would be so good to be sharing this, even if it's a bad experience, it would be so good to be sharing it with Tenny.

I don't regret doing this.

But it would make such a big difference to be doing it with her. And that's all I want to say, really.

'You look tired!'

'Huh? Ah. Yeah. We slept in a park last night. Just down there.' Mark pointed wearily down the lakeside promenade to a grassy, tree-studded park, where a group of Swiss youths were setting up a game of bowls, unaware that the green had until a few minutes ago been somebody's bedroom.

'Aha! You're going far?'

'Round the world!' we mumbled in chorus.

'Mmm. Well,' grinned the slender grey-haired lady, 'I've also been on a kind of "world tour". So, if you're not in a rush, I'd like to invite you to my place. We can chat. You can rest. You can spend the day there if you like? Stay the night, even. It's no trouble.'

Invitations like this had become a frequent feature of our journey across Western Europe. By far the most effective method of eliciting them had been to ask plainly for help – for a water-bottle refill, or, if we were feeling lucky, for a spot to pitch our tents. Mark had become the designated door-knocker after a brilliant early run in the Netherlands, where we'd made this astonishing discovery. Putting on a happily clueless face, he would unveil his goatee, put on a cycling headband that looked to the untrained eye like a fluorescent-yellow sock, and amble vaguely towards his quarry. And the sight of this pitiful creature seemed to awaken the hospitality buried in every human being.

It may also have been that he didn't take things like this as seriously as I did. For me, stopping a passer-by or knocking on a door was a sign of weakness. The journey I'd always imagined was supposed to be a demonstration of self-sufficiency, and my hesitant approaches seemed to put people off. But as far as Mark was concerned, he was just asking for help. And by doing so, he had become responsible for a staggering list of back gardens, garage floors, spare rooms and sofas on which we had spent our nights since we had vowed in that leaky Amsterdam hostel to abandon paid accommodation entirely. These encounters had been diverse; our hosts revealed a dazzling array of hobbies and professions and views on the world. And, in that way, farmers, plumbers, school teachers, conservationists, diplomats, judges, newspaper editors, blacksmiths, businessmen, translators, potters, water-polo coaches, vagrants and violinists had become part of the journey I'd always imagined would be about sweat, strain, mountains, forests, wild camps, sunsets and the purest form of independence.

Mirella's unexpected invitation was unusual in that it had arrived unsolicited – and at seven-thirty in the morning. As we waited on the lakeside wall while she ran some errands, I wondered what kind of 'world tour' she'd been on. It wasn't likely to compare to what we were doing, of course, but it would be fun to hear about it anyway. Soon we found ourselves cycling behind our unexpected host into the terraced suburbs of Montreux, where we weaved up the steep and crooked alleys to Mirella's home. We wheeled our bikes into the garage, paused briefly to admire the wizened old touring steeds that rested inside, and followed her into a house full of airy rooms and natural light; a monument to simplicity, overlooking Lake Geneva – the most beautiful bathroom on Earth, she said.

Mirella unpacked her shopping in the kitchen and quietly explained that she'd spent a total of twelve years on the road with her husband, over the course of three separate world tours. India, Australia, Tibet, China, Yemen, Oman – the roll-call went on, but without a hint that she was merely ticking off a list of countries. Her ride hadn't hinged upon big distances or impressive-sounding continental crossings, and she clearly didn't think herself superior as a result of her achievements. The Italian-born nurse was in her fifties and had only recently returned to Switzerland after eight continuous years of life on the world's back roads, finishing her ride back into Europe by following the River Danube as we were planning to do on our way towards Asia.

Her husband, she said, was in Taiwan on a photography assignment, and if the couple had children who'd grown up and left home, Mirella didn't mention them. While we slumped half-asleep in the sitting-room, not quite knowing what to make of our chance encounter, she cooked us a lunch of *spaghetti alla Bolognese* and watched in amusement as we shovelled vast quantities of it down our throats. I couldn't comprehend what she'd done, try as I might, my world already in a spin after only four weeks on the road.

Twelve years.

'So,' enquired Mirella as we finished off the last of the pasta, 'what kind of distances are you guys doing each day?'

The question came with a tilt of inquisitiveness. But there was something else beneath it. Was it suspicion? Amusement?

The question was a test, designed to reveal something about the way we were conducting our journey – something that we thought was superficial, but that would tell her a great deal.

'Hmm . . . about seventy or eighty kilometres on average?' I haltingly put the figures to Andy and Mark, still having to convert from miles. I supposed that bigger numbers would sound more credible to a world-class veteran like Mirella.

'Maybe less, actually, I think . . . sixty. Sometimes fifty . . .'

'It really depends on a lot of things . . .'

'We've never done more than ninety so far, to be honest . . .'

'We're trying not to rush . . .'

Mirella had been listening to the excuses we found ourselves making for our disappointing progress, and was nodding knowingly.

'Good!' she smiled. 'We almost *never* rode more than fifty kilometres in a day. Sometimes forty, thirty, twenty – it wasn't important.'

She sat forward in her chair. 'You know what? There's really no point in going fast, riding far. We stopped whenever it felt right, even if we'd only travelled ten kilometres. Because it's when you step off the bike that you're really *in* the place. The cycling itself is not the point. It's not the point at all.'

Mirella gazed up at the ceiling, allowing memories to flood in.

'We always took our time – camping in wonderful wild places, making friends, spending long periods of time off our bikes. We spent six months on a sailboat in the South Pacific. Another six months on a horse ranch in Australia. Wherever we stopped and dismounted, things would happen. We let people come to us – express their hospitality, be curious. Then we would see the place through their eyes. Eventually we found that we'd travelled tens of thousands of kilometres in that way. But we could never have had those experiences if we had just pedalled like crazy all the time.

'So you're really doing a good thing, guys. Keep it slow. Enjoy life.'

After lunch, Mirella invited us into a tiny study with a couple of chairs and an ancient computer, and treated us to an extended version of the slide-show she presented at public events. Image after glorious image, perfect in colour and composition, portraying all the subtleties and spectacles of her and her husband's filtration through the cultures and landscapes of the world. More than twenty thousand pictures had been captured on traditional negative film, carefully packed away, developed, and boiled down to the selection that now passed before our eyes. These spellbinding photos had been crafted with the considered strokes of a master artist, putting my own efforts at camerawork to shame. And the story she wove through the images brought a lump to my throat – as I sat in the tiny study in my sponsored T-shirt, taken far away from Switzerland to places where Technicolor characters swept through lands of colour and detail, as exotic as distant galaxies. I suddenly found myself fighting back tears.

'We might not have much in the way of money, or possessions,' said Mirella, quietly, sitting cross-legged on a folding chair by the computer desk. 'But we cycle travellers are rich beyond measure. Because we have all the time in the world.'

What to do with so much time? If time was the new measure

of wealth, I was the new Sultan of Brunei. Switzerland's cycleways were so comprehensive and well-signposted that there was little need for navigation, and we often found ourselves separated for hours. There was little to do but ride, soak up the sun, and find new ways of entertaining myself, of which my favourite was to lip-sync the mooing of cattle as I rode past. Only occasionally, when one of us grew too eager and overshot an important junction, did separation cause any problems, and even then it didn't seem worth getting annoyed about, because Switzerland seemed too perfect to spoil with disagreements, everything in sight either a sunlit green or the perfect brown of a wooden chalet, its window-boxes overflowing with colour.

I sat in the sun at the top of a pass, chatting with Mark as we waited for Andy, who'd taken a wrong turn and was having a lovely afternoon ride through the Swiss Alps on his own. He'd borrowed someone's phone and sent a text message to Mark to say that he was on his way.

'Do you think they've painted the pylons green to try and hide them?' asked Mark, nodding across at the valley.

'A view like that, and you're talking about pylons?'

The long grass was bursting with long-stemmed buttercups and purple thistles, rocking in the gentlest of breezes. Across the road was a billboard advertising 'Glacier 3000', a giant cable-car ride that would take its passengers up to an altitude of ten thousand feet. Once there, they would have the opportunity to ignore the free scenery – and fork out more cash to ride the world's highest alpine roller-coaster, and then buy a Polaroid picture of themselves, screaming.

'Did he say how far away he was?' I asked Mark.

'Nope.'

'I don't know why he keeps doing this,' I moaned. 'He knows I'm supposed to be navigating – that's why we set up these "group roles", to avoid exactly this kind of situation.'

'I think he's just excited about the riding – that's all. There's no point being hard on him. He's going to be here soon.'

'Yeah . . . I guess so.'

We basked in the sun. I tried not to feel guilty about another extended break in the riding. After all, to lie in the long grass on a warm summer's day, eyes closed, was about the simplest pleasure imaginable. But relaxing seemed to require practice.

'The thing is,' I continued, 'we're such good friends, and we know each other so well – it's kind of inevitable that you take it out on the people closest to you. And we're both unwilling to admit that we're the ones at fault, so occasionally it keeps going a bit longer than it should. But at least it doesn't end in violence any more.'

'It used to end in violence?'

'Yeah, it did.'

'OK, cool, cool . . . good stuff.'

'But that's going back a long way,' I clarified.

'Right. Well, I've noticed it's got a lot better in the last couple of weeks.'

In France we'd agreed that too much time was spent discussing the same old minutiae, so we'd decided to set up a weekly rota. This had resulted in identifying the two main chores of life on the road – meals and route-finding – and we'd assigned jobs via three rounds of paper-scissors-stone. Thus had I landed the first week-long assignment of

'Routemaster', and Andy the expedition's first 'Foodmaster'. Mark, in order that he not feel left out, had been branded with the flattering title of 'General Bitch', which was more fun than it sounded, as it encompassed directing the filming efforts, co-ordinating places to sleep, handing out Haribo, fishing when appropriate, and doing the washing up. It'd had the immediate effect of smoothing out our days, giving us more time to enjoy unexpected discoveries and meetings. It had also preventing Mark and Andy from ganging up on me the whole bloody time.

'What's that book you've got there?' I asked. Mark always kept at least one book to hand in his handlebar bag, snatching a few minutes of reading whenever he could.

'Oh, it's *Crime and Punishment*. I think you should read it.'

I could smell steak being barbecued as I dumped my bike on the driveway at the address I'd scribbled in my notebook, and my knackered body interpreted this aroma as permission to shut down entirely, even before John and Sophie had answered their door. It was nine in the evening, the last dregs of light draining from a clear sky, the silhouette of Mont Blanc tipped red on the western horizon.

I'd met the couple the previous winter in the French Alps, where I'd found a seasonal job as a chalet girl (part of that pledge I'd made to explore my options). Although it had been the worst ski-season in living memory – the snow so bad that farmers had been hired to shovel snow out of the forests and onto the ski-runs – I had hit it off with the couple and their two teenage kids, who had driven over for the week from their home on the other side of Lake Geneva, and I'd told them of my emerging plans to pedal the globe.

They had expressed huge support for the idea, as they would, having been born at just the right time to follow the original hippie trail from Europe to Kathmandu – which at the time, they said, was little more than a particularly aromatic Nepalese village.

A meat feast of hitherto-unseen proportions followed, then a night's sleep of a depth to rival the dead. And the following morning, the three of us gathered around the computer screen in order to watch the first public rendition of our unfolding escapades – episode one of the Ride Earth video series. Excitedly I loaded up the video, turned up the speaker volume, and hit the play button.

What followed was fourteen minutes of hilarity and disbelief. The skill with which the producers had sliced up our shoddy material and tied it all together with their own professional footage was staggering. For the first time in my life, I watched Tom Allen emerge into life on the screen as a fully formed character; my very own alter ego of pixels and video clips, complete with quirks and mannerisms I never knew I had. I sat between my two friends, stunned by the helpless realisation that *this* was how our everyday behaviour and speech looked and sounded to the world at large. Having summarised our backgrounds and our high-minded mission with laudable precision, the video ended on a dramatic post-departure note – a shot of me, easing myself over the edge of a low wall in Cambridgeshire in order to cool off my feet in a stream, edited cliffhanger-style to look as if I was about to plummet to my death. The title music played, and the episode wound up with the production company logo. We all stared speechlessly at the screen.

'Yes!' I cried, regaining my tongue.

'It's like you've fallen down a ravine!' said Andy.

'More please!' laughed Mark.

There was a long pause as we digested the fact that anyone with an Internet connection would shortly be able to watch what we had seen.

'I sound like a gibbering idiot,' said Andy, 'but . . .'

'What a massive relief!' I interrupted. 'It's actually taken a huge weight off my shoulders, watching that.'

'I'm slightly disappointed that they haven't included much from the journey to Harwich.' said Mark.

'That'll be in the next episode, won't it?'

'Yeah, that'll be in the next film.'

'I definitely sound like a dribbling maniac,' put in Andy again. The filmmakers had pulled together all of Andy's absurdities, stitching them together into a montage that summed him up – I thought – rather well. But I suspected he was having doubts about how it looked.

'We all seem really different,' said Mark. 'I think that works. It'll work to keep people interested.'

Mark had a storyteller's eye, and he was right. The video had done a brilliant job of establishing the protagonists of the story, their quirks and the manner of their interplay. The eccentric, athletic artist (Andy); the impassioned, hard-headed perfectionist (me); and the well-read, warm-natured eco-warrior (Mark) would be thrown together under the most intense of circumstances: a life on the road; a kind of three-way marriage that would encompass every waking hour of their lives. Sparks, surely, would fly. And that was the kind of stuff that TV producers would sell their own body-parts for.

'Well!'

'Indeed.'

'Crikey . . . it's really happening.'

Riding through endless valleys and alpine towns, leaping into lakes of crystal clarity, grinding up smoothly paved bicycle trails and swooping down from forested passes – crossing Switzerland was the very dream of bicycle travel, and with our well-oiled feeding-and-navigating machine in motion there was plenty of time for a mind to wander. In fact, there was more than mine knew what to do with.

My inner-monologue chattered incessantly, like a radio that wouldn't switch off. It began seconds after I opened my eyes, continued throughout the day, and invaded my fevered dreams. I dearly wished to pedal carefree, lapping up these sumptuous days in lands of green and plenty. But thoughts had been gathering, like dust in the attic.

The life I'd lived before had seduced my waking hours with as much *stuff* as possible, as much value-for-life as I could gather. Squeezing the last drop out of each and every minute had become my reason for living – the cause of those overly complicated route plans and obsessive attention to detail. But the result was a brain that could not sit still; a backlog of competing questions that had never had the time to duke it out. And now the fighting had begun. It was as if, by choosing to live life in a bicycle saddle, I'd been awakened from a kind of hypnosis, and the task of mentoring myself back into consciousness had been forced upon me. But I didn't want to hear these new things that I had to say.

'Would you please very kindly shut up?' I begged the voice in my head.

'Just getting started,' came the reply. Then it yammered

on about political questions I couldn't answer, foreign languages I'd failed to learn, philosophical conundrums I couldn't untie, past relationships I'd forgotten to nurture, the absurd and inconsequential brevity of my life thus far, the billion things I could be doing other than riding a bicycle; each topic chewed into mush before being spat back out into my skull. I wanted nothing more than to watch the flash and dazzle of sunlight on a waterway. Instead, the spectacle became no more than a backdrop for an internal shouting match.

'Please, for the love of god – just *shut up!!!*'

Out of the clamour rose a single realisation. I'd been half-asleep for twenty-four years, stumbling frantically forward, never stopping to look back. My world had been extrapolated from what I'd seen on flashing screens and newsprint – views of other people's creation, chosen for me by merit of their grabbing my attention first.

Mirella had been anything but an evangelist, but she'd told her tale with enough skill to keep me thinking for long after our encounter, prompting some uncomfortable questions. If reaching Istanbul, for example, was our primary goal, there was clearly a number of much faster, easier, and better ways to get there. That was why cars, trains, buses and planes had been invented – to get people places faster, easier, better. Since we'd chosen not to reach Istanbul by car, train, bus, plane or any other sensible mode of transport, then, our main objective must be something *other* than getting to our destination. And that 'something' was obviously worth investigating. Except that I didn't quite know what it was.

As we cleared the Central European Alps and followed the mighty River Danube east into Austria, two possibilities seemed to appear. The first was that I was taking on an epic challenge in order to prove something outwardly to the world. The second was that I was doing this for altogether more self-absorbed reasons – reasons which lurked in deeper shadows that I had not yet penetrated.

Panoramic thoughts drifted across the scenery. Was destination-focused travel a symptom of some deeper trait? Why did we value quantifiable achievements over unmeasurable personal growth? Was I born to forever chase after distant goals?

These thoughts made me uncomfortable. So I did what my stubbornness had always allowed me to do: alternately bludgeoning and ignoring them until they fell quiet.

Central Europe in August was green and lush and with harvest on the breeze. Refreshed by a break in Vienna, we were soon passing out of Austria and through a small corner of Slovakia, where we paused in a downtown Bratislava park for an enjoyable afternoon of watching girls go by. Balmy weather was set in, and we were more concerned with mosquitoes and heat rash than heavy rain or mountains. And the girls were stupendous. So stupendous, in fact, that they were too distracted by each other's stupendousness to notice us at all.

Into Hungary we rode. Gentle rivers meandered through bustling little towns, hot springs on their fringes, full of bathers enjoying nature's brand of health spa. We had never made such excellent progress. At this rate, we would be in Istanbul well in time for the last days of summer.

As I sat contentedly on a bench in the shade with a hunk of bread and cheese, looking out across the River Danube, my friend Mark stumbled out of a nearby bush.

'Mate, I need to get to the nearest airport.'

'What?'

'I've got to get to an airport.'

'Really?'

'Yes. Right now.'

'There's probably a toilet nearby if you just ask someone . . . ?'

I looked at him, confused. But then I saw it in his face: a whole train of thoughts condensed into a single, decisive expression. Mark was leaving Ride Earth.

He turned and trudged back to his lunchtime resting spot under a tree, river-bank shingle crunching beneath heavy footfalls, dappled sunlight stroking his new mop of hair. A mobile phone rested loosely in his hand.

Alone on the bench with my half-eaten bread and cheese, I fumed. *The girlfriend*. We'd been on this mission together for only ten weeks! What the hell had happened to the Istanbul idea?

Mark shuffled dejectedly around under the tree, fiddling with the phone with one hand, rubbing his head with the other, producing a series of dramatic-sounding sighs. There would be no convincing him to stay. On the odd occasion that did he make a big decision, it was invariably final – even if it made no bloody sense at all.

We packed up and found our way to the town's little railway station. Not only was Mark about to jet off back to flipping England, but we were about to skip a hundred miles of riding on a train to help him do it! I forced myself to keep my mouth firmly shut. And the following day, Mark loaded his bike and bags into the back of a taxi, and with a goodbye and a handshake he disappeared. I watched the cloud of dust evaporate between the gardens and cottages of the suburb where we were supposed to be staying. Staying as a *team*.

Mark had dropped everything and flown home to patch up his increasingly strained relationship. I spent the rest of the day raging to Andy about the manner of his departure and the decision he had made. I'd been extremely pleased with the way the project was going: even though a few superficial details had changed – our route had evolved, our progress had been more halting, and we'd done a lot less off-road riding than we'd imagined – there were good reasons for this. The dirt roads weren't far off now: Hungary was the bridge to Eastern Europe and the developing world. We'd soon be back on track.

And none of these minor digressions undermined the public messages we were trying to put across through our website and media coverage. We were still on target for an impressive bicycle-powered circumnavigation of the world. Part of this was our ongoing commitment to undertaking the entire trip without flying, to promote the idea of world travel with an environmental conscience. We'd even hooked up with a big environmental organisation to collect anecdotal evidence for the effects of climate change.

Later that night, I scribbled an entry in my diary.

'I have lost a significant amount of respect for Mark over his decision to fly home. Everyone has a better reason than the environment to take a plane, and his was no different. Irrational forces dominate once again.'

Andy was never going to quit. He was as stubborn as I was, and while this was often a source of friction, it also inspired a kind of silent competition when the going got tough. And that, I knew, would pull us through times which might otherwise defeat us.

But that Mark – free-riding, noncommittal Mark – had waltzed onto a short-haul flight at the drop of a hat, undermining the important anti-airline message we'd worked so hard to promote for the sake of a *girl*?

I sat down the next day and sent him a blunt email expressing my disgust. His reply merely stoked the fire.

'I was following my heart, something you are doing, and I don't blame you for it. You don't exactly have the best track record for understanding other people's thoughts, wishes and emotions, Tom, so your reactions have not surprised me. What *has* surprised me is your incredible lack of empathy regarding my decision under emotional circumstances, plus the extreme lashing I am receiving for apparently breaking one of the "Ride Earth Commandments".'

I haven't seen or heard from Mark since then. And it occurs to me that I never truly took my old friend seriously. Time off the bike to recover my strength in Sudan gives me plenty of room for retrospection, and it comes flavoured equally with nostalgia and regret.

I remember the way Mark began his email. 'Dear Ride Earth Dictator,' he'd said. Now I admire his self-restraint. 'Dear obnoxious, self-important prick' would have been far more appropriate.

CHAPTER 5

One of Wawa's elders arrives to share a meal with me and my hosts. The meal waltzes into the room on a metal tray balanced on a small boy's head. It contains dishes of stewed beans with cumin, lemon, onion, hot pepper and oil; bowls of green bean and tomato stew; a kind of bread rather like a huge, thick and dense pancake; and another thinner bread like a crepe. In typical Middle Eastern style, the bread serves a dual purpose as cutlery, and we sit on the floor in a circle around the tray, digging dollops of stew from the bowls with segments of bread folded into miniature edible shovels. Pasta arrives as a late addition to the spread – having no cultural compass for the dried macaroni recently brought in by the village store, our mystery chef has boiled it up with sugar and served it as a dessert!

After the meal, the white-haired Nubian tries to explain something to me, pointing to my stomach, but I cannot understand what he means. Everyone scrabbles around for a way of being understood, and quickly Nashradeen remembers the English word:

'Doctor!'

He points at the old man.

'Doctor?' I reply. 'Oh . . . good?'

This must have been taken as an agreement, because a mood of preparation suddenly sweeps over the room. The tray is taken away and a chair is located for me to sit on. I'm told to roll up my trousers, and while I do so the doctor hands a banknote and an instruction to the tray-bearing child, stands up and goes outside. I hear running water and hands being washed. The boy dashes off, returning a few minutes later with the change and a tiny shrink-wrapped package. As the doctor unwraps the little box in front of me, I realise that whatever I have agreed to involves a packet of razorblades.

Without a moment's hesitation, the doctor removes the folded paper wrapping from a shiny sliver of metal and begins to calmly slash at my legs. I barely register what's happening until I notice the blood, because there is no pain. But the blood is definitely coming now. With practised strokes, gentle but firm, the old man crosshatches my calves with fine red lines, giving the muscles a good squeeze to get the blood flowing. I flit from horror to bewilderment to amusement in a matter of seconds, ashamed to admit that the word 'AIDS' flashes before my eyes, despite the fact that the razors are new, and the villagers are trying to heal my illness, not to hurt me. It's as if the great incurable disease is tattooed across Africa's forehead, so that I can't think of one without the other coming to mind. This bloodletting might cure my stomach, but it also reminds me that I might still harbour a few unhealthy stereotypes.

The events of the day also serve to remind me of the line that I can never cross. It's the line between what I can communicate and what I want to express. Were I able to speak Arabic or Nubian, there would be so much to tell these people. I'd be able to point out the funny mix-up with the pasta. I'd be able to ask them all the questions I have about the way things are in this village. I'd be able to find out what they make of the country's politics. And I'd be able to answer questions about myself, about where I came from, what it was like to live in England, why I ended up in Africa instead of India or Australia. I'd be able to tell them about the girl whose photo I keep in my diary, and about the other times I got sick and why it seemed so much more difficult to deal with – why so much weight seemed attached to those very human attributes of weakness and mortality.

It had started, in fact, as early as Vienna, as we'd followed the last traces of the Danube Cycleway. The pain, a nagging twinge of discomfort, originated somewhere under the top edge of my right kneecap, and accompanied each pedal stroke, starting as a tiny sensation but deepening until I could think of little else. The health of my body was critical to the journey. And this was not just an ache of tiredness.

I ignored it. I didn't mention it. Stubbornness cured everything. The pain subsided with Mark's departure, and after a few days of rest in Budapest I struck forth with Andy towards Romania. We hadn't even made it beyond the city limits before the pain resurfaced, worse than before, each pedal stroke more and more agonising until I had no choice but to stop. I sat on the roadside beneath a gigantic billboard. Traffic barged past as I held my head in my hands, gutted by the realisation that this was probably the beginning of a significant amount of time off the bike, and – as much as I detested the idea – I should probably find a doctor.

Our host, Laszlo, was sympathetic.

'You guys can stay here as long as you like,' he said. 'Don't feel that you should hurry to leave. I'm going to be away for the winter, but I'd happily leave you guys to look after The Place for a few months while I'm gone. You're the kind of travellers I know I can trust with something like that.'

Just when we needed it most – the offer of a place to live in the outlying suburbs of Budapest; no rent, no fuss, no expectations other than to look after the place and take responsibility for ourselves while we were there. I'd known Laszlo less than a week, but he didn't attach much importance to the idea of carefully building trust, preferring to assume everyone equally good at heart. Leaving his home permanently open, key in door and welcome note on the table, was testament enough to that.

Laszlo was a member of a movement called Couchsurfing; an Internet-based hospitality exchange network that already spanned the globe and was growing in popularity. The website took the idea of relying on the hospitality of complete strangers and formalised the process, rather than leaving it up to chance. We'd heard about it back in Vienna, and I'd thought the idea revolutionary. A quick search for hosts in Budapest had turned up a man who lived in a yurt with his turtles, and seemed to have an unending stream of recommendations from other Couchsurfers who'd stayed there on their way through Eastern Europe. And so we'd found ourselves navigating the backstreets of suburbia in the dead of night, the resident guard dog population a frenzy of surround-sound barking, and we'd eventually found the famous yurt-dwelling Hungarian entertaining a group of sleepy travellers around a campfire on the lawn. Flopping down by the fire, he'd handed each of us a piece of salted pig fat on the end of a stick.

'Welcome to The Place, guys.'

And he'd continued telling the story while we'd toasted the delicious fat over the glowing embers, catching the dripping grease with hunks of bread.

'Aren't you worried that people might steal things?' I'd asked the next day.

'The way I see it,' he'd explained, 'if someone takes something from here, they must need it – otherwise why would they take it? And who am I to argue if somebody needs something? They'll probably make just as good use of that thing as me.'

His possessions were thin on the ground – a shelf full of books on philosophy and climbing and little-known cultures, an old computer in the corner, a few pans, and a Mongolian yurt full of Buddhist ornaments which could hardly be a particularly big target for the criminal masterminds of Budapest. Laszlo seemed to live as a traveller in his own home; owning only the bare essentials, sharing his life with others and encouraging them to do the same with him, embracing whatever might come of it. On the odd occasion when he did need some money, he simply found large corporate sponsors to fund high-profile attempts on the summits of the world's highest peaks. He was, after all, one of Hungary's foremost high-altitude mountaineers.

I'd never considered that the traveller's approach might be applied to a more stable existence. I hadn't realised that life could consist of anything other than either an unhealthy amount of work interspersed with brief periods of free time (like everyone I knew back home) or a lengthy escape abroad with a bit of cash in the bank (like me and Andy). Yet here was a man for whom time was the only real currency; an asset of immeasurable value, to invest carefully and wisely.

I made a foray into the city centre carrying a cardboard box which contained everything that hadn't passed the usefulness test: the so-called waterproof socks, my heavy watch, hiking maps for most of Western Europe, a handbook entitled *Pocket Mountain-Bike Maintenance*. Then I bit the bullet and paid an expensive visit to a knee specialist at a sports-injury clinic that Laszlo had recommended. I explained my new lifestyle to the doctor as he pushed and pulled at the tender joint.

'It's almost definitely an overuse injury,' he said, finally. 'The cartilage under the kneecap has been worn down by repetitive movement. So if you're cycling every day, the first thing I would do is to look at your riding position – the height of your saddle, the angle of your pedals. If some-thing's out of alignment, it'll be magnified by repetitive exercise.'

'Right . . .'

'I'm going to give you something to help the cartilage regrow. It's a powder, so you'll need to mix it with water and drink it once a day. And, of course, you'll need to rest.'

'How long for?' I asked, expecting the worst.

'Oh – two weeks, at least. Maybe three.'

Summer lingered on, so being stuck with Laszlo was hardly a chore. Travellers came and went, and as two weeks approached we all decided that a night on the town was in order. In a rooftop bar, accessible only by a hair-raising elevator ride through the innards of a dingy socialist-era city block, I met Maria and Magalie, two rosy-cheeked backpackers who were supposed to be returning with us to Laszlo's place. They were curious to know how we'd got there, and I prepared myself for another round of predictable questions.

'You're cycling?!' exclaimed Magalie. 'Oh my god . . .'

And her distinctive South London twang brought a flood of nostalgia, reminding me how long it had been since I'd heard anyone other than Mark and Andy speak with a colloquial English accent.

'That actually sounds like really good fun!' joined in Maria. 'And I thought *we* were being adventurous, hitching around Europe . . .'

'Yeah, well, cycling's pretty cool,' I told them. Then – why not? – 'Maybe you should give it a try?'

'Yeah, right – I would *never* be able to do that!'

'I think you would, actually,' I said, the beer adding to my conviction.

'Oh, come on. Look at us!'

'Yeah, you'd be fine – all you need is a bike. You've got your other stuff, right?'

'Mmm . . . I think I'll stick to backpacking! But . . . oh my god, I'm actually tempted . . . Maria, what d'you reckon?'

A sizeable quantity of beer later, Maria and Magalie were making plans to come with us. It would make far more sense than train-hopping around Eastern Europe. Where was the fun in that? Missing out on all the good bits? Sleeping in expensive hostels and paying through the nose for city attractions every day? Cycling was as easy as pie – heck, if these two jokers could do it, anyone could! Why not give it a go?

What had I done?

The next morning, the four of us walked a couple of blocks from Laszlo's to the local scrap-yard where we unearthed a large pile of vintage city bikes. Andy cast his eye over them and selected two. At the same time, I noticed a full-size adult scooter with big bicycle-sized wheels and a solid platform on which to stand whilst pushing the contraption along. If my knee injury resurfaced again, I decided, I would buy the second-hand scooter and continue my journey alone, making the first known transcontinental scooter journey in the process. But my knee had felt much better during the last week, and I decided that the time was ripe to give cycling another go.

We paid thirty euros for the bikes, took them back to the yurt, and the girls went off to the station to cash in their remaining train tickets. The horizon opened up once again, and the story took on a new tint: Ride Earth, new and improved, was back on the road.

September began with all the warmth of summer, but threatened to end with a chill in the air. Looking at a map, I traced a simple route across another couple of borders and down to a narrow isthmus of land broken by a thin strait – the Bosphorus. Strange that such a narrow stretch of water could delineate the edge of a continent. Labelled Istanbul, this spit of land was still just about the most otherworldly sounding place I could imagine. Crossing the suspension bridge to its Eastern Quarter would mark our arrival, by bicycle, into Asia.

I had two good excuses to take it slowly on my first day back on the road: not just to protect my knee, but because we would be a group of five. Sally, another young English traveller staying with Laszlo, had heard about Maria and Magalie's defection from the backpacking camp and hit the scrap-yard herself with less than twenty-four hours to go until we were due to leave. The girls were all excited, and it was infectious. Wobbling down the road away from Laszlo's goodbyes, bells a-tinkling and horns a-honking, there was a definite sense of overture to the departure. This was the furthest east I'd ever travelled. Mark had quit, and in his place was a gaggle of complete novices, and we were intensely conscious of our responsibilities to them. New territory lay ahead, and the thrill of the unknown rose up again.

We set out along flat, straight, drizzly back-roads across the Hungarian Great Plains, once an ocean floor, like the English Fens. But the dull weather had no effect on the spirit of adventure that burned within our new group. Sally rode just ahead of me on a single-speed town bike, complete with basket, her waterproof flapping. In my rear-view mirror, the dynamo light of Maria's granny bike caught my eye. Behind her was Magalie, who had cut a banner from a sheet of cardboard and illustrated it crudely: two bearded stick-men and two smiling girls pedalling cartoon bikes away from a yurt, the ponytailed figure of Laszlo waving them off on their journey towards 'The World', as depicted on a road sign. Andy, meanwhile, was bringing up the rear of the group, swinging the video camera low for an on-the-road shot of the group's first day of riding, and serving as a very visible warning to approaching traffic that there was something unusual on the road ahead.

In the early weeks of the trip, when tempers had been running high, I had worried about the moment of Mark's departure – of setting out with Andy alone. But we'd already had enough trivial clashes for us both to have grown sick of them, and the presence of impressionable females put paid to any more arguments. Life on the road, I hoped, would be just as fun as I'd promised them.

Sally, an athletic and strong-willed character, only planned to ride with us for a day. The following morning, after sharing one of our two tents with Maria and Magalie, she rode back to Budapest, picked up the belongings she'd left there, and pedalled furiously on her single-geared wreck of a bike to Slovenia, two hundred miles away. Spending her nights outside on the bare earth in a sleeping-bag from Tesco, pedalling with neither route nor schedule come rain or shine, her brief adventure felt far more raw and spontaneous than mine, and I felt a sudden pang of jealousy.

The weather improved, and as a group of four we enjoyed a few memorable days of carefree nomadism, wandering on our bicycles through Hungary's backwaters. We experienced impromptu hospitality, the joy of making sense to strangers out of charades and scribbles and dog-eared dictionaries, and more fresh air and exercise than we'd have got for years had we stayed at home. I slept beneath the stars, rather than in my tent, and there was no shortage of riverbanks and meadows in which to make ourselves at home. The girls sang and joked with us as we rode, and no hint of romance threatened to complicate the arrangement. But only a few days passed before Magalie received news that she'd have to go to France for a wedding, and we waved her off on the train amid promises that she'd be back for more adventures in a couple of weeks' time.

Andy, Maria and I rode seventy miles the next day – an unprecedented distance – to the Romanian frontier. We would begin this next stage of our journey as a group of three. So content had we become with basking in the end days of the Hungarian summer that the events on the far side of the border came as a kick in the teeth.

CHAPTER 6

A deafening explosion of white illuminated the world like a photograph: I was passing the rear end of a cow. The muddy backside vanished and was replaced with that noise of scrambled colour you get after a flashbulb in the face, quickly dissolving into utter blackness.

Rain lashed down; a million watery bullets pounding my poncho; squelching footsteps rendered inaudible by the roar. Through the wall of water I picked out the distant red dots of the police car. And I trudged forwards into the darkness, putting one foot in front of the other in a string of individual acts of faith.

I'd spotted Andy some way ahead. Maria, I guessed, was following me, though it was impossible to know for sure. My head-torch from Lidl, presented with the sudden opportunity to demonstrate its vigour, had instead chosen to die. Rivers of rainwater ran down my neck, and I made a mental note to pay a personal visit to the British Army's poncho-design department upon my return to England. I stumbled into a ditch, then leapt out of range of a guard dog that flung itself at me from the blackness, before strangling itself on its own chain.

The tail-lights reappeared through the rain, slightly to the right of where I'd been heading. *God damn it.* How the hell had they even found us? The track we'd followed on our map had seemed normal enough. Just another Hungarian country lane, we'd thought, except that it happened to end up in Romania, which suited us perfectly, because Romania was where we were going. Of course, there *had* been those big metal barriers painted in the blue, yellow and red of the Romanian flag. And the first villagers we'd met *had* kind of shouted a lot and pointed back the way we'd come. But this was the EU, where border crossings no longer existed – right?

I arrived sopping and cold to find two police vans sat wonkily in the mud along with more cars and more flashing lights. Andy was loudly making fun of the situation in exaggerated Queen's English amid a horde of Romanian policemen who couldn't have had the foggiest idea what he was talking about. But it seemed like a good tactic – play the foreign idiot, keep smiling and hope for the best. I tried to follow suit, failing of course to be anywhere near as amusing.

Then I saw that Maria was already inside one of the vans! When had she overtaken me? I was utterly disorientated. After more shouting and standing around and more radio calls, Andy and I were ordered to deposit our belongings in the back of one van and to climb aboard the other with Maria. This resulted in endless fussing with trailers and bags and clips and straps and mud in the dark and pouring rain, the damp, impatient policemen growing more damp and impatient by the minute. Nobody would explain anything. The other van lurched away, taking all of our worldly possessions with it. Finally our own van bundled off into the night, the windows steamed up and any attempt to keep our bearings became totally futile. After cycling for seventy miles, we were now soaked, frozen, starving and being carted off back to Hungary by the Romanian police. There was little left to do but laugh in despair. I dearly hoped that we wouldn't be locked up. That would be another massive blow for Ride Earth.

The three of us sat, clothes dripping and eyelids drooping, in the dimly lit waiting room of the border post, which had existed after all. Between snatches of sleep on the world's most uncomfortable wooden benches, we were shouted at by a succession of increasingly angry immigration officials whose job it was to keep us awake, miserable and confused. After an eternity in red-eyed limbo, we were given back our belongings and frog-marched out of Romania and to the Hungarian side of the border. Had we been deported? And if so, where were we supposed to go now, at god-knows-o'clock, and in the wrong country?

The Hungarian border guards glanced at our passports, gave them back to us and told us that we were free to turn around, leave Hungary for a second time, and proceed into Romania.

The Romanian border guards scrutinised the passports closely, silently, followed by a prolonged period of page-flicking and re-flicking. We waited. I fantasised about sleeping on the world's most uncomfortable wooden benches.

All of a sudden, drawers opened. Arms moved. Then came a moment of deepest possible significance.

A rubber stamp landed on an empty page of Maria's passport. *What had she done to deserve this honour?*

The documents were thrust through the small gap in the window, together with a smirk of derision.

'Velcome to Romania!'

The rain still hadn't stopped when dawn broke, exposing the

same dark clouds and pot-holed thoroughfares that had welcomed us into the country. The heady days of good living under the summer sun now seemed like a distant memory. Grim faces drifted along broken pavements, eyeing us suspiciously as we cooked breakfast in a dilapidated bus shelter and washed up in a puddle.

Although occupied by our present misfortunes, I was dimly aware that the proving grounds were coming to an end. My bike and I had survived an important test in making it this far. This was my first ever long-distance bicycle journey, and despite the relatively merciful experience I'd had until now, the learning curve had still been steep. Poised on the brink of Western Europe, I had hoped that it would begin to flatten out. Romania, though, seemed to have other ideas.

For the next few days our bedraggled trio rode through bleak plains, weaving around gigantic craters in narrow asphalt lanes, pressing on through the dreary nothingness for lack of any other option. A cloaked figure drifted through the drizzle, crook in hand, vaguely attached to a distant flock of sheep. The eastern horizon ahead, long, inexpressive and featureless, began to bubble with suggestions of approaching uplands, which lifted my rain-drenched spirits. While passing through the Alps, I'd felt a humbling sense of smallness amongst the pillars of rock and earth and ice. We are sometimes confronted with a thing infinitely more vast and powerful than ourselves: an impenetrable mountain range, a frothing ocean, a furious lightning storm. We're given the chance to look upon it, to exist quietly in its presence, and to be ignored; reminded viscerally of our own insignificance.

The rain subsided and a beam of late afternoon sunlight

came through the clouds ahead. We took off up a hillside track and made camp in wiry yellow grass on the valley's northern slopes to take stock of the previous days. Things here seemed rough around the edges, incomplete and uncared for; beaten, weary and stripped of dignity. Roads crumbled beneath the wheels of spluttering Ladas and donkey-drawn carts, weaved through villages constructed in an age of fervent uniformity, now barely holding themselves together. Dogs, pigs and chickens roamed the muddy streets freely; grass and weeds sprouted from cracks and gutters and foundations. Abandoned shelters, factories and warehouses of unknowable purpose littered the landscape away from the villages, mostly empty but a few now serving as makeshift shelters for herds and their drivers. I felt the presence of something ambitious, some enormous thrust of progress that had long since withdrawn, leaving its remnants and its people forgotten and decaying, and I wondered what memories these fading edifices held for those who might have seen them proud and gleaming, as they were in their heyday.

Desperate for shelter from the rain one evening, we spotted a little concrete platform in the middle of a grassy pasture at the bottom of the valley through which we were cycling. It was open-sided, had a little tin roof supported by a metal pole at each corner, and was about fifteen feet square. It would make an ideal place to build a fire, dry out a few belongings, and sleep in relative shelter.

Dumping our bikes, we clambered onto the raised platform and stood under the roof, looking out at the surrounding hillsides. The place immediately felt like home. There was a kind of intuition at work here that I'd felt time and time again: a sudden feeling of certainty that *this* was the place. We would pass the night in safety here. The spot might not look particularly different from any other – at least, not in a way that I could identify. But the feeling, one of immediate relief and relaxation, was palpable and welcome.

Without hesitation, Maria took a head-torch and set off across the pasture to where the river would be, venturing into the thin row of trees in the hope of finding firewood.

'Funny, isn't it?' I said to Andy, who was tying a length of string between two of the roof supports to create a drying line for our sodden clothes. 'It's like – someone says they're going to cycle round the world, and you think it means they're going to get on a bike and pump away until their legs fall off and then come home victorious. But it's not actually like that – it's not about how many miles you can do, or how fit you are.'

'Yeah. I'm really impressed with Maria.'

'Yeah, me too! And look at this place. It's so quiet. This is what it's all about.'

While I fired up our little petrol-powered stove to boil up some pasta, Andy built a fire with the damp wood, and soon we were sitting on the concrete, staring into the heart of the blaze, entranced by the flames as the world about us faded away. Soon the glowing embers were all that could be seen, throwing a dim orange cast across Andy and Maria's faces, the fire's remnants reflected in their eyes as tiny points of light. Our damp shoes sat in a row, steaming, silent additions to the campfire audience; the reeking wood smoke collecting below the roof before dissolving into the night.

'I feel like we should have some kind of story-telling thing, or something,' I said, to the fire.

'Go on then, mate. Tell us a story!' replied Andy.

'I'm not going first! I'm no good at stories . . .'

'You tell us a story then, Maria.'

She squirmed. 'Really . . . ?'

'Yeah, you can do it! Tell us something we don't know about you.'

'OK . . . er . . . well, I used to be a waitress in New York. I can tell you about that.'

'New York? What were you doing there?'

'Well, I got kicked out of England after I finished college – I went to college in London with Magalie, that's how we know each other –'

'Hold on – how did you get kicked out of the UK? You're English, aren't you?'

'Well, yes, I am! I mean, I was born there, I mostly grew up there, and I went to school there . . . but because my parents are both American, and they didn't do the right paperwork when I was born, I got to the age of eighteen – I was supposed to get my own passport, and it turned into this . . . this nightmare situation . . . I ended up in court, and the judge was like, "I can't quite believe this, but for some reason the law is finding against you, and there's nothing I can do . . ." – and they ordered me to leave the UK!'

'Seriously . . . ?'

'Bloody hell.'

'So I thought – well, I've got nothing to lose, I might as well go to America and start a new life there. So I got jobs waitressing and behind bars – they didn't actually pay me a penny, everything I earned was in tips – that's how it works in the US . . . but I didn't really enjoy it, and one day I was on the phone to Magalie, and she said the same thing about her job . . . so we both decided to quit our jobs and spend the summer travelling around Europe. And that's how we ended up in Budapest!'

'So . . . you actually have an American passport, then?' The border-crossing fiasco was starting to make sense.

'Yeah, I do.'

'No way! Go on, let's see it!'

Maria dug through her backpack and pulled out the navy blue booklet. Emblazoned across the front cover in gold script were the words 'United States of America'. How absurd, I thought, that the particulars of your little coloured booklet could so powerfully affect your options in life; where you could go, and how you'd be treated when you got there.

'But it really made me think about what I'd got. I have friends in the UK, obviously; friends in Switzerland – family, too – and in the US, and I speak French and Spanish . . . so now it's really nice to feel comfortable moving around, but still having all of these ties in different places. It's a really nice balance.'

Our route bent south-east towards the far end of Europe, and the weather settled into a pattern. Night-time and morning rains gave way to breaking clouds and the first rays of sunlight by lunchtime, followed by pleasantly warm afternoons. Mornings were a struggle of trying to motivate ourselves to begin the days' riding; they brought a dampness and a chill we'd not previously felt: the damp and chill of autumn. I was now sharing my tent with Maria, as Andy – through a campaign of weary sighs and 'clumsy' elbows in the night – had made it clear that he did not enjoy sharing his with me. The sound of rainfall on the taut flysheet always sounded far worse than it would prove to be when I finally hauled myself out, still stinking of the previous night's campfire. Turkey, which of course would be nice and warm, became an ever-more enticing prospect – and then of course there'd be Iran, which would obviously be baking hot. But two of south-east Europe's largest nations, Romania and Bulgaria, would need to be crossed first.

We followed valleys eastwards which, although tranquil, were riven with the same desperation I'd felt when we'd first entered the country. Commerce seemed non-existent; villages seemed to subsist off vegetable patches and scattered livestock, and their residents were packed three or four generations deep inside dilapidated houses and their wire-fenced compounds. A single grocery store carved out of a former sitting-room, shelves of meagre stock hidden behind counters, would constitute a village 'high street'. Tucked away down a side-street off the main thoroughfare might be a bakery, or a street-vendor selling watermelons or tomatoes out of a barrow.

On the scale of a globe, I was barely a finger's length from home, yet I found myself astounded by the ruin that I'd cycled into. Romania had recently been accepted for full membership of the European Union, and I'd somehow convinced myself that it must have made leaps and bounds forward from the days when images of orphanages filled our screens. That had been almost twenty years ago. But those with ambition had simply left the country to find a better life in the West – in Italy, Spain and further afield. I tried to imagine hundreds of thousands of Brits making the decision to pack their bags and flee the country, with no intention of ever returning, due to the political and economic climate. It was impossible to comprehend. Yet this was precisely what had happened here, and between four and twelve million Romanians now lived in the overseas diaspora, depending on whose definition of 'Romanian' you used. And this turmoil was all so close to home that I'd been able to cycle here from my own front door.

I tried my hand at approaching people, to ask for water or the whereabouts of a shop or Internet cafe. Though the Romanians were initially tough-mannered, often unsure quite what to make of our bizarre appearance, this attitude was easily dispelled with the usual tactic of an earnest smile and a bit of friendliness. We stuck to small back-roads, many unpaved, and one evening we were offered a patch of grass to camp on within the compound of a family home on the edge of a village. By the time Andy and I had scouted out their back garden for suitable spots, the old couple had become so enamoured with Maria – who had discovered that she could communicate through judicious use of Spanish – that they invited us inside their tiny two-roomed cottage, where we sat on ancient settees piled high with grubby patterned blankets and shared a delicious meal of salted pig fat with fresh tomatoes and chipped potatoes fried in lard. The sitting-room, such as it was, had been painted a loud turquoise; yellowing lace curtains were tacked to the splintering wooden window-frames; a tapestry of threadbare rugs skinned the floorboards while brown sheets of flypaper hung from above. A disproportionately grand old television set perched upon a cabinet, overlooking the low room, and the ancient matriarch switched it on when the conversation ran out of steam, filling the little room with the off-kilter brass and intricate percussion of Balkan pop, which we politely sat and watched for what seemed like hours.

As darkness fell outside, the rest of the family returned, smiling and curious – a young husband and wife, one of whom must have been the son or daughter of the old couple – and a handful of small boys who surreptitiously fiddled with the little moving bits on our bicycles and otherwise darted about in silence, clearly under orders to make themselves seen and not heard in the presence of guests. A hotchpotch of brick and mortar in one corner was identified as a stove – a *soba* – when a couple of logs were thrust inside and the door closed on a lit match, and a homely warmth began to permeate that little cottage in the hills. And we trotted out our well-practised charades, miming and foraging for words beneath the dim glow of a light bulb, as the region prepared to put to rest the harvest of another year.

CHAPTER 7

In Sebes, a dreary city of abandoned industry and loitering groups of men, we were due to be reunited with Magalie, and all of us – Maria in particular – were looking forward to the prospect immensely.

Needing somewhere to stay overnight while we waited for her arrival, and having found that the town's sole hotel was obscenely overpriced, Andy happened to get talking to a middle-aged man in a tatty leather jacket who was filling his car in nearby petrol-station. This gruff little man seemed to jump at the chance to have three desperate explorers stay the night in his home: another fantastic display of the great outpouring of hospitality that seemed to await the bicycle traveller.

Simon's wife fed us chicken risotto and prepared a makeshift bed on the floor of the living-room. A mangy dog trailed around behind her, looking forlorn. Simon was very accommodating, but – unusually – made no enquiries about our journey; neither where we'd come from nor where we were heading, which were by far the two most frequently asked questions. He seemed more interested in how much our collection of cameras and bicycles was worth. And the following morning, after his wife had taken Maria to meet Magalie at the station, Simon sat Andy and me down at the kitchen table and began to lay out his demands.

Now, an average Romanian's salary, explained Simon in a mixture of English and German and scribbles, was about one hundred and twenty euros a month. And a night in the hotel up the road, he repeated with solemnity, was a hundred euros. My heart was already sinking. I kept my mouth shut, my eyes on the scrap of paper and my face as blank as possible as Simon billed us the equivalent of two hundred euros in Romanian *lei* for the night we'd already stayed and for the second night that he had suggested we also spend in his home. This, after all, was the same as what we would have paid for the hotel.

I looked at Andy. 'What exactly are we supposed to do now?'

'I dunno, mate.'

'Well, we can't pay him two hundred euros. That's ridiculous. We don't even *have* two hundred euros.'

Which was true. I reached into my pocket, as the one responsible for food this week and thus the only one with any cash, and withdrew a bunch of fluff containing about sixteen euros' worth of lei. It was enough to feed the four of us for another couple of days.

'He's basically blackmailing us.'

'I know.'

Simon sat in silence, not understanding our deliberately colloquial English and looking intently at the bright pink of the wall across the room, elbows resting on the table, fingers interlocked and rocking gently back and forth in front of his mouth. Anger began to rise inside me. How dare this little man abuse our trust? How dare he take such extreme examples of cost and use them to justify landing us with this ludicrous bill? And how dare he destroy the trust I'd learnt to invest in strangers to help me on my way?!?

I picked up the pen and paper and tried to explain that my

daily budget was less than five euros per day, and that two hundred euros should last me several weeks, not two days; all the while drawing ridiculous scribbled pictures of globes and bicycles and calendars and annotating them incomprehensibly with calculations and sums of cash. When he stared blankly at me, I lost my patience and told him outright in English what I thought. The meaning was lost, but the tone said it all. I rose from my seat, followed by Andy, and we began packing our panniers as quickly as we could. I thrust the last handful of lei into Simon's hand – a modest amount, but still far more than our presence had cost him – carted my baggage outside into the muddy yard, and stood expectantly by the tall wooden gate, waiting for Maria and Magalie to return, to tell them the bad news: that we'd been conned, that we were getting the hell out of this dump *right now*. Softly, rain began to fall. Simon came down the little steps to the yard to plead with us to come back inside, was brushed off and so went inside himself and closed the door, came out again and resumed standing in the open doorway, looking out across the tangled sprawl of mud roads and yards and houses. The rain set in. And we all waited in this uncomfortable stalemate.

Poor Magalie: she'd been so enthusiastic about continuing her spontaneous bicycle adventure that she'd ridden trains all the way from France to Romania, somehow convincing guard after guard to let her on board with a bicycle in tow. She and Maria arrived back at our ex-host's house, opened the gate to find our sorry little huddle of ponchos and bikes sitting in the yard, expressions of doom written across our faces, and were suddenly given instructions to look sharp and get packing, half-washed laundry and all. The truth was that we hadn't had a day of rest since our stay in Budapest, which by now seemed to have taken place on another planet entirely.

Riding south from Sebes and into the foothills of the Fagaras range of the Transylvanian Alps, it became clear that we were entering a region of very sparse habitation, and 'real' wild camping – for the first time – began to look like our only option. We'd spied a network of tracks on a map of the country, and it had looked as though we'd be able to piece together an off-road route through the mountains, rather than rejoining the busy main road. This back-country route had looked remote and daunting, little evidence of settlements along the way, but we'd decided to make it the basis of a scenic detour. Now, kicked out into the rain, I could think of little but finding a spot within the alpine peaks to lay low for a couple of nights and get some much-needed rest, because the events of our first days in Romania – a new world for all of us – had been fraught and exhausting.

The sun reappeared from behind the rainclouds, only to disappear again as the valley sides rose high and steep above the little road. Traffic dried up, save for an occasional grumble from ahead and the appearance of a logging truck loaded with huge pine trunks for a timber mill back down the valley. These same pines clung to the higher reaches of the steep slopes all around us. In the well of this winding valley, our route traced the path of a narrow, fast-flowing river, and it became clear that we were gaining altitude. The air was clear, moist and deliciously cool as the climb began to make itself felt. I passed through a little hive of activity: a group of road-workers who were building the very road on which we had been riding for the last couple of hours. Amid the reek of hot tar and the surprised looks of the labourers, my front tyre rolled off the tarmac and onto the uneven gravel track that continued into the invisible depths of the mountains. A thrill passed through me; surely this was the kind of detour worth taking!

Andy stopped ahead of me and I did too while we waited for the girls to catch up. Standing in the shade, I swung my arms around to warm up, and – suddenly – accidentally flung off the beaded bracelet I'd worn since leaving home. It flew through the air and into the undergrowth. I ran after it, digging in vain through the foliage, but it could not be found.

I scrambled back out from the bushes. 'Damn it!'

'What?'

'I've just managed to lob my bracelet into oblivion!'

'Was it a special bracelet, or something?'

'Well . . . erm . . .'

The bracelet had been given to me by an ex-girlfriend. We'd been together for a few years – since university, in fact, where it had been easy enough to find ourselves heading in the same direction. But the relationship had been amongst the casualties of the Ride Earth idea. Along with a career, a salary and the expectations of my friends and family, my girlfriend had gradually been relegated to the world I wanted to leave behind, her relevance to my life dwindling beneath the magnitude of what I was planning to attempt. So self-involved had I become that I barely noticed it happening, and I should not have been surprised when, one weekend visit, she laid it bare to me: I clearly had better things to do than take our relationship seriously any more. I told her that was a load of bollocks;

she dropped me off at the railway station and then bought a Lonely Planet guidebook and a pile of expensive apparel and a one-way ticket to New Zealand; I returned home furious and continued laying my very important plans. She had, of course, been absolutely right: I'd forgotten her needs almost entirely as a result of taking myself too seriously. The bracelet's loss represented the last emotional tie I'd kept to my former life – apart from the presence of Andy himself, of course.

'. . . actually, you know what? It's probably for the best.'

The two girls eventually emerged round the bend, both on foot; Maria red in the face but smiling, Magalie sauntering casually beside her, cracking jokes. Magalie's new bike had twenty-one gears; Maria still rode the three-speed antique she'd found in the scrap-yard in Budapest, backpack strapped wonkily across the rear rack. Dressed in everyday summer clothes, happy to dismount and walk and laugh about it, they appeared to be perfectly normal people – two former schoolmates, a little older now, abroad for the summer, sharing the fun of a bike ride together. It was, I thought, almost *enviable* to be able to see it that simply. Because if they were serious about it for the long-term, they'd really need to equip themselves properly, as we had spent so long doing. It wouldn't be long now before paved roads, bike shops and outdoor equipment supplies receded into the distance, and they obviously couldn't continue in this carefree, haphazard way forever.

The day was drawing on, the air becoming chill, and we searched in vain for a concealed piece of ground where we could get our heads down for the night. Down in this narrow channel carved from the rock, it didn't look likely that we'd find the dream location we'd fantasised about all afternoon, and, as the light grew fainter, tensions began to rise.

I tried to remember how I used to think about accommodation. It was easier in so many ways. I would have decided where to go, researched hostels or hotels and made a booking, and then turned up on the appointed date, dumped my bags and followed a guidebook around for a while. Simple, predictable, safe. Fun. A break from something called 'the grind'. No chance of being lost deep in the Romanian mountains at sunset with nowhere to stay, no idea what might lie round the next bend.

Round the next bend was a village of Roma gypsies. Little roofs jutted half-hidden from the forested mountainside, high above the road to the east. On the far side of a little river, a dirt track ran parallel with our own, and lining the track was a jumbled row of walls and windows and fences and gates. Chickens pecked at the dust and dodged industrious women with brooms and baskets. Kids dashed and shouted. An untethered horse pawed at the ground and slurped from the stream. There wasn't a car to be seen, no sound of machinery; no indication that the industrial age had penetrated this remote backwater of Eastern Europe, which looked for all the world like a turn-of-the-century peasant village reconstructed for some trite period drama – save for a gigantic communist-era concrete bridge that spanned the stream.

Before we could decide whether to turn back or ride straight through we were surrounded by dozens of inquisitive faces, feet shuffling to get a better look, eyes peering out at us from beneath headscarves and dusty hats. Nerves bristling, I asked Andy what he thought we should do, but Maria and Magalie were already befriending the mob of kids who emerged from between adult hips and legs and began inspecting our curious means of transport with a flurry of fingers and thumbs. My bike, with its bulging cargo trailer, was far more interesting than I was. But neither Andy nor I was in the mood for a repeat of the previous night's extortion. We wanted to continue, to find a quiet spot and pitch our tents in peace and anonymity.

Then a young woman pushed her way through the growing crowd and introduced herself. She was around my age, somewhere in her early twenties; she carried a baby and spoke better English than anyone I'd yet met in Romania, and when we told her what we were doing and that we were looking for somewhere to camp she immediately invited us to follow her to her parents' home.

No . . . not again. I explained that we had no money and that we just wanted to camp. And at that moment, I realised with horror that it was absolutely true. I'd given my last lei to Simon, and in all of the fury and haste of escaping Sebes I had completely forgotten to withdraw any more cash. We faced a long, remote adventure through the Fagaras mountains without a penny to our names.

'Look at them, Tom!' implored Magalie. 'They don't want anything from us!'

Money was not important, the woman insisted. We were welcome to stay the night in this village. Neither she nor her parents wanted anything in return. They had everything they needed.

I was left with little choice but to let my reservations fall by the wayside. And I hoped that my faith in the kindness of strangers would, through these people, be rescued. Maria and Magalie were excitedly making their way down to the concrete bridge that looked so hopelessly out of place amongst the trees and dirt roads and timber-framed buildings. There was no backing out now.

The evening would be worthwhile, of course, and challenging, requiring mental energies that were difficult to muster after a day in the saddle. I would have to entertain the girl's effervescent father and her one-eyed mother, whose mouthful of gold teeth cut through the darkness of their tiny shelter. But this was also the point. It was why, now I'd tasted the thrill of the unknown, I could never go back to the pleasant blandness of pre-planned travel. Life would never again be so easy, so convenient, so predictable. I would forever relish not knowing what lay round the next bend.

Up through the pines, the scattered homes twirling wood-smoke into the sky were outnumbered by the abandoned ones; otherwise little sign of life existed in these eerie alpine wonderlands, the track gradually disintegrating until it was little more than a trail of rocks and scree, cut through with channels formed by heavy rainfall. We came out onto a plateau, the summit of the pass, and then the track pointed downhill.

I had almost forgotten how it felt to be freewheeling, so long had we pedalled perpetually upwards, and I was taken by surprise to find my wheels rolling without input. Suddenly the southern valley opened up, a sea of forested ridges and peaks extending to the horizon. I'd spent several days looking ahead at nothing but valley sides and the prospect of further climbs, and the sight of these endless, undulating lands produced a satisfaction that arriving here by car could never hope to reproduce. It was the most brilliant venue for lunch, and Andy, Maria, Magalie and I sat gobbling up the last of our scavenged food in the sun, looking out across the great expanse.

We'd found refuge the previous night in a small mountain lodge. The staff, taking pity on us, had fed us bean soup and given us a room to sleep in and a bundle of firewood for the stove. In the morning we'd raided the buffet laid out for the lodge's paying guests, leaving with several bags of cooked sausages, salami, bread and chunks of omelette. Munching the last fragments of egg at the highest point of this detour, which far outclassed Britain's highest peaks, the rewards now lay at our feet. Yes! And we swept down from on high, whooping with adrenaline, the bikes we'd built for precisely these conditions eating up the terrain as we sped through the untouched Carpathian forests. And, on a particularly tight bend, Maria's slender form was projected with Olympian grace over her handlebars to land in a blur of limbs on the gravel surface of the road.

'It's just a flesh wound,' joked Magalie, borrowing the words of Monty Python's Black Knight. Maria laughed. She was shaking with adrenaline, but her injuries seemed trivial, though there was quite a bit of blood on show. Miraculously, the clapped-out old bike had survived unscathed. Maria had been having so much fun on the downhill that she'd overestimated the control afforded by bald tyres on the loose surface – a beginner's mistake.

We stopped to patch the poor girl up on a wide piece of grass, strangely glad to have found a use for Andy's extensive first-aid supplies, which occupied almost an entire pannier.

Maria propped herself up on a convenient boulder, ably tended by Magalie, ever the optimist and joker. The valley drained out of the mountains, opening up as it did so, and there was a stream flowing nearby featuring a small and inviting waterfall. It was an opportunity too good to miss: I had lost track of how long it had been since I'd had a decent wash. Andy and I stripped down to our shorts and plunged beneath the torrent; it took all my strength just to remain standing beneath the icy bombardment.

The decision to take the mountain detour had hung in the air, as we'd worried that the higher passes would already be snowbound and impassable. But we'd been forced to take our chances after our unfortunate run-in with Simon. Escaping Sebes had taken precedence, and there had been no room to change our route or turn back. Now, heading back down from the silent magic of those mountains, it seemed absurd to think that there had been a real question over which option would be better: a few hundred miles of filthy motorway, sharing our journey with transcontinental freight lorries and badly-driven Ladas and four-by-fours; or an unpredictable adventure amid pristine wilderness and among people who would look after us, whose feet were planted firmly on the ground?

The detour had been a glimpse of my much-dreamed-of travelling fantasy. It would be easy to attribute it to chance, but the reality wasn't so simple. Chance could never have sprung if we hadn't put our trust in the mystery of what lay ahead. The result, I reckoned, had probably been the most memorable week of my life. Was this, in fact, the essence of adventure – something internal, intangible, impossible to describe in terms of routes and maps and schedules?

CHAPTER 8

The last time I'd looked at a map of Sudan, no road had been shown on the Nile's west bank. Nothing, it seemed, existed over there at all. But now I can see palm trees and foliage on that distant shore, just as over here. And anyway, I figure, the world needs trailblazers. For people to stop treating places and experiences as products to be consumed; to refuse to allow fear to dictate where they do and don't go.

I plan to make a small contribution to this campaign, and in order to do it I will spend the afternoon gathering intelligence in the small settlement of Faaka. This turns out to be most enjoyable, as it involves sitting in a little restaurant-hut for several hours, eating fried fish and chatting to anyone who wanders past.

'There is nothing over there,' says an Egyptian telecoms construction manager who pulls up in a pick-up truck. 'There is no boat to cross. It is a wild place. No people. For at least one hundred kilometres, there is just sand.' He laughs, clearly pleased to have put me off this ridiculous idea, and shows me pictures of his girlfriend's breasts on his mobile phone, expecting that as a European I will approve of his progressive sense of sexual liberality.

His supervisor, an engineer from Khartoum, disagrees. 'Well, it is beautiful over there,' he admits. 'There are a few people. Small villages . . .'

But he too seems to think I'm going to suffer riding a bicycle – or, more likely, pushing it through the sand for the next few days. The restaurateur appears with another huge platter of flour-coated fish steaks, lights a cigarette and fires up a small gas stove upon which is balanced a huge frying-pan full of oil. A wonderfully decorated old single-speed bike rests against the wall; someone's pride and joy, no doubt, but the owner decides not to show up. And I have heard enough to convince myself that I am going to travel the rest of the way to Dongola, the first decent-sized town on my route to Khartoum, on the opposite side of the Nile. I'm pretty sure it will beat another few days of dodging roadworks in the desert heat.

Mr Abud, a plump and ageing Nubian with a densely wrapped headscarf and a comical bug-eyed look, regards me with a mixture of curiosity and suspicion and eventually shrugs me off as a madman. He starts the outboard motor of his tiny wooden boat and we speed off towards the midstream of the broad green river, leaving Faaka far behind amongst the receding palms. With the wind lifting my matted hair and the river spray in my face, I think back over the day, and about the spontaneity I'm finding in travel, of the way I'm starting to say 'yes' when the chance comes to divert into entirely unknown waters.

Like all of the nations I've cycled through since I found myself alone, I have deliberately done as little research as possible about Sudan. If I know two pieces of essential information (how to get in, and how to get out again), that's all I want to know. I'm tired of the opinions I never chose to have, and I'm tired of being proved wrong, time after time after time. I don't want to arrive in a country I've never visited and expect to find myself in danger. I just want to arrive and to see what is put in front of my eyes. I don't want to know what someone else thinks the cheapest or cleanest hostel is, or where I can get the best street food in town. I want to find my own way, and whether I end up at the same place or not is irrelevant. And I don't want to know how old the ruins are that rise up from the sand, as impressive as Egypt's yet devoid of tourists. I want to wander around them in complete and utter ignorance, having stumbled across them by chance. I don't *care* whether or not I 'understand'. It's no longer important. It's not the point.

Mr Abud drifts away from the shore. I push my bike up the bank and through the palm trees, the buzz of his outboard motor receding behind me. Wandering through the undergrowth, I stumble across a faint trail and, following it, I find myself in the middle of a tiny hidden village in the sand, on the far side of the river's fringe of trees.

I stop amongst the buildings and honk my horn. The first Nubian to peer from a shady doorway gapes in disbelief; I wave and act out my sleeping-in-a-tent mime routine and, without a moment's hesitation, he welcomes me to camp under the tree outside his front door. The tree is infested with millions of tiny fruit flies, so I set up the tent with my eyes closed and run away from the swarms to see who I can find. Wandering amongst the brightly painted walls that sprout from the sand, I meet another man, who suggests that I sleep in the small mosque where the insect population is less zealous. I thank him, and he gives me his head-net to wear for protection from the flies. And, on returning to strike my tent and move into the mosque, I find a little silver tray on the sand by my tent. On the tray is a pot of tea, a trail of steam drifting from its spout, and next to it a small glass, a bowl of sugar and a little silver teaspoon. I stand beneath the tree, looking about, but there is nobody to be seen.

Magalie had decided to accept an offer from a university in England, and so Andy, Maria and I stood at Bucharest airport by passport control, waving goodbye to a fellow traveller who had become a friend.

Then, just across the border in the northern hills of Bulgaria, Maria failed to show up as we stopped to regroup. It was some time later that she appeared on the back of a small truck, unloaded herself and her bike, and told us that her knee had seized up and that she could barely ride. She was a person of purpose, and her lack of fear sometimes came across as recklessness rather than bravery, but it was obvious that she could not continue in this state. I was disappointed for her, knowing from experience how frustrated she must be. But she showed no trace of it, having already decided to hitchhike the few hundred remaining miles to Istanbul with only her bike for company. Soon she had flagged down another pick-up, Andy and I had loaded her bike, and she was waving at us from the passenger window as the vehicle pulled away.

'Look after each other! See you in Istanbul!!!'

And off she went, barely batting an eyelid at her sudden change of plan. Almost without warning, our merry band of travellers had been disbanded; the end of a period of time on the road more enjoyable than any I can remember. For all the heroics and hard riding this journey was supposed to be about, these sudden separations were numbing.

Andy and I rode onward though thin green woods towards the Bulgarian coastline. A short while later I spotted him up ahead, dismounted and standing on the roadside. He had ridden ahead as usual, his natural athleticism still outstripping whatever fitness I'd gained from cycling across Europe. At least it would give us both some much-needed time to ourselves.

I pulled up beside him.

'Mate,' he said dryly. 'We have a problem. A really big problem.'

I looked down. After only a few thousand miles, his dream bike's rear wheel had – with a dramatic cracking sound, he said – exploded. A six-inch split ran along the rim, and the inner-tube was bulging horrifyingly from this jagged aluminium maw.

It was the latest in a merciless run of unfortunate events. We'd had so much fun in Bucharest, and then, leaving the city, I'd discovered my wallet had gone missing. I'd even taken a taxi back to our host's apartment and turned the place over, revealing nothing. And now the bikes we'd spent an entire year designing were disintegrating before our eyes. We'd barely even taken the bloody things off-road!

Short of the frame snapping clean in half, a cracked rear rim was just about the most critical failure possible. Along with the shock came a jolt of nostalgia, a memory of a time when bicycle technology actually used to be interesting. When my bike had spent more time in the garage than actually being ridden, it had been easier to believe that this or that amazing newfangled engineering innovation might make me a better rider or improve my sex life. Indeed, the entire mountain bike industry revolved around convincing people with cash that this was in fact true.

Four months of living in the saddle had evaporated all interest in shiny bits of metal, especially when confronted with a couple of girls who had rescued old bikes from a scrap-yard and proceeded to get on just as well as us – if not better, as they hadn't had to worry about expensive bikes breaking.

After discovering that staring at the crack would not cause it to go away, we elected to continue carefully in the hope that the wheel wouldn't fail completely and render the bike unrideable. Paranoid and painstaking in our progress, dodging every pothole and rumple in the asphalt, we eventually came to a little seaside town perched atop a rugged promontory. Since there was no bike mechanic in town, we attempted to remedy the situation by getting fairly drunk in a bar and talking to anyone who would listen.

Quickly realising that nobody was even faintly interested in us, we bought some overpriced street food and wobbled back downhill in the dark from the peninsula to an empty beach we'd seen earlier, setting up camp for the night on the decking in front of a boarded-up beach hut. Bulgaria had been the only nation whose inhabitants had failed to offer us a night under a roof. Perhaps the sight of two serious-looking blokes with beards invited less sympathy than two pretty girls and their 'boyfriends' – or, previously, a blond guy with a goatee and a fluorescent yellow sock on his head.

Somebody had kindly left the dregs of a bottle of whisky and a pile of firewood in plain sight in front of the little hut. As we helped ourselves to both, I realised that this was the first night that Andy and I had spent on the road with nobody but each other for company. And, as the nostalgia of group riding faded away, there came in its place a strange sense of finally having *begun* – as if the previous four months had been one long goodbye to Europe, the places we called home, and only now were we setting out on the mission that had begun all that time ago with that text message. In Romania I'd received an email from one of the veteran cyclists we'd met at the Royal Geographical Society:

'I've just calculated that at this rate it will take you eight years to cycle round the world!' she'd written. If we were going to be taken seriously by the long-distance cycling community, it was time we stepped up our game.

'I bet this beach is actually really beautiful,' said Andy, breaking the campfire silence. 'Especially at sunrise, with the sun over the water. Might go for a swim!'

'Mmm – that'll be romantic!'

'Probably about as much action as I'm going to get with a beard like this!'

In the run-up to our departure from England, Andy had been dating a Czech girl who lived in the nearby town – though I'd never met her, and he'd never brought her along to any social occasions, which was not entirely unusual for Andy. He had ended the relationship before we set off, knowing that Ride Earth would occupy his life for several years to come. I tried to imagine how that conversation over a candlelit dinner might have gone:

'I'm really sorry, but I'm leaving you.'

'What?! Why?'

'Er . . . because . . .' – utter deadpan – '. . . I'm going to cycle round the world.'

'What d'you reckon's going to happen with Maria?' Andy asked. She'd be well on her way to Istanbul, if not already there. The journey already felt quite different without her; the circumnavigation sidling back into view.

'Dunno, really,' I said. 'It's one thing saying, "Yeah, I'll cycle with you to Romania on a fifteen-euro bike from a scrap-yard" – it's only a few hundred miles, and it's only one country. Cycling onwards with us to *India* . . . as soon as we leave Istanbul, there's no decent bike shops until New Delhi. That's the best part of five thousand miles!'

Back in the Romanian capital, we had made a tough financial decision. Our video camera was beginning to grow faulty and unreliable; a message had arrived from the film company that a whole batch of tapes had proved unwatchable due to recording errors. We'd had a long and difficult discussion, and – with the producers in London unable to help with funding – had eventually decided to put more than a thousand pounds of our savings towards a brand new video camera. It was superior in every way, and would produce fantastic quality footage. But it had eaten over a year's worth of our budget in a single purchase, and I began to feel that despite the encouragement Ben and James were no longer quite as enthusiastic about our story as they once had been. But things were just about to start get interesting. They needed to understand that.

Europe passed into history with the wave of a soldier's hand, and smiling officials beneath big red and white Turkish flags welcomed us to their country and gave us permission to stay for three months. We'd never need that long, of course, but it felt good to have been given plenty of breathing space for the new wheels to arrive from England. The road from this remote border-post passed through misty wooded hills and suddenly opened out into an immaculate highway, three lanes wide on each side, without the slightest hint that a motor vehicle might ever have driven upon its pristine surface. Simultaneously the woods came to an end and the landscape turned into a brown, rolling, uninhabited expanse, and as we descended to the plateau the warming air somehow smelt and tasted exotic.

We rolled into the first small Turkish town. White-haired men with moustaches and flat caps raised teacups aloft in salute as we passed by, shouting encouragements. Clearly we were only the latest in a steady trickle of travellers headed for Asia. The road was far better than I expected, fully paved, no less – in better shape, even, than roads at home in England. Towns were frequent and sprawling and a lot more modern-looking than back in the Balkans, and the Sea of Marmara appeared on the horizon like a mirage, seeming to confirm, finally, that we had come to the far end of Europe.

The coast was heavily developed, one settlement blending seamlessly into the next, suburb after suburb of comfortable-looking apartment blocks painted in pastel shades, built to a standard blueprint, interspersed with shiny shop-fronts and furniture superstores and Internet cafes and eateries boasting trays of steaming stews and rice we couldn't afford to eat. The reappearance of the Roman alphabet – extended by a scattering of unfamiliar dots and swirls – was comforting after Bulgaria's indecipherable Cyrillic, and English words littered the urban spaces, shouting loudly in bright colours about *paket servis*, *taksis* and *sandviches*. Symbols of modern-day prosperity appeared in every direction. Turkey, it seemed, was not a developing nation at all – it had caught up with and overtaken its recovering Eastern European neighbours. Or perhaps Turkey had always been a developed, powerful nation. After all, hadn't the Ottomans reached the gates of Vienna? Why had I assumed that leaving Europe would be like going back in time?

Andy, now possessing the sole remaining source of funds, was thrilled to discover a drive-by cash machine in a little booth on the roadside – so convenient! Deciding that this would be an opportune moment to withdraw enough funds for the weeks ahead, we watched speechlessly as the machine swallowed Andy's card and settled into a lifeless, unresponsive torpor, leaving us with nothing but a few quid's worth of lira and the entire width of Asia to look forward to.

Andy began to physically beat the machine. Just as it looked like he might be winning, a security guard from a nearby building came over to see what all the fuss was about. But despite everyone's best efforts, and a number of confused phone-calls to various equally confused helpline operators, it finally became clear that we would not be getting our last remaining cash card back. I'd heard that my own replacement cards were now on their way to Istanbul, along with two new wheels for Andy. I hoped they would all arrive in good time.

For the time being, though, it seemed that we would be living off the remaining contents of Andy's wallet, which amounted to worryingly little. As we pedalled east along the coast towards the looming promise of Istanbul and a place to sort ourselves out, I remembered Laszlo, our host in

Budapest. Laszlo had been a man who seemed to float above the passage of time like some omniscient philosopher, quietly evangelising what he'd dubbed 'The Process'. He'd cultivated this idea as a result of spending half a year as a barefooted beggar in India. The thrust of Laszlo's theory was that the ever-unfolding procession of all things was better simply accepted as it was than shaped to one's needs. As part of this trust and acceptance of the unknowable and unplannable, Laszlo encouraged us as itinerant travellers to shake off the need to assume dominance over the world, and instead to let things run more loosely, because only then would we be able to concentrate on the experience that was being . . . well, experienced. Only by forgetting about abstract goals would we be able to see other opportunities dangling under our noses.

It sounded like a lot of new-age whacked-out hippie nonsense. But since my idea of new-age whacked-out hippie nonsense was a preconception anyway, I started to wonder whether behind the mere words lay something clearer and more honest, which could hardly be more relevant to the mission that had brought me to Laszlo's home (or, as he put it, the place where he and his turtles happened to be living). And an opportunity had arisen to put it to the test. Could we continue travelling with next to no money whatsoever?

Now that our poverty was real, rather than self-imposed, we approached a series of roadside restaurants closed up for the coming winter, assessing whether or not we thought we'd get away with sleeping surreptitiously under an awning or in a doorway, there being no open land to camp on. It wasn't until we began to investigate the ruin of a construction site, fallen into decay halfway to completion and already adorned with graffiti and vagrants' paraphernalia, that we struck it lucky: an attendant from the petrol station next door suggested we sleep on the floor of a small kiosk in the parking lot. The kiosk was dusty and had evidently been out of use for some time, but the brick hearth full of ash identified it as once having been a handy little kebab hut. As we unpacked our sleeping-bags, the kindly attendant reappeared with a stack of broken-up cardboard boxes for us to sleep on, and this confirmed, beyond all question, that we were now fully qualified tramps.

Lying on the floor of that dusty kiosk, listening to cars and trucks thundering to and fro, Andy snoring quietly next to me, Asia just over the horizon, I found myself with plenty to wonder about. How could Turkey be defined? Was it Europe, the Middle East, or somewhere in between? How would the winter affect our continuing journey? And would we *really* get by on such a tiny budget?

And what about this religion, Islam? Because I wasn't sure that it could all be about beards, burkas and bombs – or that it had anything to do with those things whatsoever.

I rose at sunrise, packed my makeshift bivouac on the quayside and began to cycle behind Andy along the hard shoulder of the enormous coastal highway towards Istanbul. The road signs indicated that it was still over seventy miles distant. Today would be a long and gruelling day.

Sometime after midday, the signs for Istanbul vanished. They were replaced by signs indicating our passage through new settlements, but we could not really distinguish between one and the next. And, as the afternoon wore on and the suburbs showed no sign of diminishing, we realised that we were already in Istanbul. The signs were for its districts. We had, in fact, woken up in Istanbul that morning. It seemed that the city would never end. But this was the home stretch, the heroic arrival at the end of our home continent! Adrenaline and an overpowering sense of finale kept the pedals spinning and our grins spreading, despite it being almost midnight before we arrived in the downtown districts, met Maria and were taken to the house of our host for our first night in Istanbul, almost eighteen hours since we'd set off from the outskirts of the city.

Istanbul wasn't Turkey's capital, and hadn't been since the years following the First World War. However, it was still the hub of the nation's cultural life, and by far its largest city. I was overwhelmed by the scale of the place, and the complexity of the public transport was brain-melting. It took, literally, hours to get *anywhere*, the logistics of a city centre split between two continents being something I'd never really considered before. Cycling in the traffic-clogged streets and up and down its precipitous hills was an ordeal.

None of this mattered while I could escape inside the welcoming confines of an apartment, and Couchsurfing once again provided no shortage of willing hosts in central Istanbul. Despite its location in the far north-west corner of Turkey, Istanbul and its liberal, educated youth were at the epicentre of what they saw as their country's progressive and essentially European future. Turkey, they said, was the success story of the Middle East, relatively unrestrained by fundamental religion, confused conflicts or illegitimate leaders.

Once the obligatory period of rest was over and we'd satisfied our itchy feet by wandering the backstreets in search of nothing in particular – god forbid we stumble upon a tourist attraction! – Andy and I sat with our hosts and discussed our plans. Our ambition was riding high, bolstered by our successful crossing of the entire European continent by bicycle, and our sights were set on something altogether greater and more heroic than cycling to India: a crossing of Central Asia during its bitterly cold winter, crossing the Tien Shan Mountains at the earliest opportunity and entering the Far East via Tibet. I'd just received an email from another young Englishman who had spent the previous three years cycling from Siberia to England via Australia, offering us advice on the routes ahead that he'd just covered. His email brought with it renewed desire to accomplish a similarly grand journey. Tibet, China, the Far East . . . what an achievement that would be!

First, though, there was the small matter of a thousand or so miles of Turkey during winter. TV news reports were already showing pictures of mountainous Eastern Turkey gridlocked by blizzards to a dramatic orchestral score, and it was still November! Selen, our friendly host, suggested visiting her home town of Adana. The weather would be better down there; we could then cycle along the south coast, most of which was apparently a major tourist destination. But we soon put her right: we weren't *tourists*, Selen; we were eternal, nomadic travellers! We wanted hardship and authenticity, not pizza and beaches!

'In that case,' she said, 'I suggest you try the Black Sea Coast.' And, with a casual gesture along the top edge of a map, Selen sealed the fate of Ride Earth. We would cycle along the far quieter and less-visited north coast of the country, and see what we would find. It would take us much longer, certainly, than a direct route across the Anatolian plateau – by all accounts it would be a steep, remote, rain-lashed place. But speed didn't matter too much as long as we had momentum.

Leaving Istanbul was easier said than done. After three weeks of making friends and partying and exploring the city on foot, Andy's new wheels still had not arrived. A full day of investigations uncovered the fact that they'd been sitting for a fortnight in a customs compound somewhere in suburbia, waiting for import tax to be paid on them.

Meanwhile, Andy had struck up a relationship with a girl we'd met through our first hosts in Istanbul, and we'd eventually moved into the flat she shared with two other girls. I never really managed to get to know this new love-interest of his, despite living in the same building for several days and being roundly thrashed at backgammon by her over several litres of tea. Her English was practically non-existent, and I wondered how that left any room for she and Andy to enjoy their fleeting romance. Andy was careful to sidestep the topic of the relationship, and I saw him less as he spent more and more time with her. He was always cagey when it came to discussing such things. Even though we'd been best mates for over a decade, I'd never been treated to more than the briefest of updates on the basic factual aspects of his relationships. A wall went up at the slightest hint of any deeper enquiry, leaving me wondering if it was something about me and my listening abilities, or if it was simply Andy being Andy. Either way, I was – as usual – left in the dark. He was somehow involved with a woman, and beyond that fact I would have to make my own guesses.

At the same time, I discovered that one of her flatmates had something of a crush on *me*! Not only that, but she wasn't shy about expressing it when the hour grew late. While I wasn't averse to the idea of a casual fling, I had no qualms about making absolutely sure it went no further. After all, I had a new purpose in life – cycling round the world, living permanently on the road – and a relationship certainly had no place in that. Which was why, when it came to making guesses about Andy's shenanigans, I came to the conclusion that it was foolish and stupid to be getting emotionally entangled with a girl. In the grand scheme of things, we had barely even left home. We had most of a planet still to ride! Andy was setting himself up for a whole world of hurt, because we were duty-bound to leave Istanbul – and with it, the girl.

In the end, the inevitable was forced on us. The third young lady in the flat, clearly feeling left out, announced one day that she wanted us gone. Or, more correctly, her father wanted us gone. Immediately. Running out of places to stay, Andy and I found ourselves loitering guiltily outside the entrance to a block of flats, rolled-up sleeping-bags under our arms, looking with concern at the black clouds approaching across the Mediterranean. Soon enough the latch clicked, a middle-aged man exited the stairwell with a quick glance and started off down the street. Andy jammed his foot in the door and we dashed up to the top of the building. The open roof was flat, surrounded by low walls, with grubby rings on the floor where water had pooled and slowly evaporated. There was a discarded table in one corner. Nobody would come up here. At least, we hoped not! And we cackled like the pair of naughty schoolboys we'd once been.

The full-on thunderstorm was an impressive thing indeed – more so than any man-made light show or concert. A few curious souls watched from between parted curtains in the little orange-lit windows that lined the street below; meanwhile I shivered as the first moisture seeped through the lining of my sleeping-bag. The table had only been big enough to shelter my upper body. Rain lashed down. The roar of the torrent was deafening, even without the peals of thunder rolling across the sky.

What the bloody hell am I doing here?

Water began to penetrate my clothes. We had been here too long. We had outstayed our welcome, and the city was kicking us out. We had to leave Istanbul. Now.

CHAPTER 9

I followed Andy north along the Asian bank of the Bosphorus Straits, then – when the city started to recede – we headed east on the smallest through-road we could find. My sleepy muscles brought the world into movement again; the simple pleasures of fresh air and perpetual motion mine once more. Soon we were climbing a quiet lane through wooded hills, all orange and brown with the passing of autumn, just like it would be back home; the air suddenly damp and cool and clean-smelling after a month of city life. I can barely remember such a pleasant shock to the senses as clearing the eastern outskirts of Istanbul.

It was already the second day since departure, correctly speaking. The previous day had involved rounding up a few things: primarily Andy, who'd been with his girlfriend and whom I hadn't seen for some days; secondly a piece of mail that sadly proved not to contain my replacement bank cards; and thirdly our bikes and possessions, which by this time were scattered about the city in the basements and living rooms and cupboards of the Turks with whom we'd stayed like the spoils of some bizarre treasure hunt. Riding towards the edge of this colossal city as darkness fell, the usual kind of thing had happened: we'd met a chain-smoking Robert de Niro lookalike in a betting shop who'd given us a bilingual dictionary and a cheese pasty and introduced us to a one-eyed tramp who'd offered us one of his secret back-alley hideouts for the night. It's OK, he'd said; he wouldn't be using it that evening. Andy had taken up residence under the table outside (since I'd won the table on the rooftop), while I'd shared the floor of a shed with the tramp's accumulated clutter and the local rodent population, my feet protruding from the narrow doorway as I slept.

Riding through the Turkish countryside, everything damp and quiet and sun-speckled, I wrestled with the value of the previous month; thirty days that had so easily disappeared into Istanbul's vast underbelly. Most of that time, I felt, had been frittered away, waiting to leave. The delays themselves felt self-inflicted. Had it really been necessary to have new wheels posted all the way from England? Couldn't a bike shop have been found, selling a half-decent wheel, in a city of nearly twenty million inhabitants on the edge of Europe?

Now we were finally leaving I had a heightened sense of a new chapter in the story of this journey. I was keenly aware that Andy and I were now forging ahead into the Middle East – alone. Maria's part in the journey had come to an end; no familiar sight remained but for each other's grubby and increasingly hairy faces. I'd barely seen Maria since she and I had parted ways on the second day of our stay in Istanbul; lack of space in her friend's apartment meant I'd ended up staying on the other side of the city. Weeks had passed, contact had grown dimmer as we'd each fallen deeper into the distractions of the city, and Maria had quietly dropped off the map. Just before leaving, I'd heard that her Iranian visa application had been rejected, and this had extinguished the last remaining possibility that she'd be rejoining us as we rode on from Istanbul. Despite the fact that Andy and I would now have to confront our differences, I found myself curiously unmoved that Maria had gone her own way. It seemed somehow inevitable, after those hedonistic months in Europe. Now we had a serious mission to tackle – to Ride the Earth proper – and as gutsy as Maria was, she would only have slowed us down.

Andy's new wheels seemed to glitter crazily, spinning in the sunlight ahead of me. But it wouldn't be long before they gained the same coating of dirt and grime as our bikes and luggage had accumulated over the last few thousand miles. With life back in perspective, and with nothing better to do but stare at the evolving landscapes of Anatolia, I performed a few calculations based on our remaining cash and the distance we had to ride. With six weeks of cycling and camping to reach the Georgian capital of Tbilisi and retrieve the second set of bank cards that would be posted there, we'd have more than three euros a day to spend on food. Suddenly I felt rich. Imagine how much bread and cheese and pasta that would buy!

The low hills flattened out into a humdrum coastal carriageway taking goods traffic between a handful of small cities. It was forgivingly easy riding for two out-of-practice cyclists, but it wouldn't last for long: Zonguldak was the location of the first big climb. It was late in the day and by nightfall we had barely cleared the city on its uphill side; completely drained, having not yet re-adapted to the daily pedalling routine, or to the calorie-heavy diet we needed to sustain the exercise.

Stopping at a petrol station for a rest and a snack meant putting on the increasingly slick 'Tom and Andy show' for

severe upper-body deformations. My winter gloves, 'borrowed' during my brief stint in the TA, were thick leather specimens which became drenched with sweat as I rode, rendering them useless. With winter drawing close, it would have been fair to say that I was ill-equipped. But there was no money to spare, and no outdoor equipment shops in which to buy appropriate clothing anyway. I would have to grin and bear it.

I awoke one particular night and peered from my sleeping-bag, wondering why the bloody hell my legs were so cold. They were throbbing with pain. I screwed up my eyes, blinded by the orange glare of a streetlamp. The sky was completely dark. Then memories came drifting back: we had gone to sleep on the floor of a bus-shelter. I was lying in a sodding *bus shelter*. The air, I saw, was somehow hazy. I blinked, and realised that it was full of swirling snow.

I closed my eyes and kicked my frozen legs in an attempt to get some warm blood into them. It didn't work. I would have to get up and jump around. But the thought was so hideous that I elected to block out the stone-cold numbness in my shins, pull my hat over my eyes, and wait the darkness out. And I drifted back into a feverish sleep.

It was light when I awoke – just in time to notice some feet by my head. Then a low roar grew, stopped with a hiss, and the legs disappeared with another growl and the sound of slush being parted by heavy tyres. I sat up suddenly – it was daylight; time to evacuate, get warm, grab a quick breakfast and venture into the new, white world that had quietly descended; which had ushered out one season and brought in the next, literally overnight.

Then I looked round.

My boots.

Had they been six inches further beneath the canopy, it would have been fine.

But it wasn't fine.

My boots were now full of wet snow.

'Bollocks!'

Andy seemed fine when he awoke, still having a fleece and dry boots, and having won the inside spot in a game of paper-scissors-stone. I imagined he might have something to say about having woken up in a mountaintop bus shelter to find the world blanketed in snow. But when I pointed the video camera at him, he pretended not to have noticed and began silently packing his sleeping gear.

'Well . . . ?'

'Well what?'

'D'you want to say something?'

'Oh. Right. We woke up in a bus shelter, and it was snowing.'

'Right . . . how about making it a bit more interesting?'

'What do you want me to say, exactly?'

'I don't know – something about how you feel about it, perhaps?'

'Well, that's it, isn't it? We woke up and it was snowing! I'm freezing my bollocks off! What else is there to say?'

'Well, that's not going to make a very interesting video, is it? What happened to making an effort to . . . to communicate?'

I didn't want conflict; I wanted to film the bus stop and the snow, because although it might be fairly normal for us to sleep on the floor of a bus shelter at sub-zero temperatures, it might one day be entertaining for people back home. But now it seemed that Andy wasn't interested.

Filming had been his idea from the beginning. Andy had jumped at the chance to team up with the production company, convincing me to give it a try. I'd been reluctant, more interested in the idea of photographing and writing about the journey, but I'd agreed to give it a go, and Ben and James, the company's founders, had driven up to my village for a two-day pre-departure shoot and again for the leaving day before leaving us to our own devices. We hadn't had a clue what to do with our video cameras, other than what everyone else did: press the red button and point the lens at anything remotely interesting. The subtle art of story-telling was something about which we'd never paid a thought. I'd eventually taken to the process, though, and I was determined to do the best job I could. Granted, it was rapidly becoming the story of the most confused, interrupted, ill-prepared round-the-world bicycle journey of all time! But if that was going to be the story, then so be it.

Andy'd had reservations about the first episode, but he seemed to have come to terms with his portrayal now that four more episodes had been released. We'd also seen how much the material itself had improved since our awful early attempts. So I couldn't understand his touchiness when I decided it was a good moment to get out the camera. Maybe he was under more strain than he cared to admit. Could the mysterious backgammon-girl, left behind in Istanbul, have something to do with it?

As we gingerly nosed down the slushy switchbacks towards the town of Amasra, damp brakes squealing, the snow began to thin and the air grew less biting. I looked east from Amasra's picturesque lagoon along the coastline, counting the endless ranks of steep promontories that slid into the ocean, noticing the green ribbon of the lower slopes and then a definite band of white which disappeared up into the clouds. We had no elevation profile for the route ahead, but my eyes could fill in the missing data very well.

We followed our noses through the empty streets of Amasra to a bakery and, while eating breakfast on its doorstep, were invited into a nearby tea house as its owner arrived to open up for the day. We'd been invited into countless Turkish tea shops; indeed, they had become shrines in our heat-seeking pilgrimages as the temperature dropped. Approaching one particular village, we'd made a deliberate decision to decline the inevitable invitation. We would accomplish this by cycling through at high speed – we needed to make progress more than we needed another free shot of caffeine. But upon hurtling past the village tea shop, an elderly patron had burst forth and charged down the street after us, bellowing in protest and brandishing in one hand what appeared to be an old shoe. He was just about to rugby-tackle Andy from his bicycle when we decided that tea might be a good idea after all.

These village *chay salonu*s followed an endearing formula: large misty windows making way for a large and sparsely decorated room set with square tables and wonky-legged classroom chairs, heated by wood-burners whose tin-pipe chimneys followed artistic routes around the walls to the point of escape. The village's elderly men would sit in groups playing card games and backgammon, overlooked by little hanging pendants – a royal blue stone depicting a cartoonish eye in black, white and yellow – and at least one portrait of Ataturk, who would also be found loitering in the toilets.

Hours would pass in a blur of wood-smoke, warming our toes while being fed endless glasses of the sweet brew and holding identical conversations in bad German with the retired members of what must have been the entire Turkish merchant navy. I have never met so many ships' captains or so many flat-capped old dudes who'd sailed the seas for a living. Africa . . . America . . . Panama . . . Dubai . . . Liverpool . . . the seafaring experience contained within the tea shops of the Black Sea Coast appeared to be matchless.

We wrenched our bikes up and down the tiny roads with the Black Sea crashing against the rocks below. Far beyond that northern horizon lay another of the growing list of places I realised that I knew nothing about whatsoever – the Crimean Peninsula. More miles inevitably highlighted what I *didn't* know, and what I *did* know found itself increasingly outweighed. Cycling the Black Sea Coast didn't mean I'd later be able to say I 'knew Turkey' – my experience here and everywhere else would be nothing but a cross-section; a snapshot in time. But extrapolations were so easy to make. Every day I watched fears germinate in this way: newsreaders on tea-shop televisions delivered hourly reports of insurgency and violence over a stirring orchestral score; computer graphics depicting F-16 fighters and guided missiles; slow-motion replays of targets exploding in fuzzy lo-fi; exultation at the successful Turkish repulsion of yet another terrorist threat from just over the border in Kurdish Iraq or Armenia or Greece or Syria. Between reminders that the whole world was out to get poor Turkey, singers crooned emotively charged refrains in a multi-sensory reinforcement of Turkish fortitude in the face of perpetual threat. And, wherever I looked, fluttering white-on-red flags flew proudly, and the annoyingly benevolent face of Mustafa Kemal Ataturk, the country's beloved revolutionary, stared out at me.

Meanwhile I rode with Andy through lands of peace and tranquillity. The hills made us fitter than ever before, and together we pondered some of life's big questions, such as exactly which was the best packaged biscuit from Turkey's vast array. We eventually settled upon Tutku – a vanilla-chocolate shell enrobing a luxurious inner treasure of chocolate fondant.

December arrived, and the daylight hours continued to shrink. One night, setting up a makeshift bed beneath a table in an abandoned beach complex, my ailing head-torch finally broke and the temptation to continue into the night in order to cover more distance was severely dampened. We would now have to share Andy's equally puny head-torch between us for the fourteen or fifteen hours of nightly darkness. I made do by holding the torch's remains between my teeth while writing my diary; globs of unstemmed spittle joining the splotches of rain that began to fall onto the pages.

The rain continued all night, unrelenting and deafening. As the morning grew after what seemed like the longest night that had ever passed, Andy and I stared out at the dismal torrent. Somehow, without speaking, we both knew that we wouldn't be riding today. The thought of voluntarily setting off through that amount of flying water was too depressing. Anyway, it was time we took a rest day. Scouting around the sorry little refuge, we found a wood-saw and took it in turns to dash out into the rain to collect logs, with which Andy started a fire in a rusty old barbecue. We kept it burning all day, building it absurdly high and hot, feeding it long into the evening as a kind of cathartic distraction from the rain.

The following morning the weather had not changed; in fact it appeared to have grown worse over the course of a second night. Resigned to misery, we headed off along the hilly coast once more, and within an hour we were soaked to the skin. Despondently we continued pedalling, and then the misty windows of a tea shop appeared in the crook of a valley. Off came drenched ponchos, jackets and trousers, and in a moment of pity the owner set us up in a back room with a stove and suggested we stay the night. We had covered a pathetic twenty miles. I dreamed of fancy waterproofs that would have cost me half a year's food budget. And during the following impossibly wet days we found refuge in the most unlikely places: the changing rooms of a football ground, a concrete bunker beneath a radio mast in the hills, a wooden holiday cottage, another seafront ruin, a hotel run by a kindly middle-aged couple – and a government-run hostel for visiting teachers attached to the secondary school of the town of Turkeli. I had caught a cold, and the teachers decided that this was sufficient cause for us to take a day off. But first, they dragged us into the school to appear in front of four morning English classes (all in the same room, and at the same time).

Knowing how much I hated being the centre of attention, Andy volunteered to film me squirming in front of a hundred teenage school pupils. The boys wanted to know my favourite Premiership football team, while the girls wanted to take each others' photographs with me on their mobile phones (goodness knows why; I'd neither shaved nor had a haircut for five months and was wearing a bright red skin-tight racing jacket and a pair of filthy linen chinos tucked into my ski socks), and everyone wanted to make sure I knew who Mustafa Kemal Ataturk was and why he was such a complete and utter legend. Then we joined some of the youths for a game of lunchtime volleyball before one over-eager player walloped the ball over the fence and into the sea. We stared forlornly through the mesh at the ball, as the current carried it slowly out of sight.

Turkey's northernmost tip appeared on a brighter day over the brow of what I dearly hoped would be the last hill I ever climbed, and we decided to take a detour along the little peninsula to the historical fort town of Sinop to find an Internet cafe and contact our families as we tried to do every couple of weeks, and perhaps find somewhere to sleep, seeing as it was already getting dark again. I also secretly hoped that I would get the opportunity to spend some time on my own. Andy and I had only been travelling together as a pair for a few weeks, but petty tensions peppered our time on the road. We had shared almost all aspects of our lives for a full half year, and biking across Europe in the summertime had been no preparation for this really quite miserable ride. Perhaps cycling as a pair shouldn't be treated as a given. So much of what we'd originally planned had, after all, already veered off course. Perhaps, since we had each deliberately equipped ourselves for life alone on the road . . . perhaps the time was now coming for these two old friends to try their separate paths?

Turkey, however, was not ready to release its friendly grip. Led astray on the way into Sinop by the aroma of freshly baked loaves, we had barely polished off one boulder of dense white bread when a cafe-owner dragged us into his establishment for a second lunch of delicious red lentil soup and a session of questions and answers between grateful slurps. Now painfully bloated, we trailed the quaysides of Sinop for hidden tramping spots. Coming upon an Internet cafe, I sent an email to one of Ride Earth's equipment sponsors, asking if they'd be able to send out some warmer sleeping-bags. *Should be fine*, came the reply. I just hoped we would get them soon – the nights were only going to get colder, and we could spare no money for indoor accommodation.

Running out of tramping ideas, Andy popped into a hotel to find that the rates were extortionate; meanwhile I walked into the tea shop opposite and walked out again with the former national skin-diving champion of Turkey and the keys to his fishing boat. This did not seem in the slightest bit unusual, and soon Andy and I were helping to haul the small launch in and heaving our bikes aboard. There was almost enough space in the cabin amongst the jerry-cans of diesel for the two of us to stand up; the berths were almost long enough to lie down on, too. We thanked our new friend profusely; he shrugged.

'Stay as long as you like.'

We told him we'd stay a night and then press on, and thank you very much – *teshekkur ederim!* And we hopped back to dry land to try and walk off the epic bread with a romantic little evening stroll down the quayside.

This, it turned out, was a mistake. Within minutes we'd been accosted by an overenthusiastic young man with too much time on his hands, who appeared to know everyone and everything about Sinop. There was absolutely no convincing Berk to leave us alone without appearing outright rude, so off we trailed, trying to appear grateful for his hospitality while secretly wanting to lock him away in the fishing boat. I could barely contain my horror as we were led into a cafeteria and presented with two more bowls of soup! I peered at the bowl; this was a new variant. Our new companion passed me a bottle of garlic sauce and indicated that I should season what I now identified – with a stifled groan – as tripe. The chunks of furry white stomach lining floated obstinately in the greenish-yellow liquid, stinking of the sheep from whose interior they'd recently been extracted. To this day, I am unable to qualify exactly how I reached the bottom of that bowl without redistributing the contents all over my newest friend and the restaurant floor.

But the gauntlet was far from over, for opposite the cafeteria lay a patisserie. Berk asked the shopkeeper for a box of assorted *baklava* – a treat, under normal circumstances. I accepted the gift with a quivering smile and a repressed heave, explaining that it would be a shame to eat these little pastries right now – they would make such excellent on-the-road snacks, you see? Berk was oblivious to my discomfort, sauntering casually, hands in pockets, extolling the virtues of this pretty little town by the sea, and we wandered the streets together, Andy and he babbling away incoherently, me trailing a short way behind and wondering exactly when the torture was going to end. Some semblance of relief came when Berk suggested we visit a nightclub, and I was able to sit for half an hour watching young people dancing and drinking and smoking too much and not being able to hear what anyone was saying as I carefully hid the fact that my bottle was still entirely full.

On leaving the club, Berk presented the final hurdle in his diabolical challenge: it had been at least an hour since we'd last eaten – how would a pizza or two go down? We politely declined, which was interpreted by the Turk as a resounding acceptance. And so I staggered to a seafront restaurant where I meticulously concealed an entire pizza somewhere within the tubing of my throat. Gasping for air and doubled over with pain, I thanked my host for the evening, who smiled and said we were welcome, and let's do it again some time.

Anyone wandering the streets of Sinop in the early hours the next morning might have seen a figure in a skin-tight red windstopper leaping ashore from *Mert Tugay II* and jogging – buttocks clenched – along the harbour to the nearest public facilities, all the while uttering a series of disturbing groans. I believe it was on my fourth visit I decided I'd paid enough to have earned lifetime membership.

CHAPTER 10

'Somewhere in Africa . . . like Kenya . . . yes, that would be nice,' I was thinking. Passing streetlamps flickered into life through the drizzle, the nondescript sky deepening into murky blue.

Andy strapped on our shared head-torch and we gingerly pressed on along the highway's hard shoulder. Following his silhouette into the night was an act of blind faith. We had one rear light between us, and no front lights at all. There was nowhere to buy any, and we could not have afforded them anyway, but we simply had to keep going. We were both desperate to get out of Turkey. We'd been in the country for almost three months and were beginning to tire of the sheer uniformity of the huge nation; each coastal town a changeless clone of its predecessor.

A car passed, bringing a few seconds of respite. The road was illuminated for an instant by the sweep of the headlights, debris and texture harshly accented in a blinding white, and I memorised the road surface ahead for perhaps ten or twenty metres. Then the darkness returned and the sound of the motor faded into a background of crashing, invisible waves. Only the chill air on my cheeks betrayed any sensation of movement. I might as well have been riding on the moon.

I heard a squeal of brakes. Snapped out of my trance, I

grabbed at my own brake levers, unable to see, before colliding with the back of Andy's trailer. I was thrown forward by my own momentum, ending up bent double over my own handlebars, the back of my right leg stinging sharply where it had absorbed the bike's weight through the teeth of a pedal as the heavy three-wheeled vehicle came to a sudden halt.

'God's *sake*! What are you *doing*?'

'What do you mean?'

'Why the hell did you just stop like that?'

Andy sighed heavily. 'I was just . . . stopping!'

'Well, why didn't you say anything?'

'Well, why weren't you looking where you were going?'

'You're aware that it's the middle of the night and I can't see a bloody thing?'

'Well, what do you want *me* to do about it?!?'

Being in charge of filming for the week, I decided to capture Andy at his most unreasonable. Nothing else I'd tried seemed to have worked. I quickly flipped open my handlebar bag, pulled out the camera and its big long-life battery and slid the two together in a well-practised motion. Toggling the power switch with one hand and opening the screen out with the other, I pointed the lens at Andy and flicked the night-vision mode on. He flashed into view on the screen in a sickly shade of green; a lanky, helmeted figure astride his overweight bike, stood by a roadside crash barrier, body half-turned to look at the guy who'd just ploughed into the back of him.

'What . . . what are you doing?'

'Getting the camera out. So you can see what you sound like in these kinds of situations.'

Andy looked back at the road ahead, exasperated.

'Isn't it obvious that this is probably not the best time to be filming?' he asked after a while with faux diplomacy, knowing that his words were now being recorded.

'No, I think this is absolutely the best time to be filming.'

'So you want us to end up being arrested?'

Andy was referring to an incident earlier in the day, when we'd set up the camera on the side of the road and filmed ourselves cycling past in the rain. This had attracted the attention of the Turkish police, who had turned up with a number of squad cars and a van, made a huge fuss, and demanded to see the contents of the tapes and of our digital cameras, as if they believed themselves foiling some kind of major international terrorist plot. Then a local diplomat had happened by in a blacked-out Mercedes with Turkish flags flying from the front corners of its bonnet, waved the gormless cops away, and told us with a wry grin that we were free to go.

'Don't be so paranoid!' I replied. 'How are we going to end up being arrested if nobody can see us?'

'You're . . . you're just completely reckless!'

'The world isn't out to get us,' I said, 'and if there's a problem . . .'

'I *know* the world isn't out to get us – I didn't think that in the first place! I've been cycling with you for six months . . .'

'And you think I'm reckless?' I asked.

'Sorry?'

Lorry.

'You think I'm reckless?' I repeated.

'Occasionally, yes.'

'*Occasionally* reckless?'

'Yeah.'

'OK . . . look, can we just *go*?'

We rode onward into the night. Some time later we came to a town. Andy spotted a taxi rank and we took shelter in a little heated den by the road with a huddle of smoking taxi drivers, before wandering surreptitiously over to the pedestrian subway beneath the highway, rolling out our sleeping-bags, and silently preparing ourselves for another sleepless night outdoors.

The following day I had something to distract me from this rigmarole. A message had popped up unannounced in my inbox: an email from Ben, one of the video project's producers.

'Without beating around the bush,' he'd written, 'the simple fact of the matter is that we have not been able to secure a sponsor for the podcast and because of this we have to stop work.'

We knew that episode six had been delayed. A hard drive failure. No backup. It was the editor's fault. They'd already recut it and were just putting the finishing touches to it all. Ben and James had been ploughing more than a thousand pounds a month into the on-line series, dwarfing the budget of our journey. But the reality was that the funds had now run out.

It seemed unfathomable. Everyone had been so enthusiastic. Even Mark, after returning home, had taken a job with the company in order to help with publicity and sponsorship. The first five episodes had been entertaining; the editor had done an admirable job with the early spools of horribly amateurish footage, and we heard nothing but occasional blasts of optimism when we'd asked how it was all panning out. But we'd never been party to the audience figures or the publicity strategy – all that had been hidden behind an increasingly corporate wall. For all the upbeat talk, the series had failed to make a splash, and all the excuses and changes of tack couldn't hide the fact forever: nobody was really that interested in watching our journey unfold. And, consequently, nobody wanted to foot the bill for a series without an audience.

Lying on the floor of a subway on a cold winter night, a few thousand miles from home and with no money, it seemed an appropriate moment to try to look at it all objectively. The fact of the matter was that Ben and James had tried to get the British cycling community interested in the story of three hopelessly idealistic middle-class university graduates on an extended holiday in Western Europe. We made slower progress than even the most uncompetitive gaggle of Sunday-morning roadies. We were slightly less entertaining than Ewan McGregor and Charley Boorman (though of course far more heroic and adventurous). The camerawork was worse than in the shakiest home video. For all we'd imagined that would be impressive and noteworthy about the journey, it had turned out to make for rather uninspiring viewing.

'Of course,' Ben had gone on to write, 'none of this affects the documentary film, and so the most important thing is that you keep shooting. I'm sure you will anyway. But don't for one second feel that all of this has been a waste of time. This project has always been something of an experiment, and we've all learnt a great deal along the way.'

The comforting words rang hollow. For weeks we'd been

posting packets of tapes into oblivion, and there was no evidence that anyone had even watched them. The final episode had finished on a sour note somewhere in Austria, featuring Andy and I coming to blows one morning over the mysterious issue of a broken trailer.

'I strongly believe that every end has a new beginning and that this situation is no different,' finished Ben's message. 'It just may take a while to materialise.'

The north-east coast of Turkey was famous for its unique take on the national cuisine; also for its tea and hazelnut plantations. Huge cheese-filled pizzas swimming with molten butter and chunks of spicy sausage; great platters of grilled meat with rice; stews of aubergine and tomato and green peppers and chickpeas: these delights sat tantalisingly behind big glass windows in restaurants that we were too sodden and grubby and poor to enter. We celebrated the shortest day of the year by cranking out the longest day's ride of the journey so far, but the internal disorder which had afflicted me so memorably in Sinop had still not subsided after almost a fortnight, and when we finally arrived at the historic fortified city port of Trabzon I threw in the towel and declared that – for the first time in a quarter of a year – it was time we rented a room. I was sick of stopping at every petrol station and dashing for the toilet, and Andy was probably sick of waiting around for me, although he acted with admirable patience and never said as much. The facilities were invariably of the squat-and-hosepipe variety. I couldn't even sit down to be ill.

We'd heard that the three-day *bayram* festival – the 'sacrifice feast' – was now under way in Turkey, and that custom dictated that half of the spoils would be given away to the destitute, the homeless, and to travellers, which sounded like a cracking way to spend a day off. We found a twin room in a hotel-hostel in Trabzon city centre, all dull lino and pastel shades and greenish fluorescent lighting, which to us was a luxury of the highest possible order. But first, we had important chores to attend to. And so, after the obligatory luggage explosion, we headed out into the small city and Andy called our friendly equipment sponsor for the umpteenth time, pouring yet more of our precious and dwindling cash down the line to England. It had been more than a month since they'd agreed to help get new sleeping-bags to us, and the delay had become particularly acute on the many nights we'd had to spend in the open, tossing and turning all night, waking bleary-eyed and frustrated, frozen to the bone. That we'd resorted to sharing a single tent was a measure of how desperate the situation had become.

'It's ringing!' said Andy, as I listened in from the door of the booth. 'Hello there – it's Andy from Ride Earth here. Can I speak to Dominic, please?'

A female voice twittered back.

'OK, thanks . . .'

There was a pause while the whereabouts of Dominic, our contact at the company, was identified.

'Erm – probably not,' replied Andy, having been asked if he could hold the line. 'I'm in a phone box in Turkey at the moment. So I don't know whether . . .'

'Tell them it's urgent!' I interrupted.

'It's pretty urgent,' continued Andy. 'Er . . . we've been trying to get in contact with him . . . a fair amount, recently.'

This was the diplomatic understatement of the century. I

began jogging on the spot for warmth, attracting stares from passers-by. On the other end of the line, the chattering continued.

'Right . . . well, basically, we're planning to cycle across Central Asia in the winter, and then across Tibet. So it's going to be really cold. And we were talking to Dominic about the possibility of getting some, erm, warmer sleeping-bags sent out. Because at the moment we've only got summer ones. And we're getting a little bit chilly.'

'Tell them it's snowing!' I interjected.

'It's starting to snow and stuff, so . . .' Andy swung round to look at the phone booth's little screen, where our calling credit was gradually counting down to zero. The receptionist, doubtless, was now desperately looking for a way to wind up this unexpected call from West Asia and resume the nice quiet game of Solitaire she'd been enjoying.

'Is, er, Jeremy there?' asked Andy.

Jeremy was the managing director of the company. I remembered our first meeting with him, in which we'd reeled off our pitch and he'd told us that he thought we were complete idiots. While Andy waited, muttering under his breath, I looked around the little square. Bare trees surrounded a central plaza, once hosting outdoor cafes, now empty, scattered with the winter leaves. Figures in thick dark coats, flat caps and tightly bound headscarves traversed the damp stone tiles; traffic circled the square beneath a dismal sky.

'OK. Alright, then. Well, er, drop . . . drop us an email, then, if he's still on the phone. I mean, is he going to be on the phone for a long time, d'you think, or . . . ?'

'Tell them we'll ring back!!!'

My fingers were finally beginning to warm up, and I stuffed them into my armpits, so that they could warm up as well.

Andy grimaced. 'OK, no worries. Well, if you could, er, tell him when he gets off the phone that I'll call back in five minutes . . . Alright then. Thanks very much. Bye!'

He hung up the phone. The glass double doors of the booth slammed shut behind him.

There was an outdoor equipment store on the eastern outskirts of Trabzon. As far as we knew, it was the only such thing between here and Beijing. Now, at the end of December, I had finally decided that a replacement fleece pullover was worth the huge financial outlay. But the expensive imported sleeping-bags were far beyond our budget, and we'd decided to give our sponsor one last chance.

'We just need an answer, really. Just an answer,' Andy was saying to me.

'I know. It's ridiculous. How long does it take to say yes or no, for god's sake?'

'I wish we could just go and buy some sleeping-bags, or another blanket, or something. So when it's snowing on us in the night, we're not freezing our tits off.'

'Dying of hypothermia, more like.'

'Or we could just go and get some geese, pluck them, then get some plastic bags, fill them with feathers and stitch them together. That might work!'

'Hah! Maybe!'

'It's a religious festival – do they slaughter geese today?'

'I think geese is – er – Christmas?'

'Oh yeah, of course . . .' Andy's face broke into a grin. 'Hey, it's almost Christmas, isn't it? Brilliant!'

Andy entered the booth again in a last-ditch attempt to save ourselves a five-hundred-pound outlay for two brand-new sleeping-bags. Five hundred pounds was supposed to get us from here to China. Meanwhile, two small boys, attracted by the sight of a hairy Englishman doing aerobics to keep warm, had decided to make a nuisance of themselves.

'Can you tell the kids to go away?'

'Bye!' I barked at them. They ignored me.

'Hi there, could I speak to Dominic, please?'

'Yeah, don't do that,' I said. The boys were trying their damnedest to get into the phone booth.

'Oh, hi! It's Andy here. From Ride Earth.'

One of the kids wore a baggy hoodie and had a streak of blond at the front of his black hair, making him look like some kind of eight-year-old gangster-rap superstar. He stood at my feet and – incredibly – started frisking my pockets!

'*Yok! Yok!*' I snapped, brushing the marauding hands away. '*Para yok!* No money!'

'Why!' he squeaked back up at me.

'Yeah, I'm in a phone box.'

'WHY!!!'

'Shut up! He's on the phone!'

'Shut up!' shouted Andy. 'Go away! No, I'm not talking to you, there's some kids hassling me. Erm, basically – how's it going?'

Andy forcibly shut the doors on the kids, who turned their attention to me.

'*Para! Para!* Money! Money!'

They yammered at me in Turkish. Then the rapper-child reached up and stuck his hand into my left trouser pocket.

'*Para! Para!!!*'

'No!!!' I fumed.

'Why!'

'I don't have any money!'

'Why!'

'I don't have any money!'

'Waaahh!!!'

'Can someone please help me?' I shouted to everyone nearby. 'I'm being molested by children who're trying to get money off me!'

In desperation, I turned and set off in the direction of two men who looked like they had nothing better to do than scold street urchins. I felt a tug on my left arm. The elder of the two, pale and scrawny in a puffy red jacket, had grabbed on to the sleeve of my fleece and was now jumping and yanking aggressively.

'Why! Why!'

'Why, why, why – why, why, why!!!' I shouted back. I felt another hand go into my right trouser pocket. Turning, I grabbed the arm and pulled the thieving little fingers away.

'*Para* why!' yapped the discarded rapper-child, rubbing his fingers together tauntingly in the globally understood sign for cash.

'*Para yok!*'

'*Para!*'

'*Para yok!!!*'

'Why!!!'

'It's none of your bloody business *why*, is it?!?'

'*As-salaam alaikum!* Ha-ha!'

We set off from Trabzon the following evening to avoid wasting any more money on accommodation, no closer to obtaining our sleeping-bags than we had been a month before. We rode single file in yet another hideous highway night ride. It felt schizophrenic – an eternity of pitch darkness interspersed with the blinding roar of passing lorries, whose drivers would arrive in Georgia, warm and dry, in a few short hours. The pressure to keep pedalling was becoming exhausting. In order to get ourselves invited to some kind of Christmas Day celebration, we would need to cover the hundred and forty miles out of Islamic Turkey to Christian Georgia by Christmas Eve, which was just two days away.

As we rode, I couldn't shake a feeling of utter dejection, of suddenly hating this life that I'd chosen for myself. The riding sucked. The weather sucked. And I was forcing myself to cycle through it towards some dream of Christmas in a nation that I knew nothing about, and in which I would know nothing and nobody. I was driven by a memory – of all the other Christmases I'd known at home; of the smell of cinnamon, the twinkling fairy-lights, something good in the oven, and the faint hope that it might just snow this year. Well – this Christmas would be nothing like it. It would be freezing cold, and it would be no less lonely than today or any other day.

Maybe the source of this misery lay beyond the weather and the tedium. Maybe it was the way in which all the support had seemed to drop by the roadside as we drew further and further from home. Everyone had been so positive, so encouraging, as we'd laid our plans. But these voices had fallen silent. Mark had left to pursue another kind of life. Maria and Magalie had had their shot too, but had also gone their own ways. Then the film company had pulled the plug on our story, just when it felt that we were finally getting somewhere. And now, despite the platitudes, I knew that our equipment sponsor was letting us down. Nothing would come of these promises. They would sink into oblivion, and if we weren't careful they would drag our mission down with them.

And I couldn't help laying the blame for all of this upon myself, and my foolish ambition and idealism. It had been my and Andy's decisions that had ultimately got us to where we were now: out of money, riding pointlessly through the grim bleakness, hopelessly unprepared for a winter which had already begun and would only get worse as we forged inland and across the Caucasus mountains. The idea of Turkey being nice and warm had been laughably ignorant, and it would be just the same for Iran.

I suddenly resented Andy for not saying anything when I'd tried so hard to insist the journey looked like the one I'd always planned, when really I should have stopped and taken a step back.

And I resented myself for still being the same stubborn old Tom, for getting angry when things didn't go the 'right' way; for forcing all those square pegs into all those round holes, for verbally bludgeoning my best friends into silence as I made mistake after mistake.

I found it impossible to talk to my riding partner about all of this. We were both struggling; too stubborn to admit that this was more of a challenge than we'd expected. Our tempers frayed easily, and there was nobody to take it out on except each other. The tiniest aspects of Andy's behaviour seemed to irritate the very centre of my being: the way Andy sucked noisily, habitually, on the corners of his lengthening moustache; the way Andy cleared his throat all the time with an unnecessary shouting sound; the way Andy broke into a rhythm of abrupt little coughs whenever he was trying to hide being angry or annoyed; the way Andy would sing the same repetitive inanities while riding behind me; the way Andy would reduce any disagreement to some philosophical twaddle about the true meaning of 'knowledge' or 'perception'. Instead of the comradeship I'd expected, my best mate was now simply pissing me off. And – after half a year in each others' shadows – I had no doubt that I was doing exactly the same thing to him. Andy had not been his usual self since his encounter in Istanbul with the backgammon girl. Yet, if he was missing her, he never uttered a word to me about it. Then again, given how I'd reacted to Mark's relationship troubles, perhaps I shouldn't have blamed him for keeping silent, or for our ability to communicate to have broken down.

So I did something else. I took the video camera, found a secluded spot by the sea, and tried to talk to the lens instead. It was difficult to begin with, and I felt uncomfortable opening up with my thoughts. But at least the lens would not argue with me. It wouldn't bitch about my personality defects, or suck the corners of its moustache. It would just listen.

I've recently found out that the video series has been cancelled. I feel a little bit sick, really, because a very fundamental part of what I'm doing has just been taken away – just like that.

It's not really what I wanted to hear. And I'm not feeling great. I've had a pretty hideous cold, and I feel completely and utterly drained – physically and mentally – by it, and also by the cycling, which is just very very tough, and very cold, and very difficult to try and stay warm and dry, and . . . just . . . get the distance done, in such short daylight hours. And the nights are just getting ridiculous – it's so cold, now, that it's actually becoming painful . . . and I'm missing my family and friends a lot, and . . . yeah, I've got to deal with this news as well.

I'm definitely going to keep filming, because there might still be a documentary to be made – and it's an incredible record of my journey. But it's not nice to have to deal with it all in one day.

The first tunnel took me off-guard. It had been recently bored directly through the small rocky headland. Two tunnels of half a mile each came in rapid succession, only just completed and still without any lights. Andy was nowhere to be seen when I arrived at the mouth of the first tunnel, and after a few pedal strokes I was riding blind. He still had the head-torch. Had he forgotten that we only had one between us?

I gingerly got off the bike and dragged it up onto a narrow sidewalk, less than a metre in width, and began to walk. The paving slabs covering the wide drainage channel wobbled musically beneath me like a giant concrete xylophone. A roar filled the air: vehicles had entered the tunnel and high-speed floodlights swept along my path, screaming past in an explosion of whiteness. This was no place for people to be exposed, trapped blind in a concrete tube full of hurtling metal, as if injected into some futuristic video-game.

After fifteen minutes of shuffling in the darkness, with container lorries thundering past a couple of feet to my left and a solid wall of rock and concrete on my right, I emerged into the daylight at the end of the second tunnel, irritated and not at all sure what my riding partner must be thinking.

'You know you're the only one with a head-torch, right?'

Andy stared blankly at me, headphones still in his ears, unmoving and silent. So I continued past him and along the road, wondering what I'd done this time to end up at the bottom of his priority list. Yet another argument an hour beforehand probably hadn't helped.

A few miles later, another unlit tunnel appeared. By this point I'd calmed down somewhat – after all, arguing would get us nowhere. Andy was out of sight behind me, so I stopped and got off my bike to wait. Turkey's highway-building fervour was impressive, but it was no comfort to the long-distance cyclist. I began to miss the early days in Turkey – those silent hills, steep enough to snap my chain, and the bright, quiet freshness of the coast. It already seemed so long ago. Here, we had to detour off the highway into a pickle of backstreets just to buy a loaf of bread! Dynamite-blasted cliffs on my right, sea-defences on my left, and nowhere to go but forward or backwards – either way, I'd have to take my chances in another tunnel.

I gazed once again into the gaping black maw.

Then a cyclist whizzed past me and disappeared headlong into the blackness, ears plugged with headphones, pumping the air with one fist in a mocking dance, and was gone.

It was Andy.

I couldn't believe my eyes.

Speechless, rage building inside me, I stared into the blackness where Andy had now stopped, and a smug, taunting voice called:

'Are you coming?!'

I screamed obscenities. I wanted to turn round and cycle off in the other direction, never to see that arrogant arsehole ever again. That'd teach him to make a mockery out of what could be a matter of life and death!

But I couldn't cycle off in the other direction. This was our challenge, our shared mission! We relied on each other! We were supposed to be a *team*!

I marched into the tunnel on foot.

'What the *fuck* do you think you're doing?!'

'I don't know what you mean, Tom!'

'Are you – are you out of your fucking mind?!'

'What? I stopped, didn't I?'

'D'you think that's funny? Do you think this is *funny*?!'

'Here you go, then! Here, look, here's the head-torch! Off you go!'

'Fuck you.'

I stormed back out of the tunnel, knowing my best mate was enjoying this. We'd known each other for twelve years. He knew *exactly* how to provoke me.

Well, I'd show him. Oh, yes! I'd show him exactly how expensive his little 'joke' would be!

I jumped furiously back on my bike and pedalled blindly into the void at top speed.

The head-torch lay on the ground at Andy's feet.

I didn't see the three missing paving slabs.

'Er – hello? Er – my friend Tom . . . has just fallen off his bicycle. Erm – he hit his head on the concrete. On the floor.'

Even before the ambulance arrived, as I lay on the roadside and Andy dug through his first-aid kit in search of surgical tape to glue my face back together, everything seemed to snap into focus; all these concerns that had built up, unvoiced, which were easy enough to avoid as long as the forward momentum remained. I was surprised to find myself not particularly bothered about the feeling that my face had grown to twice its normal size, nor the pain in my head and the ringing in my ears, nor the fact that I seemed to be almost blind; but instead to be wondering why it had taken an accident like this for me to acknowledge that what I was doing was completely and utterly pointless.

I wondered how it had happened. I'd kept pedalling with the mantra that I simply should, because – given enough time – something would happen that would bring a little more understanding to things. Well, something had indeed happened that had done exactly that.

'Problem? No, no, no – no, it wasn't a car accident, no. It – he just fell off his bike, and hit his head.'

I was not a cyclist. I rode a bike because it fitted with my aims, not because I intrinsically enjoyed riding it or had built an identity out of doing so. I had set out from England to learn about myself and about the world. So why was I still pedalling all day with nothing left to do or think about? I gained no pleasure from the act of cycling, especially not down the hard shoulder of a highway. I had crossed eleven countries by bicycle power and felt no need to celebrate the crossing of a twelfth. I hadn't frozen to death, or been dissolved by the rain, and no amount of coldness and wetness would ever teach me any more about how to deal with being cold and wet than I already knew having cycled along the Black Sea Coast of Turkey in the winter. No amount more pedalling would bring a change of conversation with the locals or any further cultural insight. And it was now starkly obvious that no amount of time on the road would cause the deteriorating relationship between myself and Andy to suddenly, magically improve. I was gaining nothing, and – if the events of the day were anything to go by – had lost my way so badly that I risked losing everything. Something had to change.

'He's got a headache. Erm . . . he's just being taken away in the ambulance now, so . . . '

As the front wheel had fallen away – as momentum had carried me through the black air, as I'd suddenly gone from upright and seated to lying in a disoriented heap on the floor, without any recollection of the moments in between; as I'd picked myself up matter-of-factly and walked the few remaining yards to the end of the tunnel, warm liquid running down my cheek, touching my face and finding it numb and wet – something within me woke up. Some voice in my head gave me permission to realise that Ride Earth was no longer important.

I heard that voice. And I breathed a huge sigh of relief.

CHAPTER 11

I promise you this camera is on its way out. I give it another . . . I give it another three weeks.

Having now cycled in temperatures approaching fifty degrees Celsius, and comparing it to cycling in temperatures of around minus thirty degrees Celsius two winters ago, I have to say – it's definitely better to be too hot than to be too cold. I suffered a lot more that winter than I have done here.

Yes, it is very hot, and it is uncomfortable, but in the extreme cold it's a real . . . I dunno . . . you're aware of your mortality, and the fact that these are seriously dangerous temperatures, and that without shelter and without the right equipment you won't last long. At least in the heat, as long as there is water around, it's probably not going to kill you.

I know I'm putting it in a very general sense. But it's better to be too hot than too cold. Definitely.

There's another reason why I've been doing really long days recently. And it's because Tenny and I have been in touch with each other by email. And it's given me the motivation to push it a little bit further every day. Because I do miss her a lot. I mean, there isn't a day that goes by when I don't think about her.

It's not something that should distract me from the experience I'm having here. But it's something that's keeping me going, and it's giving me focus. And therefore . . . therefore, it's got to be a good thing.

I think that before I met Tenny, Andy and I – I think that there's a danger when travelling to get lost a little bit. There's always a danger that you . . . there's a saying that 'you can be so open-minded that your brain falls out'. And I think that might have applied if we'd carried on. There's no knowing where we'd have ended up, and how long we'd have travelled for.

In the end, it does become more self-indulgent than anything else, I think. There's always a natural end to every stage of one's life.

The heat sits across my back and shoulders like a cloak. My route has swung south-east on a newly built tarmac road. Khartoum, the Sudanese capital, is behind me, and I will soon arrive at the Ethiopian border, the remainder of Sudan still being out of reach for the independent traveller. The south is preparing for a referendum, and Africa's largest nation looks set to be cleft in two. By the time the sun dips below the horizon I've cycled a hundred miles, and it is clear already that an entirely different atmosphere shrouds these lands. Gone are the pretty, friendly, brightly painted villages. Gone are the reassuring sprouts of palm branches that told of closeness to the riverbank. The most enigmatic period of travelling I can remember has come to an end, and the road heads out into the featureless wind-blown gravel plains of the Sahara, which is beginning to look increasingly like the ten million square kilometres of purgatory I'd always seen in my childish imagination. I snatch a few hours of sleep beneath my mosquito net, and am back on the road an hour before sunrise, head down, face shaded beneath the sunhat I've tied to my head with string to prevent it being taken by the infernal wind.

These are the longest days I've ever spent in the saddle.

My body had never been so attuned to the task of cranking out sheer distance. But the newly paved surface is not here to help. Dotted occasionally alongside the tarmac are collections of sad crumbling shelters, some inhabited, some ruined and empty, none resembling a community. I revert to eating alone from my supplies, carrying as much water as possible. Lonely figures shuffle across the wastes between forlorn huddles of houses, sometimes wandering the empty desert, like sickened animals looking for some place to finally give in to the unrelenting heat, sand and god-damned sun.

I stop briefly at a tiny shop with a fridge full of Pepsi, Sprite and – my personal favourite – Stim, something similar to Appletiser. The owner's existence depends on selling a few bottles or a packet of overpriced biscuits every day to passing buses and pick-ups travelling the long road between the bigger towns. He doesn't ask why I'm alone in the desert on a funny-looking bicycle. An old woman shoos me away like a stray dog when I approach to ask to camp within the perimeter of her village. Nobody smiles or waves. The atmosphere is heavy with oppression. And, knowing nothing but odd snippets of hearsay about the history of Sudan and her internal conflicts, I can only pass by. That night, as I lie on my back in the sand, sinking into sleep's oblivion beneath the clearest starscape on earth, I can't help but wonder why it has to be like that. But, for now, I am about to leave Sudan behind. And, as always, I will leave with more questions than answers.

'Hello Mister!'
   'Hello.'
   'Are you fine?'

'Yes, thank you.'

'Where are you from? Germania? Farrance? America?'

Ah, the Germans. Great travellers indeed.

'England, actually.'

I wonder what name my home country is known by here. Anything beats the Arabic 'Br-r-r-itannia', or previous incarnations: 'Ingilterra', 'Anglia', 'Angle', 'Inglestan'.

'Ah, my friend! England! Wayne Rooney! Margaret Tatcher! David Beck Ham!'

'Er. Yes. I couldn't agree more.'

'My friend, you like football, no? I very very much like Chelsea.'

'Really? Why?'

I haven't the foggiest clue about football; if I had, I would still be somewhere in Egypt having a stimulating conversation in a tea shop about the ins and outs of the English Premier League.

'Before, I like Liverpool. Everybody like Liverpool. Very, very good. But not now. Now everybody like Chelsea.'

'Oh, right . . .'

'My friend, maybe you need help? What are you look for? Hotel restaurant-bar-change-money?'

Yes, I was waiting for this, and I'm sure you have friend who has very good hotel-restaurant-bar-change-money.

'No, thanks, I'm OK. I'm just walking. I like to look around on my own.'

'Why? Mister, you need help! I have friend, he has very very good hotel-restaurant-bar-change-money!!!'

One expects an arbitrary frontier on a map to bear little relevance to what one sees on the ground. But borders are often established where they are for good reason. In many cases there really is some major geographical distinction – mountain ridge, significant waterway, deep valley – that was fought over at some point or other in the past and which was too defensible or treacherous to allow either neighbour to overcome the other. And, once past this historical boundary, modern-day social and economic influences shape the landscape on each side: differences in land-use alone can mark drastic changes in the space of a few metres.

The Ethiopian side of the river is greener than Sudan's scrubby desert, bristling with strained, ambitious flora; a hazy backdrop of distant peaks telling of the high-altitude ride ahead. Ethiopia, the continent's most mountainous nation; rarely remembered for that reason. Those I'm still in touch with back home doubtless harbour the same guilt-laden images of Ethiopia as I do: dusty skin stretched over sunlit ribs, bellies swollen with hunger, flies gathering around staring white eyes. It's been two decades since the awful pictures of that famine reached British screens, so I'm hesitant to guess at what I might find as I take a pedal-powered cross-section of this wounded place.

But these dismal thoughts are quietened by the unadulterated sense of life that radiates forth as I stare up the wide gravel road in front of me. Lined on either side with unkempt rows of tumbledown shacks that extend beyond the reach of sight, as if carelessly scattered from on high by a distracted creator, Metema's street scene is absolutely crawling with people. Men. Women . . . women in public! Children weaving among adults like rivulets down a streambed. Rickshaws. Donkeys. Wood smoke and freshly baked bread. Honking and yammering and a cacophony of competing sound-systems – music! How long has it been since I last heard music played in the street? I eagerly push my bike up the track and into the fray, Islamic Africa and the Middle East already a relic of my mind.

As a rule, I've avoided hanging around national frontiers. These settlements evolve to tempt newcomers with their trade, to extract the maximum possible cash before moving guiltlessly on to the next punter who comes their way. The tricks of the trade are ever-changing and easy to be duped by, but the rule of thumb remains: there is no free lunch in a border town. Yet for every rule of thumb there is a contrary little pinkie to be found.

I follow Nega from his office across the road, and we duck down an alley between grey, rickety wooden walls and emerge into a small yard decked out with a couple of little tables and stools. Nega has a centred, confident air about him, applying himself to each task as it comes with equal quantities of calm and concentration, whether giving the waitress our food order, making a path through crowds of street-vendors and loiterers – or finding a particular page in a medical textbook in order to show me a magnified image of which of the four strains of malaria he has just diagnosed me with.

Malaria. . .

It had been that unusual ache in my legs, together with the very beginnings of fever, that gave it away; that groggy feeling you get when you stand up quickly and the world seems to glow slightly, lagging a split-second behind. A little twinge at the back of the throat rounded off the symptoms I needed to send me in the direction of Metema's sparsely furnished clinic and into Nega's treatment room for a blood sample. While the smear of red on the glass was left to dry, he'd asked me to accompany him across the road to one of the many eateries, and that was where I realised that I was in fact about to get a free lunch in a border town. Then I'd sat in the clinic's waiting room, reading the bold, lavishly illustrated posters on the walls that detailed the fundamentals of condom use. He'd delivered the news to me shortly after with the same friendly, plodding diplomacy that he employed in everything else he did. Don't worry, he'd said. This is just the first stage.

Still not sure what to make of having malaria, to be honest. I feel very weak . . . and . . . mentally weak, also. I feel . . .

I don't know, really.

In Sudan, the temptation to do very very long days, day after day after day, was too high, and I couldn't pace myself. And now I'm paying for it. I've just run myself into the ground, basically, by pushing it too hard.

My – my body just feels like it needs a rest, and I don't mean a couple of days in a city, rushing around trying to do chores – I mean some proper rest, where I do nothing but stay in one place and have some serious recuperation time.

It's just what to do while I'm waiting, really, because resting while you're ill is not really resting, if you see what I mean – it's being ill. I don't really know what I'm talking about, to be honest – I did start this video diary with something in mind, but it seems to have gone astray somehow. Erm . . .

I think I've talked too much, now. I think I'm going to stop.

I return to the hotel in which I'd spent the previous night to tell the staff that I won't be checking out just yet. I'm clutching a small packet of multicoloured pills and instructions to rest throughout the three days of heavy medication I've been prescribed. I'm not planning to argue with this – after all, I've just learnt that the world's single biggest killer has taken up residence in my bloodstream. I should be terrified. I have *malaria*, for goodness sake – the disease that kills one African child every forty-five seconds. So why do I feel so flippant? I have a bit of a fever, sorer-than-usual legs, a handful of pills, and a couple of days off to look forward to. What's missing is any sense of the gravity of having being diagnosed with a potentially fatal disease. Why is that?

Here's the thing. I have already accepted that what happens to me on this journey is mostly outside my control. I prepare for a balance between expected and unexpected. I'd taken anti-malarial drugs, for example. They hadn't worked. I'd covered up and slept beneath mosquito nets: a couple of bites got through anyway. Bad luck. I've already dealt with so much in the way of unpredictability, of being exposed and vulnerable, on this journey that is rapidly proving the biggest test of my life. Learning precisely how little grasp I have over the way these elements of life play out, I long since stopped trying to fix the odds in my favour, or wasting energy on emotions like fear or frustration or anger which have absolutely no positive effect on the cards that have been dealt. And I suppose it is the same with this. I know that a reaction will not change what has already come to pass. So why bother? Why waste energy on tears or terror or panic when that energy would be much better spent taking the medication, hoping for the best, preparing for the worst, and making a quick check that – were things not to go my way – I had at the very least been pursuing a life that was authentically mine?

I rediscover the glory of fresh fruit juice, abundant in Egypt but missing in the parched deserts of Sudan. Mango, orange and pale green avocado puree are the staple beverages here. I happen upon the quite heavenly combination of mango and avocado together in the same glass, and, with my new friend and fellow hotel resident Mike, we brave a twice-daily road-crossing to this little eatery, where we gobble endless plates of spicy spaghetti Bolognese, washed down with freshly blended fruit.

Mike is not a scavenger; he's a well-educated and ambitious private-school teacher from Addis Ababa. He's waiting for a colleague to arrive before travelling on to Khartoum, where he teaches the children of the well-heeled in the city's international school. Heavily built but smartly dressed, with an impermeable smile, he's as gentle as a lamb, despite his reservations about returning to Khartoum for another two-year contract. Having returned to Addis after his previous contract carrying savings totalling several years' local salary, his family had grabbed the sudden windfall and blown it all at once, leaving him with no choice but to head once again to Sudan to earn yet more money to keep his lazy, selfish relatives lazy and selfish.

'I can honestly say that they have ruined my life,' he says, sitting on the concrete outside my room as I offer him a serving of tea in the cut-off bottom half of an old water bottle. And then he breaks into a trademark laugh – long, wobbling, and from the belly. His eyes are already glazed over, cheeks full of the narcotic leaves known across tropical East Africa and Arabia as *qat*.

'It makes everything in the world look OK,' he says through a mouthful of little green flecks, '. . . when really, it's not!!!' Another belly laugh.

Mike had been an aspiring screenwriter, a hopeful creative mind in the big city. But he'd soon discovered that Ethiopia's film industry simply didn't exist. There was no money, neither to earn nor borrow, in order to fund it. So he forgot about building something; there were no foundations upon which to build. He forgot about travelling to Hollywood, or even Nollywood; immigration laws, he'd found, were not designed to favour the African on the street. And so he'd quietly dropped his ambitions and taken the only work he could find. At least, he says, teaching is a relatively noble and well-paid profession, even if it isn't quite what he'd dreamed of.

There's one big difference between me and Mike. I had the choice to follow my dream, when he did not.

If riding gave me too much thinking time, being holed up in a tin-roofed mud hut with malaria is a recipe for insanity. But it's the other people in my life I'm more concerned about. The ones I left behind. How would they feel if they could see me now, sweating and feverish, knowing there was nothing they could do to help? I thought about my parents, back in long-forgotten England. I thought about my best mate Andy, who by now must be somewhere in India, or perhaps Nepal. And I thought about the girl who crossed my path in Armenia, for whom I made so many sacrifices, and who I left in tears in order to do this. What if I never get to see her again?

I won't tell her about the malaria. Not until it's passed into the canon of travellers' tales. And I can think of nothing but her, as I lie in the hotel-brothel. Outside in the yard, the matriarch haggles with Herculean force over the price of a soft-drink delivery. Another resident slouches on a mattress beneath a papaya tree, fiddling with a mobile phone. And I lie on the bed, thinking about our story together, about that chance meeting in an Irish pub on Valentine's Day where it began – and all because of a sponsored sleeping-bag.

CHAPTER 12

'Tom?' The voice crackled in my ear.

'Hey, Artur! What's happening tonight?'

'So – I have one friend who is organising some Valentine's party. It's at Cheers. You remember Cheers, I think?'

I laughed. 'Yeah, I remember. Just about.'

'Anyway, I'm thinking I will go to this party there, later tonight. If you want to join?'

I had met Artur some days previously at a gathering in the home of the young Italian volunteers who were hosting me in Yerevan, the capital of Armenia. He was a native of the country, about my age, who had shunned the status quo and now kept a big mix of company – European volunteers and NGO workers posted to Yerevan; Westerners of Armenian descent who'd floated to Armenia on dreams of some lost homeland; and the country's own hippies, eco-warriors, vegetarians and cyclists; all of whom drifted together into an eddy marked 'outsiders' that I was very happy to find myself occupying.

Artur was serious, almost military-looking, with close-cropped black hair and a matching beard, but behind it was a calm and softly spoken character. He was unnaturally thin, to an extent that you'd imagine would make it difficult for him to lift himself out of bed. His clothes always hung baggily from the corners of his frame, full of air, as if he were a life-sized puppet. Yet there was nothing lethargic or clumsy about Artur – instead, he exuded vitality, as if all that fat and muscle that the rest of us had was just unnecessary baggage, weighing us down and stilting our actions. Artur would dart and sweep through the streets, like a bike messenger in traffic, then melt into the shadows and simply exist there, observing, scanning the crowds and surroundings for some moment of beauty or intrigue or irony.

He would rarely be seen without one of his collection of ancient cameras. Despite never appearing to take any photos with them, he in fact had a habit of constantly capturing images – only he took them when nobody realised he was doing so, until a few days later when the resulting prints appeared, catching the subject off-guard. And, like an artist who can capture the essence of someone's soul with a few strokes of pencil lead, the photos he developed seemed to contain nothing at all, yet at the same time miniature universes.

Artur's unique perspective on the world made for interesting company. So when he suggested heading to a party on the evening of St. Valentine's Day, I didn't hesitate to agree. I was free, and I was single, and I was preparing to leave Yerevan for the next stage of my journey – this time, alone.

After eight weeks, the scars on my face were slowly beginning to heal, though I imagined that a faint souvenir of the event would remain beneath the hair of my eyebrow for the rest of my life. Even before I'd left the scene of the accident on a stretcher in the back of an ambulance, I'd quietly quashed the idea that anything mattered except for my most immediate circumstances, least of all Ride Earth. Time had proved that prediction and planning made no real sense. This life was not a business, or a holiday, or an event, with some big, abstract idea floating above it. It was a guy, on a bicycle, somewhere, with the stuff in his bags, and the thoughts in his head. And that was it.

Andy had arrived at the hospital with the police while I'd been having the stitches put in above my right eye, and had gathered all of our belongings and convinced the authorities to put us up in a hotel for the night. The following morning, I'd decided that I'd try cycling tentatively onwards. My face was in agony; my right eye closed up and patched over with a dressing, my left eye swollen and purple. I'd had a deep, throbbing pain in the centre of my forehead, and I'd blacked out twice that morning. But it was Christmas Eve, and the border, after all, was only a few miles away. And that afternoon, at the border-crossing, I discovered that Georgia's version of Christianity was an Orthodox one, and that Christmas would not be taking place until the seventh of January.

Meeting another bicycle traveller in the seaside resort town of Batumi absolved me from any further decision-making. Having ridden alone from the Arctic Circle of Scandinavia, Marek proposed we ride the three hundred miles through the snowy interior of Georgia to Tbilisi together in four days in order to celebrate New Year in the capital. Andy had agreed enthusiastically with the Polish cyclist's plan, and I was happy to fall in. And as soon as we arrived in Tbilisi, having seen almost nothing of Georgia, I drifted off, met new people and made different friends. Days passed during which I neither saw nor spoke to Andy at all;

he disappeared from my life and embarked upon another shadowy romance – this time with a French girl we'd met on New Year's Eve. It was exactly the break I'd needed. But – again – it made leaving the city quite difficult.

On the morning of our planned departure, I sat down at our host's kitchen table. The house was empty, and, finding myself once again with nobody else to talk to, I began to confide in the lens of my video camera.

Today, erm, we are going to leave – well, I'm going to leave. I don't know where Andy is. He's found a distraction – he's basically got involved with a girl, and he's let it basically rule his . . . rule his life for the last couple of days. And he hasn't really been thinking about anything else, so . . . basically I wanted to leave yesterday, and I would have done if – if he'd been here to pack up and to go. And today we arranged that we'd leave in the morning; last night he didn't come back, and this morning it's already gone eleven o'clock in the morning and there's no sign of him, so . . .

What do I do? Do I just wait around, and waste more time and money, because, er . . . he . . . because he can't see the consequences of his actions? I don't know. I might just go off on my own, tell him which way I'm going – tell him to catch me up, and that I'll see him on the road.

It's snowing again. There's no delaying the leaving any longer. When we do leave, it's going to be bloody cold, and it's going to be very difficult. You can't get away from it, you've just got to face it, and get on with it. I'm looking forward to the challenge, myself; I want to get my teeth into it, and go – get out on my bike – now.

I want to finish my porridge, get on my bike, and leave.

Andy had reappeared the following day. I hadn't enquired,

he hadn't explained, and we'd set out through the mountains towards Armenia, crossing the border the following morning on the snowy mountain road to Iran, with less to say to each other than ever before. We'd collected our visas to enter Iran during the three-week layover in Tbilisi, and we would finally collect two brand-new winter sleeping-bags. Having given up altogether on the useless sponsor, my mother had driven to an outdoor shop in Milton Keynes and posted the two sleeping-bags she'd bought to a contact in Yerevan.

And rather than on clear terms and under sensible circumstances, it was on the second day in Armenia, halfway up a long climb in the freezing winter sun, that my journey with Andy would come to an end.

'Waiting for you,' he said as I pulled up behind him, 'is really starting to grate.'

This, I knew, was a prelude to what Andy *really* wanted to say. He'd never been one to express his emotions in a straightforward way – not about our early bickering, not about girls, not about the escalating arguments in Turkey. The meaning was always hidden behind vagaries, taking pressure and mediation to come forth, or was never communicated at all. He'd been thinking about this for some time, and, looking for an excuse to justify cutting the rope, had used a thinly veiled nod towards my inferior fitness, knowing that five thousand miles of cycling hadn't closed the gap. I found myself suddenly annoyed by Andy and his idiosyncrasies. Why could he never just *say* it? *Spit it out!*

And at the same time, I knew that I'd been waiting for *him* to do this, because I could not. Though I'd made noises about leaving Tbilisi without him, I was unable to say it to his face. I was paralysed by pride, immobilised in the face of the inevitable. I was equally guilty of this indirectness; this inability to communicate my concerns.

He continued cycling, pulling ahead quickly. I followed at my own pace, and a few minutes later I caught sight of him talking to the driver of a stopped car on the road ahead. The car pulled away, and he turned and began freewheeling slowly towards me, stopping on the roadside opposite me in the shadow of the white mountainside. *Finally.*

'Erm – I'm going carry on to Yerevan on my own,' he said. 'I think it'll be kind of a good experience for both of us, to . . . to see what cycling alone is like, and stuff.'

'Yep.'

'So I'll give you half of the money, and half of the food – whatever's left, anyway?'

'Sounds good.'

'That driver said he could help us out in the next village.'

'Oh . . . ?'

'Here you are, then.' Andy offered me a torn-off piece of paper with an indecipherable phrase written on it.

'What is it?' I asked.

'It's the address of a shop where he said we can go and eat.'

'Right.'

'Obviously I've tried to copy it as best I possibly can.'

'OK. Well,' I said slowly, 'it's kind of your adventure now, so . . . I probably won't see you there.'

'Right . . .' he replied. A moment of uncertainty flashed across his face. 'I'll . . . see you in Yerevan, then.'

'Yeah.'

'Yeah,' he said. 'OK – see you later.' It was as if he was stepping away from the doorstep of my house in Middleton.

'Good luck,' I added.

'Yeah, you too.'

I held out a hand. He shook it, mounted his bike, wobbled into the road, turned uphill and began to pedal. His legs span quickly, yet – in first gear – he edged away with comical slowness, wiping his nose with a ski glove, sniffing in the cold air. Then he was further off, weaving gradually along the icy roadside, his breath still visible in the sun; my best mate Andy, tall, lean and broad-shouldered, trusty old blue and silver helmet strapped to his bushy head of hair, cargo trailer close to bursting with sacks of equipment, pedalling silently into a future entirely his own.

Andy had done something brave. He had acknowledged that the time had come to take action. And – even if he hadn't said all that could have been said – at least he'd done it. He had done what I was too stubborn and afraid to do myself.

As the solitary figure disappeared round the bend in the distance, I felt a kind of crazed elation, as if someone had just thrown open all the windows on a windy autumn day, letting all of the world into a stuffy space that had been closed off for too long. A mere speck on a bare white hillside, I could be anyone right now – do anything at all! I could change my name, fabricate a new personality out of thin air, and nobody would have the slightest idea who I really was as I passed into and out of their lives. I could get on a plane to the other side of the planet, disappearing from sight completely, leaving the Ride Earth website to fester and my email account to fill up with unanswered messages. And it wouldn't matter one bit, because the last remaining thread of my previous existence had just been cut away.

More than two years would pass before Andy and I would next travel together by bicycle.

In Yerevan, Artur and I walked down the long, sloping boulevard, three lanes wide in each direction, the pavements lined with brittle, empty trees. Frozen slush crunched beneath my feet, a grey mess of footprints captured by the plummeting temperatures of night.

I was talking to Artur about Andy, who I'd heard had gone back to Tbilisi from Yerevan.

'I just don't understand it,' I said. 'Why, when he's got this . . . just this *ultimate freedom* – he could do whatever he wants, go off, cycle wherever, travel exactly how – in exactly the way that suited him . . .'

Artur listened. He was good at that.

'. . . why, now, has he decided that the best thing he could possibly do is to get involved with another girl?!?'

I had only seen Andy a couple of times since arriving in Yerevan, as we'd stayed with different hosts. But Artur was a friend that Andy and I had made in common. So I felt able to voice my thoughts on my best mate's latest movements, conquests and errors of judgement.

'He is wanting to travel by bicycle again. With you. You know that, right?' said Artur, eventually.

'Yeah, I know.' I sighed. Andy had said this in an email a couple of days previously, as part of a discussion about the ongoing sleeping-bag saga, which had now grown even more complicated. I'd arrived in Yerevan, alone, to find them impounded by the customs department. That had been over three weeks ago.

'The thing is . . . I really don't think I'm ready to do that. I mean, it's not because of *him*, or our friendship, or Ride Earth, or whatever. It's just . . . I feel like, right now, I'm doing what I want to be doing, making my own decisions.

And that feels good. And I want to keep it like that for as long as it still seems right, and then . . . and then meet up later on. If it still feels like the right thing to do.'

We were passing the monolithic headquarters of the American University of Armenia, which sat like a massive window-filled brick at the top of a broad expanse of steps to our left.

'The building used to be the centre for Communist Party conferences,' said Artur. 'Now it's the centre for a capitalistic education system!'

The next plot was home to the British Embassy compound; a wall of pinkish stone topped with silver spear tips, housing a modest little Greco-Roman mansion with a wrought-iron maquette of the crown perched on its head. Tomorrow, one of the bureaucrats would resume work on the long-winded process of getting our sleeping-bag parcel re-addressed as diplomatic mail – thus avoiding the seven-hundred-dollar tax bill we'd received for their import into Armenia.

We arrived at Cheers, found a photocopied note on the wall outside, and deduced from it that there was a gay and lesbian party in full swing inside. Banging techno pulsed into the dark empty street, causing nearby windows to vibrate in protest, and this was soon joined by the sound of muffled screaming. The bouncer peered up at us as we stood in mild confusion at the top of the basement stairs, and slowly shook his head.

I asked Artur what he suggested. Snow had begun to appear in the air – the lightest kind of snow, almost imperceptibly fine.

'I guess I got the wrong message,' said Artur. 'Wait one second – let me call some people.'

Our next stop was another basement joint called Red Bar. It was already late, as Artur kept strange hours, usually going to bed around dawn and then getting up again in the early afternoon. The peacefulness of the city at night, he said, was calming and relaxing, and suited him better than the rowdiness of the day.

We trotted down the steps into the crowded little bar. It was dark and the music was frantic and uncomfortably loud. The dark red walls seemed to suck the little remaining light out of the atmosphere. A bar counter lined with neon stood in front of the side wall, and in the space opposite a dozen shadows jostled for dancing space amongst sofas full of figures shouting into each other's ears, desperate to make themselves heard above the din.

Three girls squeezed past on their way out. Their faces were vaguely familiar. But then they seemed a uniquely recognisable trio. One of them was so short that if I hadn't looked down I'd have missed her completely, tiny even beside her dark-eyed, kindly-faced friend, who could barely have been five foot tall herself. And the third, a young, sweet-looking girl, towered above the two of them like a matriarch. They hollered something up at Artur as we moved aside to make room on the stairs. Artur shouted something back as they disappeared out through the door. A magnanimous blast of ice-cool air swept into the bar, dissolving instantly in the fog of sweat and smoke and spilt beer that permeated the room.

As my eyes adjusted, more familiar-looking faces began to surface – others who I'd half met or shared a self-conscious dance or a spot at the bar with during the many revelries of the previous month, and of whose names and circumstances

I had lost track. I tried to make conversation. But I couldn't hear a bloody thing.

I stared around the bar, fiddling uneasily with my hair. Swishing elbows and bouncing handbags hinted that I was taking up valuable room for groups of gyrating females who I didn't recognise, and who, I noticed, were carefully ignoring me. Then, as my fingers traced the outline of my scar, I remembered what I must look like. An injured, bulbous eye peering through an overgrown hedge. A fleece riddled through by campfire sparks. A pair of navy nylon sports slacks. And enormous military boots.

'Sod it,' I said out loud to nobody in particular, nodded at Artur, and we trotted back out into the street.

Shamrock was one of those fall-back bars; the places you go when all other options have failed to deliver, and you just want to sit out the rest of the evening somewhere familiar and comfortable, where the bar staff at least know your face, if not your name, and you can relax and stop peering around the room so much. It was a short walk away, so that's where we went.

I pushed open the door, dearly hoping for a full entourage of friends and acquaintances and attractive women to herald our entrance. Instead, there was nothing. The barman, tapping away at his mobile phone by the glass-washing machine, ignored us completely. The door swung closed, revealing the bar's only three customers, sat at a table in the corner behind it. It was the three girls we'd briefly seen leaving the previous bar. They nodded, half-acknowledging our presence, before returning to their conversation and glasses of wine.

Artur headed over to the other side of the room and

greeted the barman, who looked up in surprise, then smiled and reached out to shake Artur's hand, glancing briefly at me as he did so with an expression somewhere between customary warmth and mild fear. I smiled back, again wondering whether I was actually fit for appearance in public at all.

I took a seat at the bar. A tall glass of beer arrived. Artur, who didn't drink, was exchanging a few words with the table in the corner.

'These girls are asking if we want to join them,' he said, turning to me. 'I know them.'

'Sure – why not?'

The rectangular table was pushed up against the wall, across which two high-backed benches faced each other. One of the girls, who faced her two friends across the table, shuffled up the bench towards the wall, and I took a seat next to her in the space she'd made, immediately feeling thrust into the spotlight. Artur, meanwhile, was giving the girls a quick introduction to the world of Tom Allen in Armenian, and I watched their faces with amusement, waiting for the all-too-familiar moment at which he mentioned the words for 'bicycle' and 'from England', and the penny dropped.

At this point, I knew, the three listeners would each break into their own version of confused laughter, looking at each other for some kind of cue, and the most forthcoming of the group would quickly ask Artur for some point of clarification, checking that no misunderstanding had taken place and that this guy had indeed ridden through the mountains in the middle of the coldest winter for a generation in order to be here. Meanwhile, the shyest member of the group would dip her head slightly in embarrassment, covering the manoeuvre by taking a sip of her drink, and surreptitiously looking over the rim of the glass at the third girl for support, which would be delivered via an almost imperceptible raising of the eyebrows.

And this is precisely what happened.

Artur lowered himself onto the bench opposite me with a grin.

'And . . . how . . . how long it took, this journey?' asked the girl next to me, the kind-eyed, dark-haired one from the previous bar. She was curious; there was no hint that she was asking out of politeness. But she was obviously hesitant with her English, so I tried to keep my words simple and intelligible – easier said than done while speaking through a wall of moustache.

'Erm . . . eight months,' I said, 'from England to Armenia.'

Her eyes widened in disbelief. '*Eight months?* Oh my god – I would die!' And she repeated the sentiment to her friends opposite. At least, I assumed that was what she was saying, although she might have been making a hilarious joke about the fact that the missing link between modern man and early hominids was seated next to her. They all burst into laughter.

'And are you continuing your trip?' asked the girl opposite – the short one, Serineh, whose dreadlocks must have been an even bigger novelty than my own greasy mane. Calm and straightforward, she had the kind of perceptive manner that seemed to cut through any woolly language and see what was going on beneath.

'Yes . . . I'm going to Iran. I've got the visa, so . . .'

'Oh! We're from Iran.'

'Sorry?'

'We're all from Iran.' Serineh nodded towards her two friends.

'You mean you're Iranian? Persian?'

'It means,' explained my neighbour, 'we're from a small community – well, a big community – of Christians in Iran. Armenian Christians.'

'So you speak Armenian – or Farsi?'

'We speak Armenian, at home. And with friends we speak Armenian.'

'But . . . you speak Farsi as well?'

'Yes – we study at school. And it gets more and more, as we go to . . . higher classes. And then all the teachers are Muslim Iranians.'

'Er – can you write down some phrases in Farsi for me?' I asked, standing up to retrieve the notebook from my back pocket and knocking the table in the process, spilling wine and beer across the polished wooden surface. 'Oh, crap – sorry!'

'Doesn't matter!' said Serineh, jumping up to fetch a cloth from the barman. The tall girl, still shy to speak to me in English, said something to my neighbour, who translated:

'Arpa is saying not to worry, because the wine is free. For women.'

'Hold on – that's not fair!' I laughed, and realised that I didn't know her name, and that I couldn't remember whether or not she'd been introduced. But I wanted to know it. And so I entered that unfortunate state of semi-distraction when you're trying to hide the fact that you're waiting for an opportunity to slip into the conversation the line, 'By the way – sorry – what was your name again?'

'Have some of the cheese.' She flashed a smile and pushed

a little terracotta pot along the table, containing what looked like little crunchy breadsticks but were actually strips of rubbery cheese, which came apart in strings when you picked at them.

'Oh – thanks!'

I nibbled at one of the bizarre cheesy wands with the feeling that I was being studied.

'These are . . . these are *weird*.'

'They were free also, so you might as well have some!'

'Why do women get free stuff on Valentine's Day, anyway?'

'Don't they get free stuff in England?'

'Er . . . I dunno, really,' I said, too quickly, realising how unromantic and ignorant I must have sounded.

'Where in England are you from, then? I mean, which city?' she said, taking a sip of her wine.

'Oh, you wouldn't have heard of it. It's a village, actually. Kind of in the centre of England. Only about five hundred people. It's pretty small.'

'A village!' she said, seeming taken aback. 'What is the name?'

'Er – Middleton.'

'Mmm,' she replied. I guessed what she might be thinking.

'I should just clarify – villages in that part of England aren't really like the villages in Armenia. Or in Iran, I imagine.'

'Yes, yes – I was wondering – you have . . . I mean, you have a normal life, in your village, right? Electricity?'

'Oh, yes! It's very comfortable. We have electricity, services, good roads . . . everything is very normal.'

'Oh, good! I was thinking maybe you live on a farm, or something!' And she laughed, clapping her hand to her mouth like a cartoon character.

'No, no, no! Well, my mother grew up on a farm. And my

granddad. And there are a couple of working farms in the village. But no – I'm not a farmer!'

I wasn't sure quite what this young woman would make of my description of middle-class rural England. But she didn't enquire further. Artur, Serineh and Arpa were chatting away in Armenian at the other corner of the table. I began to contemplate the bar snacks, slowly rotating the little pot and its contents between my fingers.

'So, don't you like the cheese, then?' she asked.

'No, yeah, I do! It's just the flavour – it's interesting . . .'

'It's, er . . . smo . . . sm . . . *Serineh-jan – tskhvats, che?*' Serineh looked over, nodding. 'Smoked?'

'Oh – that's what it is . . .'

I studied the ridiculous rubbery strand, pulling it apart and watching the tendrils unfurl from each other as they were separated.

'They are not really . . . for eating. I mean, they are, but you have it with beer – it's like . . . something to play with, or something to do while you are drinking.'

'Delicious!' I grinned, holding a stick aloft theatrically and snipping off a length with my front teeth. She laughed.

'So . . . d'you reckon you could let me know a few useful things in Farsi?' I asked again, tapping the cover of my notebook with my fingertips.

'Er – excuse me?' she replied. I looked at her quizzically. 'Oh, no –' she continued, worried I'd taken offence, 'I didn't mean . . . I have to say that . . . I really like your accent . . . but I find it a bit difficult to understand. But I really love it!'

'Oh! Thank you! Er – well, I wanted to ask if you could write down some sentences in Farsi. So I can know a few . . . basic things . . . before I arrive.'

'Yes! Of course! What do you want to know?'

'Just . . . basic stuff. Like the words for "hello", "food", "water", "thank you" – things like that. By the way – sorry – what was your name again?'

'Tenny. I am Tenny.'

Now I'm on my own I should probably start doing a few more video diaries. And talk a bit about what's been going on the last few days. Where to start . . . erm . . .

So today was a very long and eventful day.

This morning, after I got up, I had an email from the embassy – from the British Embassy – saying that my sleeping-bag was available for collection from the airport, and would I like to go with the driver to the airport?

So I arranged to do that. And I thought in the meantime I'd go and buy myself a new head-torch, which is something that I've been lacking for . . . well, several months, actually. I'm not sure how long this one will last, but nevertheless I think it was a pretty good buy, for just over a quid.

I also bought a lighter for lighting my stove, which also conveniently comes with a digital clock, that you can't change, and that has the wrong time on it.

After that, I went to a second-hand shop and got a down jacket. So, together with my new hat, which is made from real rabbit fur, I'm prepared for the cold mountains of Iran, and hopefully for the coldness of any Central Asian mountains I might venture through. And all for the bargain price of about six quid.

And after that I went to the British Embassy, and while I was waiting I met the French couple who Andy was staying with before he went back to Tbilisi. And – hah! – unbelievably,

Vincent just happened to have been given my bank card by Andy! I haven't had a bank card since September in bloody Romania!

And so I went to the airport with the Embassy driver, and I was so pleased that everything was going really well. And then we were told that the computers weren't working, so we'd have to come back tomorrow! So I got as far as the airport – I was even in the same building as these bloody sleeping-bags, after three months of trying to get hold of them, including one month of waiting here in Yerevan – and I still don't actually have them!

So, tomorrow – fingers crossed – I'm going to get them. And I'll probably be a hundred quid worse off for the privilege. Which is about as much money as I need to cycle across the whole of Iran to Turkmenistan, so it'll be a bit of a financial blow. But it just means I'll have to spend another week picking peaches in Australia or wherever, so I'll just try and think of it like that.

Because I saved up enough money to cycle round the world. In reality, at the rate it's going, I can probably get to Australia or New Zealand, as I'm spending no more than two or three pounds a day. I've had to pay for accommodation on . . . what, nine nights out of the two hundred and fifty or so since I left England? And things like this down-filled jacket – well, I found it for a fiver in a second-hand shop. It's got a bit of paint on it, but – you know – it doesn't really matter, does it? It's going to keep me warm. That's the important thing.

So tomorrow I'll try one more time. And if I don't get these bloody sleeping-bags tomorrow, then I'm going to go to a party, get very drunk, and pass out in a ditch. And if I do get them, then I'm going to celebrate. By going to a party, getting very drunk, and passing out in a ditch.

The next morning felt like the morning before my first driving test, when success felt so close yet still so tantalisingly out of reach, because it depended on everything happening a tiny bit more perfectly than was reasonably possible.

I was outside the Embassy gates at nine-thirty, in time to watch them creak open, as appointed, and the friendly Armenian driver to emerge in one of the British Ambassador's big luxurious four-by-fours. We sped along the highway leading south towards the airport and the cargo depot. It was a glorious late winter's day, the sun vigorous and confident, the sky a blemish-free blue, the roads and pavements licked with meltwater. The objects of my last quarter-year of travail drew closer. Soon there would be a box in the boot and we would be speeding back to the city, and I would realise that winter was already ending.

'I can't actually believe it. I can't actually believe it's *there*.'

I stood, hands on hips, looking down at the cardboard box wrapped in packing tape in the middle of the living room floor. My mother had obviously paid a visit to Lidl and nicked one of those packing boxes that they leave there for the shoppers too stingy or environmentally-conscious to pay 2p for a plastic bag: the box's exterior advertised not sleeping-bags but Ecuador's finest bananas.

'It's . . . it's not real.'

I gave the box a tap with my foot. My Couchsurfing hosts Lucila and Anton stood around in their slippers and tracksuit bottoms, having just got up, watching with amusement as the hairy Englishman's dreams came true in front of their eyes.

'Did you check what's inside?' asked Anton.

'Er – well. I really should have done. But the driver said

that . . . if there's diplomatic mail, then what they do is they put it in the car, lock the doors and windows and then drive really fast back to the Embassy without stopping, because . . . it might contain something sensitive.'

Lucila handed me a pair of scissors and I began to hack at the layers of parcel tape.

'How the hell do I get into this box?' I laughed. 'My mother – as usual – has packed it rather too well.'

Ironically, it was my dear unwitting mother's diligence that had created the one-month hold-up. Worried that falsifying the price of the bags would be an insurance risk, she'd ignored my pleas to declare them at a tenner each and instead written their true value on the customs declaration form – which, unfortunately, was several hundred pounds; easy prey for a hefty bill of import tax.

'Carina, you're missing this moment!' called Lucila to the third housemate, who was still getting dressed.

'Exactly!' I shouted, slicing away at the box's seams. 'This is something monumental!'

And then it fell open and two tightly stuffed bundles rolled out onto the floor.

'Tooooommmm!!!'

'Woohoooooo!!!'

I leapt up and punched the air – someone's camera flashed. 'YES!!! Oh my GOD!!!'

I picked up one of the bundles and tossed it into the air, catching it with a flourish – 'Yaaaayyyy!!! Amazing, amazing, amazing . . .' – while the three Italians watched in disbelief. They'd clearly never seen a fully grown man get this excited about a sleeping-bag.

'Sleep in comfort at minus twenty-five degrees!' I said,

reading the label on the bag. 'Well, that'll be useful *now*!'

'There are other things in the box,' said Anton, pointing, as I pulled the sleeping-bag from its sack and measured it up against myself as if it were a shirt on display in a clothes store.

'Oh – yes.'

Alongside Andy's sleeping-bag was a padded envelope containing a book of some sort, and a thin envelope with my mother's handwriting on the front. I carefully opened it and unfolded the handwritten letter. Something slipped out and fell to the floor.

'Ah – what's this?'

Putting the letter on the sofa, I reached down for the folded piece of paper. It was a newspaper cutting. I stood up straight, opening it out.

'It's an article. Oh dear . . . hah! I don't believe it!'

The piece had been cut from the *Harborough Mail*, my local newspaper. At the top of the full-page spread was a big picture of me, sat on the floor on the left, and Andy squatting down on the right, grinning widely, both of us cuddling the giant toy panda that sat between us: the mascot of the WWF, whose office we had visited in Istanbul. Below the photo, the article's words painted a picture of two intrepid young Englishmen from the Midlands living a dream of adventure on the open road, in which each day was filled with acts of heroic defiance and fortitude, winning over foreign lands and people, forging ever onward. Their mission, it seemed, was going from strength to strength. What could possibly stand in their way?

CHAPTER 13

I stood by the road. It was cold. Old, crunchy snow lingered here, at the crux of the pass that went down into one of the series of yawning valleys along the mountain road that led to Iran.

I leaned my bike against the concrete barrier at the edge of the mountain-top lay-by. Beyond the barrier, a sheer wall of ice-clad rock dropped off into an invisible gorge, hundreds of metres below. I fished my feather jacket from the enormous dry-bag that was strapped to the back of my bike, containing everything I'd need to survive the rest of the winter outdoors – a new sleeping-bag, an inflatable mattress, extra clothes procured from flea markets in pursuit of the dream of pedalling onward alone. I'd been climbing all day, and now, having stopped at the top, I was rapidly growing cold. My toes began to throb, my skin sweaty and shivering.

How ironic that – having spent over three months chasing a god-damned winter sleeping-bag – I would finally set off and discover that winter was already releasing her grip on the lands beneath these peaks! By now it would probably be warm enough to camp down in the valleys with my old gear, plus maybe a cheap fleece blanket or two that could be given away later on, and while I might shiver for a few nights, it would be getting warmer day by day. The road drew south, to Iran and Pakistan, and it was early March, almost nine months after I'd left home, which now seemed an unimaginably long time ago.

But something fundamental had changed. And in this new light, all the plans I'd laid from the comfort of my bedroom seemed so ridiculously irrelevant, formed from such idealism and inexperience, with not the slightest grasp of how it would feel to leave my life on a wealthy island in the Atlantic and convert, literally overnight, to one of wandering, permanent vagrancy in unfamiliar lands where not even life's essentials could be taken for granted – let alone what would happen if one day I found a reason to change my mind.

'Hope to see you again soon!' she'd said, as we'd parted ways at the end of that evening in the Irish pub – and I'd hoped so to, though I'd feared it was relatively unlikely. But a few days later, at a leaving party my friends were throwing for me in Cheers, I'd spotted two diminutive figures sat at the bar: Serineh with her dreadlocks, Tenny with her long, thick, dark hair – the shorter two members of that Armenian-Iranian triple-act with whom I'd spent such an enjoyable Valentine's evening.

Tenny turned to see the newcomers, and fixed her eyes on mine. This was one of those awkward moments when you are aware of having been slightly over-enthusiastic when you'd previously met someone. And you don't want to appear too forward, in case the other hasn't spent as much time as you have imagining how it might be to meet again. And you know that you'll end up giving the exact message you *don't* want to give because of this over-analysis and resultantly clunky behaviour.

My insides shrivelling into a walnut-sized ball in my

stomach, I waved to her as I closed the door, feigning a carefree and confident smile. Tenny waved back, returning the smile, but I was already striding with an air of forced nonchalance towards my friends in the opposite corner of the room. Nervously, I glanced back to check whether Tenny was still looking at me, but by this point she'd turned away to say something to Serineh. I spent the next few hours re-playing our previous conversation, wondering if the thrill of the chase I remembered feeling was real, and worrying that I was attaching too much meaning to the encounter; that I'd imagined an undercurrent of flirtation that wasn't actually there. To pass the time, I half-engaged in conversations with the people who'd organised this 'sleeping-bag leaving party', all the time beating myself up over the fact that the subject of my fixation was still sitting across the room, probably thinking what a fool she'd been to assume I'd be as sincere and laid-back as I'd first seemed, no doubt making a mental note to avoid bearded English men in the future. Why wasn't I over there talking to her? I was leaving Yerevan tomorrow. And she was sitting right *there!!!*

A few hours and a few drinks later, I could no longer ignore the fact that my window of opportunity to speak to Tenny again was closing fast. By now she must think me two-faced or a complete wimp (or both). Out of the corner of my eye I could see that her friend Serineh was putting on a thick winter coat, ready to head out of the bar and into the snowy night. It really was now or never.

'You're going?!?'

Tenny had dismounted the bar-stool and looked as if she was about to follow Serineh out of the bar, which was now almost empty. It was almost two in the morning and I was supposed to be riding out of Yerevan in a few dismally short hours.

'Well . . . all my friends are going now . . .'

'But I haven't talked to you yet.'

'I've been here all night!'

Which was true. She had been sitting at the bar for the entire evening, wondering why I'd asked Artur for her phone number, invited her to my leaving party, and then spent several hours completely ignoring her.

'Look,' I said, desperately trying to claw back the fragments of my utterly ruined reputation, 'I'm not going anywhere right now. I'd really like it if you stayed a bit longer for another drink.'

She looked at Serineh, who said something I didn't understand, waved goodbye to us both, and left. Then she looked at the barman, who was behind his laptop lining up a playlist of music for the last vestiges of the night. He was clearly a friend, and shot her a look that I could not interpret. A few more seconds passed while she weighed up her options.

'OK,' she finally said, and smiled. 'OK. I will stay.'

We sat at the bar and talked, undisturbed. She attempted to teach me to dance the tango, and failed. We laughed. I told her I was meant to be leaving the following morning, and she wrote out a poem in my notebook. It was four lines long and it was beautiful. We shared a taxi home.

I looked down the road. The cold air stung my nostrils. Frozen snot formed mini icicles that hung from my moustache, salty-tasting and revolting. A truck grumbled up the incline, passed slowly with an annoyingly friendly honk, and rounded the bend that would take it down the far side of the range and onward to the Iranian border, a hundred and fifty miles away. It would take three days to ride there. Three days of solid, solitary pedalling through the furrows of the South Caucasus in order to get a rubber stamp in a little burgundy booklet that told disinterested men in uniforms where I'd been born. And then I'd be spat out into a place where people used a different set of unintelligible noises to communicate, went to work in a slightly different setting, raised families in slightly different-looking houses and drank a slightly different version of tea, on my mission to cycle round the world.

I thought I'd allowed for flexibility. I'd been fairly sure that the plan would need adjustment, that I'd need extra equipment sometimes, that timescales would vary out of necessity. But I'd been too short-sighted to consider that I might one day come across an idea more desirable than pedalling practically non-stop round the planet. Nine months of riding – all the thousands of miles I'd come since then – had given me time for reflection. And now a clear alternative lay before me.

I had delayed my departure for several days in order to spend more time getting to know Tenny. She'd had no idea what she was doing, but the contentment of her life as a student in Yerevan had forced me to ask myself one simple question: did I really, honestly, still want to cycle round the world? Was that neat-sounding phrase to be the sole determining factor in where I would take my life from this point onward? Exactly whose dream was I trying to live up to – my own, or that of somebody else; some figure, no doubt real, who had already made a longer, harder, better, more adventurous, more worthwhile round-the-world bicycle journey than I ever would?

Following the truck down into the next valley would seal my fate. Yerevan would become another old chapter in my story, my promises to Tenny that we'd see each other again would be quietly forgotten, her memory fading in the face of new adventures and encounters. Descending the far side of the mountain would be a commitment to an open-ended, unknown future, cycling endlessly onward in pursuit of that impossibly faraway goal.

The alternative lay back the way I'd come, back down the six-hour climb, back across the dreary flatlands beneath the shadow of Mount Ararat and into the peculiar, charming, frustrating stew of existence that was Yerevan, to the top floor of an unremarkable Soviet-era apartment block where lived a girl – a girl who had single-handedly delayed my departure for ten days after the leaving party, showing me a glimpse of a very different life that could be mine. It might not be quite as action-packed or unpredictable or dynamic – which didn't mean it would be any less meaningful or satisfying, as I had by now grown up enough to realise. But it would require such an indelible compromise: I would have to proclaim to the world that I had failed; that I had other priorities now; that I would end this mission here and strike a new and better path. Was this the truth? And, if it was, was I strong enough to do it?

It seemed that I had come to this mountain top, halfway between Yerevan and the Iranian border, to find the answer to these questions. Only now, faced with two tangible and opposite roads, would I be able to choose the right one.

The western sky was decked with cloud and the hint of

orange that announces the end of another day. I paced up and down the narrow lay-by, reeling at the disconnect between the dilemma in my head and the obliviousness of the traffic trundling past. Tenny would be coming home from a university lecture, buying supplies for a dinner alone in her lonely little seventh-floor apartment on Aram Khachatrian Street, wondering where I was, what I was doing, whether she'd see me again. My future pivoted upon this moment; yet I was still just a guy on a bicycle, somewhere, with the stuff in his bags and the thoughts in his head.

OK. This is difficult. I am really, really, suffering. My knee is absolutely killing me. And . . . it's freezing cold again. I've got no water left. I'm running out of food. And . . . I've just . . . I dunno . . .

I think I've just made some big mistakes. I've trusted far too much in other people to do my legwork for me. So now I've got this winter sleeping-bag, which I'm going to absolutely roast in – I'm never going to bloody use it until next winter! And it's . . .

And I'm in so much pain about this girl Tenny. Because . . . I've basically left her. I've left someone who . . . was the most . . .

Who I felt so fucking close to after such a short amount of time, and all because I've got this fucking visa, which cost me a hundred euros, and I'm too . . . I'm too fucking set in my ways to say, 'Well, OK, fuck the visa, let's wait with this girl for a few months, 'til she's finished her studies, and then she can come with me.' Why don't I just do that? Why am I killing myself?

I've got . . . I could go back there – I could be happy, with this girl – I could jettison all this pointless shit that I'm carrying with me. And I could set off again in two or three months' time, and . . . and

I would be so happy to do that. And there's always this nagging doubt that if I go back there I'll never leave, but I have to. I – I – I'm . . . I have no doubt that I will continue travelling by bicycle. But right now, I don't see what I'm doing, I don't understand why I'm here . . .

I've got nobody to talk to apart from this bloody camera . . . there's absolutely no friendly people on this road; nobody's stopped, usually, like, people stop every five or ten minutes but absolutely no-one's stopped to even say hello . . .

(OK, that's the first car that's actually had people in who've waved at me, so I take that back completely.)

I'm at the top of this hill. I'm at the top of this hill now – I can either. . . I can either go down the other side, and that'll be that, carry on like I am, or I can go back down this way and cycle back to Yerevan, which will probably completely and utterly kill me, but then at least I'll be able to . . . think about . . . what I'm doing . . . I'll be able to . . . I'll be able to make the most of this fucking opportunity that I've got!

I'll be able to . . . I'll be able to do something about this girl that I've fucking met that I'm just throwing away, and I don't know if I'm going to see her again if I keep going! Why the fuck am I doing it?

I mean, OK, I can say goodbye to people who I just make friends with, because there's no element of love there but . . . I actually love this girl, and . . .

Oh my god.

Exhausted, I dropped the still-rolling camera into my lap and took a deep breath. I'd been in the dismal little mountain-top lay-by for almost an hour. The pale late winter sun was descending fast towards the orange horizon; the colourless plains of what was once known as Western Armenia stretching a hundred miles into the distance of modern-day Turkey, infinite and empty from my vantage point at the top of this pass, dominated by the unmistakable outline of Mount Ararat, Armenia's most enduring icon. A few plumes of smoke rose from points on the plateau; farmers burning scrub, I guessed, though it was impossible to be sure.

Trying to play out the consequences of a return to Yerevan in my mind, I saw that the biggest obstacle would be my ego. Though I'd relinquished the notion that my journey would be earth-shattering in its significance, I still despaired about the consequences of pulling a U-turn. It wasn't just my friends and family who'd lined the village streets to see me off, nor the followers who read my occasional website articles and said nice things about my photographs; but the project's sponsors, too. I would have to write to all of them, explaining that I'd put Ride Earth on hold until I'd figured out where things were going next. But so what if a few people didn't understand what I'd been through, how I felt after nine months of self-inflicted vagrancy? Had I begun all of this just to ignore the only set of standards to which I was truly accountable – my own?

I was sick of endless goal-chasing – the next milestone, the next city, border, calendar month – of always striving for a distant point that never came closer. I craved something more rooted, I craved involvement and sharing and a respite from all the goodbyes; and above all I craved Tenny, the kind-eyed, dark-haired Iranian-Armenian girl with whom I was falling helplessly in love.

Yet the wanderlust was impossible to ignore. I knew – I *knew* – that if I turned back now, I would spend the rest of my life wondering what would have happened if I'd carried on.

Why did I always take myself so seriously?

I knew what I had to do. Of course. It was obvious.

I marched over to my bike.

Do what's right, you idiot.

I swung my leg over the top-tube. I took a deep breath, poised on a knife edge between two opposite futures – and steered onto the ice-smeared asphalt. The wheels began to roll, and the bike quickly began to pick up speed.

CHAPTER 14

I look around at the unfolding landscape; low undulations divided carefully into a patchwork of fields; deep blue overhead with a few wisps of white, the air pleasantly warm against my skin; well-kept tarmac beneath my wheels. Trees sprout between fields, and small streams make their way amongst the lulls and rises of the earth. It's so quiet, but for the birdsong. And it's obvious why I feel so bizarrely at home here. I could almost be riding in the back-roads of Derbyshire on an unseasonably warm Sunday in March.

But the low undulations are part of a plateau nearly a mile above the oceans. Divided up with low walls of piled rocks, these fields have been tilled by hand and by workhorse. The elevation offsets the climate here; other parts of this nation hold the average record for the hottest inhabited place on Earth. The tarmac will soon peter out into a track of bulldozed rubble. And the lush greenery in the distance is of a species that I have never seen before. Derbyshire this is not. This is Amhara.

'You!'

I smile weakly at the children who abandon a game of football to check out the latest *ferenj* to pass through their territory, and I roll uncertainly to a halt on the broken gravel road.

'You! You!!!'

Sprightly figures leap the piled earth and rock on the roadside; boys in faded cloth trousers and dusty ill-fitted shirts, sleeves rolled up, some with shawls of light linen draped across their shoulders; girls in absurdly pretty frocks plucked from an English Sunday-best wardrobe a half-century past; all running up to me, barefoot. They're maybe seven or eight at the youngest, twelve or thirteen tops, all lean and stringy, fit as fiddles, staring and jostling for proximity to the weird white-skin on a bicycle.

'*Ferenj.*'

They're just little humans, I tell myself. And I try to make friends, smiling and talking about my journey, pointing ahead and behind – 'Gondar! Bahir Dar!' – smiling some more. Some of the kids respond hesitantly, slowly repeating my words, staring at me as if I am an alien, or some kind of grotesque museum exhibit. I frown.

Then it dawns on me that I am.

I am an alien.

Attempts at rapport miserably trampled, I hesitantly make as if to continue riding. A ripple of havoc. The crowd, which by now has swelled considerably, attempts to part in order to let me through, and the domino effect lifts the smallest kids off their feet, sandwiched, others stumbling, and the wave of faces sways in front of me, as if Moses was warming up before attempting to part the Red Sea. Amidst the milling bodies and sudden yelps of amusement, I attempt to ride, reluctant to run anyone over. Gradually I gain momentum on the flat road. Then the hairs on the back of my neck stand on end.

'YOUYOUYOUYOUYOUYOUYOUYOU!!!!!!'

Shit.

A stampede of footfalls. Sixty Ethiopian children simultaneously lose all self-restraint and belt hell-for-leather after the wobbly *ferenj*, chasing me down the road.

Quick – can I grab a strap on this bag? How heavy is the bike? How much would it take to slow it down? What a hoot!

A few of the lazier members drop back; they can't be bothered, it's gone now – back to the football.

'You!!!' Pant. 'YOOUUU!!!!!' Gasp.

Heels hammering dirt. Flying gravel.

I pedal as hard as I can. To no effect; I'm going uphill! I cannot outrun the mob! But suddenly the bicycle's momentum wins through and the remaining crowd is receding in the shattered remains of my rear-view mirror. And I keep my eyes on the road ahead. I don't want to know what's co . . .

Thwack!

Clang!

The first stone hits a pannier. The second glances off the metal rail at the back of my saddle. More stones sail through my vision and bounce off the road ahead. I hear more dull impacts on the track behind me. The surge of adrenaline is fading by the time I come to terms with the fact that a gang of kids has just thrown a load of rocks at me.

For fun.

Here, children are going to throw rocks at me, for fun.

I've seen a fair few versions of normality, now, but this is the first in which I am a mere toy, whose only purpose is to provide target practice.

And money.

'Money!'

'Give me one birr!'

'Money!'

'You!!! YOOUUUUU!!!'

'Highland!!!'

What the hell is Highland?!? I wonder as I continue to cycle, alone and vulnerable, wearing a stupid grin on my face like I'm still cycling across fucking Derbyshire. And at the next village I collect a following of at least two hundred children, who are already standing in the middle of the dirt road as if they're waiting just for me.

I don't stop. They dive this way and that, giggling, recovering quickly to give chase, and I blank my mind as more rocks come hurtling in my direction. I blast downhill at full speed to the next village and dash into a small building with a garishly painted 'Hotel' sign outside. I hand over a couple of dollars' worth of birr for a shoebox room facing the yard and its resident goat, stow the bicycle safely inside, sit on the heap of blankets, and try to collect my thoughts.

What the hell?

I tiptoe gingerly towards the gate by road. There's a cafe of some description opposite the hotel, tempting me with its fresh fruit juices. Looking up and down the street, I can see no children at all. Adults go about their business, ignoring me completely. And I am awash with a feeling of purest serenity.

When I return to the hotel room, I find that the four empty water bottles I'd been keeping in the end-pockets of my panniers have disappeared.

Hold on . . . water bottles . . . Highland . . .

Highland!

It's a local brand of bottled drinking water.

They'd been shouting at me for my empty water bottles!

My cycle-computer had been stolen many weeks previously. That day, I'd left my accumulated mileage count in the dust. The thief had unwittingly freed me from one of the few quantifications of my travels I'd kept hold of. I had been reminded how irrelevant mile-counting was to everything that the lifestyle had come to mean, and had begun to judge my days in terms of my feelings and experiences, rather than through the numbers on the little grey screen.

Hitting the road the following morning, I leave the safe haven of the village and immediately begin to crave distractions from reality. I *want* to have a little grey screen to stare at, numbers to think about, statistics to manipulate in my favour. I *want* to return to calculating how much more impressive my kilometre-count sounds than its mile-based equivalent, likewise for my average daily distance; whether I should express altitude climbed in feet (impressive) or metres (not so) in the next website article; whether I should translate the upper extremes of temperature into Fahrenheit for added effect. Because the unavoidable alternative I am faced with is to remain in reality and come to terms with what I represent to this culture in which I am now inextricably immersed.

Then I glimpse a sight on the road ahead that fills me with incredulity. As the shape nears, growing more distinct, I gawp open-mouthed: here, in some nameless valley of rural Ethiopia, I am about to cross paths with another fully loaded bicycle traveller.

One of the defining features of my journey has been the complete absence of other foreign travellers. This life has offered no network of peers to tie oneself up with, no moral support back at the hostel after getting lost or swindled, nobody with whom to slip into that comforting world of companionable chitchat. There is no escape from escapism. There is no way of brushing under the carpet the fact that beneath the itineraries and plans, the guidebooks and tours, the modern traveller is actually deeply insecure, flitting briefly through someone else's world with a stupid smile and a camera before returning to a pre-purchased haven of safe, comfortable familiarity.

No. My journey is taking place on a plane of inner solitude, whether I like it or not. I have had to become secure in my insecurity, married to nothing but the ground beneath my feet, tracing a slow line across the surface of the globe. My life on this path has become a thing uncommunicable; I live it alone, no matter how many people I meet. And I know I will go home and discover that the brief messages and updates I have sent back will add up to little more than a list of highlights, a prompt for stories that will ramble on too long or break off abruptly. I can't help remembering those three unimposing-looking veteran cyclists at the Royal Geographical Society – despite my best efforts to share this peculiar nomadic existence, the very attempt to break it down into bitesized chunks of time and space is not just inappropriate, it is almost completely meaningless. I understand, suddenly, why their advice had been so humbly delivered; I understand how pointless it had been to judge their journeys on miles pedalled and continents covered. Their journeys, just as mine, had been entirely personal, the statistics just a way of piquing the layman's interest. And I wish that there was a way to share this realisation with my friends and family without them having to go through the stressful and lonely self-indulgence of a long, solitary journey themselves.

The figure is close now; a sunhat, an unhurried rhythm, the familiar outline of a heavy bicycle with panniers astride its wheels. He's a young, long-haired *ferenj* like me, and he grins as he approaches. I grin back.

'Hello there!'

'Hey!'

'How's it going?!'

'Things are supposed to chill out when you get out into the countryside, right?'

'Ha-ha! Not here!'

He has a look in his eyes of hard-earned wisdom: he knows exactly what psychological hurdles I've leaped to get to this meeting. In fact, it's almost as if the entire conversation itself is surplus to requirements, and that we might just as well share a moment of silence, taking in the surroundings and the present moment, without the hassle of discussing the riding conditions and the weather and the availability of water. We could swap stories of hardships overcome, but what would be the point? Anyone else in the same position would have sweated and toiled in just the same manner, given no alternative but to grind away, pedal-stroke by pedal-stroke, until the self-inflicted suffering in question had passed beyond the horizon.

That said, Jared has a Canadian accent, and the opportunity to talk in lazy, colloquial English is too good to pass up. We talk about his route, which will lead him north via the Middle East to Europe in a reversal of my own, although I suspect he'll be slightly quicker: it is approaching two years since I began that journey. And, as we talk, children abandon their herds and pad silently across the fields towards us, as if drawn by some unseen magnetic force.

We have both become used to this relentless attention, if not entirely comfortable with it. So we continue talking and ignore the growing circle of boys and girls. They stand with their goat-whacking sticks; an occasional whisper passes between smaller splinter groups. Yet more individuals gravitate towards our little party from afar. A shift of weight from a *ferenj* sends undulations through the crowd; again I have the feeling that I am some dangerous creature on display, a being of such unfamiliarity that the slightest movement is treated as a prelude to a potential lashing out. We're all the same on the inside, I want to say. But it certainly doesn't look that way to a small boy who has seen nothing of the world but the fields and herds and neighbours and the inside of his family's hut. Our audience is on tenterhooks as we stand leisurely by the roadside. We are two wise and well-travelled adventurers, enlightened as to the common nature of all people. We are two Martians, talking bullshit in an unknown tongue.

'I just ramble at them in English,' Jared says, 'saying any old rubbish – song lyrics, poems, random crap that comes into my head. They don't understand a word I'm saying, but at least it keeps me amused . . .'

This is when I notice the hand. The hand is midway through the careful extraction of a small yellow bottle from one of the rear pockets of Jared's panniers by the time I shout: 'Oi!!!'

The bottle clatters to the ground. The lanky teenage boy and his errant hand whip back into the crowd, giggling nervously. Murmurs echo through the ranks. Isn't this a funny game!

'What the . . . ?'

'He was taking something out of your bag.'

'Oh shit.'

Jared dashes round to the back of his bike to inspect the bag; glares at the crowd; tries to calm himself while he rifles through the pocket.

'Man, they've taken my tablets . . . I had some purification tablets in here. And . . . oh, man, my spare shoes have gone . . .'

'At least we rescued the sun cream,' I say, pointing at the bottle on the floor.

What the hell is an Ethiopian teenager planning to do with Factor 30?

'Shit . . . *shit!!!*'

He stands with his hand on his forehead. I'm not sure what to do. I know he's trying not to get angry at having his personal belongings re-appropriated under his nose. I'd be doing the same. There is nothing in my bags that I can't live without; and what I once did I have long since jettisoned: army-issue poncho, clothes, books, and other accessories (hip flask, solar battery charger, brass rabbit snares) that had seemed like a good idea at the time.

I look around. There are now at least a hundred children surrounding us. Again I am staggered by the sheer number of people who wander these lands. There are no office jobs, no sedentary professions. The crude, temporary appearance of buildings reflects this: stick-walled, grass-roofed little roundhouses jutting in small clusters from the green-brown hillsides – as far as the eye can see – are the quintessential image of rural Amhara; functional shelters in which to sleep and perform a few household chores.

Most of the children have sticks, and doubtless know how to use them. I am acutely aware of what an act of aggression in this situation might provoke. I imagine the pair of us being set upon by the kids, cowering on the road in terror until the next truck happens by – the adults, of course, would jump out of the cab and throw rocks at the scattering children, which I've seen happen several times. I can't help feeling something raw and violent in the air when these staring, suspicious faces surround me. Children don't hide their prejudices. I have already seen the wildness that can overcome such a mob, watching chases unfold in the smashed remains of my rear-view mirror, and I don't want to see that kind of energy bent into a confrontation.

Nor does Jared. He musters an admirable amount of diplomacy and offers a handful of birr to the crowd in exchange for the stolen shoes and tablets. Plenty of hands reach out for the cash, but the offending items fail to materialise. The pannier pocket had already been opened – maybe the robberies had occurred earlier in the day?

'Look,' I say, 'I've got some water purification tablets myself – I hardly ever use them, so you can have them if you need them.' Jared politely declines, saying I must need them, but I really am too lazy to bother using them. And so I dig my little first-aid kit from a pannier and give him enough iodine pills to get him to Gondar where he will be able to get some more.

We bid each other farewell and continue our separate ways; it is difficult to muster a smile, now that our meeting's been tainted by this episode of daylight robbery – my composure and spirit deflated once again by a bunch of little kids.

I'm safe!

I'm safe in a hotel room. They can't get to me here. At least I don't think they can!

I'm just completely knackered. I'm absolutely exhausted. By . . . just . . . being in this country.

It's just an exhausting experience. And I guess the main reason is that I never know what the next person is going to want! Half of the people I've met on the road have just stuck their hand out and demanded money, or whatever. As if the whole purpose of my existence as a white foreigner in their country is to supply them with whatever they want. In an incredibly demanding fashion. Without – without even saying 'hello', or . . . it's as if . . .

It's almost as if some white people came along in the past and dished out loads of stuff and money!

The other half have been amazingly helpful and friendly. I just turned up at this hotel in this tiny village and got dragged around a whole load of different houses, trying lots of different things to eat and drink. Not all of which I was particularly keen on. But I kind of had to eat and drink anyway. There were some, er . . . some moments where I had to control my, er . . . my, erm . . . what's it called . . . oh my god, I'm so tired . . . for goodness' sake . . .

I had to control my gag reflex a couple of times . . . but I managed it! I didn't vomit all over somebody's front room, as a guest, so that's good!

But yeah, it's just so exhausting. And . . . in some areas, the kids kind of get carried away, and before you know it . . . er . . . there are rocks the size of your fist flying past you along the road. I think partly it might be something to do with the fact that the adults seem to discipline the kids by throwing rocks at them. So a moving target – especially a random white guy on a bike – is pretty much all they need, I guess, to liven their day up a bit.

It just gets really tiring, though, not really knowing what to expect from the next group of people. And it's horrible to generalise, and to assume that everybody is just going to want – is going to demand money, or pens, or food, or whatever, off you, because an awful lot of people don't; an awful lot of people are very genuine, and they just want to help and they want to know what you're doing and . . . you know, just normal human beings!

But with some people it seems to be completely the opposite. And it's that, and the frequency with which it occurs, that's made riding here so incredibly tiring. Mentally. And physically, too. The road is . . . just . . . crap; it's the worst road I've ever ridden on, without a doubt. The mountains are extremely big . . . the altitude isn't enough to cause me problems at the moment, but the road will be going up to nearly twelve thousand feet above sea level before too long.

On a side note, for the first time today I saw wild monkeys, which is – you know – it's a nice experience. A little bit of kindred bonding going on there. I stopped to have a wander around amongst the whooping hordes!

It was lovely. It was really, really beautiful, actually.

The asphalt reappears sporadically as the route weaves across the gentle plateau of dry fields; brooding mountains appear once again to the east. I am already approaching a mile above sea level, and it looks like I'll be climbing higher still, as my turn-off has finally arrived. This faint track leading off to the east, as far as I had been able to make out from pixellated satellite images back in Gondar, will take me off the standard overland route down through Africa; instead bisecting the heart of the Amharan highlands and spitting me out in the far east of the country on the edge of the Afar Depression. That diabolical sub-sea-level desert, I've read, is commonly considered by palaeontologists to be the very region from which all human life sprang forth – not to mention being cited as the location of the hottest continuously inhabited place on Earth.

Turning eastwards will be more than an interesting-sounding detour. It will also be the moment at which I cease to sail away from the distant harbour I left behind, instead tacking around to bring it back into view. The natural onward route from the far side of the Afar desert is to Djibouti, the biggest port in East Africa. And from there, I may find myself able to catch a boat away from Africa to the Arabian Peninsula. A few weeks of riding through another of the great infernal deserts – the Empty Quarter – will bring me within striking distance of Iran.

Coming down with malaria has given me plenty to think about. And the thing I keep coming back to is that continuing through Africa is not the only way to live this life on the road. Cape Town is nothing but a convenient target, riding to it as romantic a notion as any that drove a journey; sticking to it will allow me to hold a steady course while I do what I have to do. But other targets would serve that purpose equally well. And a target of Djibouti, then Dubai, and then Iran, will let me hold my course – but also make a concession I've surely earned, after an illness that might have ended everything: to allow the chance that I might see Tenny again, if only briefly, as I pass by Tehran. And afterwards, I will continue as I had long ago planned: to ride through Central Asia, Tibet and the Far East. For though much has happened, and much has been learnt, the itch that drove me here has still not been scratched.

The stone-throwing mobs and the highway robbery are still fresh and raw in my mind, and it is not without a little trepidation that I continue to ride, as I am quickly learning that challenges are coming thick, fast and unprecedented on the road through Ethiopia. And challenges, of course, were exactly what I'd hoped for, as I'd set out on the journey that would finally put me in my place.

I gently ease the handlebars to the left, leaning slightly into the turn. Negotiating the junction, I straighten out, take another few pedal strokes, and roll off the asphalt and onto the rocky trail. The sun moves behind me: from today onward I will spend the mornings shielding my face, the afternoons chasing my shadow. And I look up at the road ahead, where a crowd is waiting patiently.

'You!!!'

Mount Ararat's outline floated in the west, lopsided crater atop its shallow-sided volcanic body, motionless and bold against an orange late-afternoon sun, the smaller twin cone of Little Ararat to its side like a child clutching the hand of a parent. I lapped up the descent, cackling and singing at the absurd distance I'd climbed – in order to relive it in reverse. Rock and scrub blasted past on either side, interspersed with grey patches of slush, the occasional sliver of white snow still hiding in crevices and in the shadows of boulders. As cars crept past, their drivers peering with incredulity at the sight of a heavily loaded cyclist taking an uninterrupted twenty-five-mile downhill at full speed, I could feel the frigid air warming as it blasted my exposed lips and cheeks, the atmospheric thermals passing behind in clear-cut layers as the plateau loomed up below. Handfuls of desolated buildings drifted past, perched on the edge of the precipitous mountain road overlooking the flatlands of west Armenia and Turkey. The same flatlands I'd spent the entire day climbing away from.

I had made my decision. My Iranian visa would expire, unused. I was going back to Yerevan.

Nothing would be the same now. The future lay wrapped in uncertainty. After nine months of focusing on the huge and distant finishing line of cycling round the world, I could now see no further down the road than the distant cloud of smog on the horizon.

I knew that something like fifty miles of pedalling awaited me. It was already growing dusky, the days still short and bleak. But I didn't care. An interminable traverse of the city's suburbs would come afterwards. Past the great central landmarks with which I'd become so familiar. I wouldn't give them a second glance. A last giant hill climb towards the northern suburbs of the city, and a metal door on the seventh floor of a post-Soviet apartment block. After that?

I didn't care. I truly didn't care what would happen next. At that moment I felt such an utter sense of purpose, my actions and desires in fantastical alignment, that I gave thanks to everyone and everything that had taken me away from my home, out of the world I knew, across Europe and into West Asia and to this strip of tarmac running through the overlooked post-communist nation of Armenia in which someone had taught me that I didn't want to live in a structure any more. I didn't need to pedal in a gigantic circle in some desperate attempt to make my life *mean* something. The idea of 'going back' was ancient history. There was nothing to go back to. Life as I'd known it had been vanquished forever. And as for 'finishing the journey'? I might as well sit on an exercise bike in the gym and crank out another thirty thousand miles while admiring myself in the mirror for all the relevance it had.

And so I plummeted earthwards with a smile on my face, because something had happened – something more remarkable than any tale of adventure – and I would be a fool not to take that giant leap and to see where I would land.

At eleven-thirty that night, after ten and a half hours of pedalling, I found myself slumped in a lift as it clanked and squealed its way to the seventh floor of a crumbling apartment block in the northern suburbs of the Armenian capital. What might happen next was anyone's guess. But I had made my peace with uncertainty, and I was going to embrace it, open-armed.

The concrete stairwell was dim and cold, and I could barely make out where I was putting my feet. But it didn't matter, because through a tiny peephole there came a welcoming glimmer of light.

Chapter 15

We love the idea of being in control of our own personal universe. It gives us reassurance to think that we are capable of exerting an influence over the objects and events and people around us. To help us believe this, we often attribute far more significance to our actions than they deserve. We have all walked up to a lift, seen that the call button is already illuminated, and pressed it anyway. Why? Do we believe that the effort might somehow contribute to the lift's safe and prompt arrival at our floor? It is an entirely futile manoeuvre, and rationally we know this, but we are often not particularly rational beings.

Especially in modern society, we have a habit of creating systems to ensure predictable outcomes. Whether it is the stashing of large amounts of money in bank accounts for the future, or the forging of careers in the assumption that doing so will mean we're able to make ends meet until retirement, we are fighting a world of immense unpredictability. But our positions are tenuous. We call it 'planning' when it is nothing but guesswork. And this guesswork transforms us from dreamers and artists and romantics – children – into the parts of a giant life-support machine that is dependent upon itself. And we are so tied to this machine that we're paralysed when it breaks down; when we're made redundant, when the bank collapses, when there's a fuel shortage, when things don't go as planned.

It is so difficult to accept how little can be guaranteed about life, other than its ending. We would perhaps be more motivated to question our journeys if we were each given an exact date and time at which they would all end, the precise moment at which we would cease to be here. Although I'm reluctant to borrow other people's words, I remember an interview with the musician and humorist Tim Minchin, who put it so nicely:

'It's awe-inspiringly *awesome* . . . the idea that – after all this space – there's You, and then there's Not You . . . and you're faced with the question of how you're going to spend that time.

'People don't even know how to spend their Saturday afternoons.'

'Barev dzes? Duk ek hayt'ararutyun t'vel Gindum? . . . Duk ek Gindum hayt'ar . . . er, da der azad e? Isk concrete k'asek Brusovi poghots vordegh e linum? . . . Komitas e, che, Komitas? . . . Ayo . . .'

Right . . . so I'm going to have to learn this?

' . . . che, che, yes yerevi shpotel em indz tvum er Komi – vortev Komitasi verevn e . . . Inchits? . . . Sirkits minchev nerkev . . . Eghav.'

I sat listening as Tenny talked on the phone to a prospective landlord in her native Armenian, a language related to no other tongue still spoken. I'd had no idea that my decision to return to Yerevan would lead to spending the next half-year living in the city, renting my own apartment for the first time, watching through my very own post-Soviet window-frame as someone flicked a switch and the city transformed from a cold bleak monochrome dump into a warm and lively hub of culture and sunshine and life. I could never have known that I would one day find myself above the Arctic Circle, pedalling alone along a road of solid ice in the dead of a midwinter's night, or on another occasion crying into a vodka glass at a funeral wake in the wild and empty plains of Northern Mongolia. I could never have allowed for the possibility that I would one day become a citizen of another country and carry a little blue booklet alongside my little burgundy one – all because of a single decision I'd made on a mountaintop. How could I possibly have known that these things would happen, and how could they have happened at all had I not taken off the stabilisers I'd attached to my bicycle journey, allowing it to roll freely and naturally into the unknown?

Maybe it was the simplicity of the itinerant lifestyle that had done this. I wasn't sure. Reducing existence to its barest material and emotional demands had stripped away all of the layers of abstraction that I'd always been taught came with modern adult life. Seen at that level, maybe it was obvious why I'd chosen a simple human relationship over my globally proportioned ego trip.

For the time being, then, I was staying put in Yerevan. And with staying put came the fantastic luxury of being able to reminisce and digest. I suddenly had so much time! Living costs in Armenia were hardly a great strain on my wallet; the monthly rent payment was my biggest single expense. After the frugality of my journey to Armenia, I never enjoyed the moment that the friendly old landlord would knock on the door to say hello, tut noisily at the state of the wiring and collect his handful of banknotes. But by living on a diet almost exclusively composed of bread, red lentil soup and *borscht*, which was far more exciting than what I'd been eating on the road, I was able to subsist on practically nothing, and a good thing, too, as I had no source of income and no idea how much longer it might be before I did. My expenditure each month struggled to top £100. And so I had the great privilege of almost limitless time to dedicate to working through the collected photographs, video footage and diary entries of the previous year's adventures, which proved extremely satisfying. It seemed bizarre that such freedom, such a feeling of completeness and wanting for nothing, was a direct result of embracing a poor, unemployed and itinerant way of life, while those I'd known at home were striving for precisely the same feeling by working themselves to the bone and becoming wealthy, career-driven and settled.

Life in one place also featured a host of fantastic novelties such as taking off my clothes before going to bed, preparing meals that required more than one pot, not permanently stinking like a PE lost-property box, having taps, not beginning diary entries with 'Day X', putting my padded shorts away in a drawer, definitely having toilet paper, condiments, being able to refrigerate things, removing the metal plates screwed into the bottoms of my shoes, shaving, having clean fingernails, and collecting names that I would remember and phone numbers that I would call. I enjoyed going out on foot and not having to squeal to a halt several times a day and explain where I was going (to the next town), where I was from (England / Anglia / Inglestan / Britannia), why I was riding a bicycle (because I couldn't afford petrol), whether I was married (no) or had children (no), why I wasn't married (erm . . .), if I was sure my tyres were quite firm enough (yes), really (yes), if it wasn't very difficult to travel like this (sometimes), how much my bicycle had cost (one hundred dollar), what I did for work (photography / writing / programming / nothing), whether I was crazy (yes), and any number of other far too frequently asked questions I received whenever I turned up somewhere with a bike and a load of bags of stuff (all day, every day).

There were so many things about life that I had never imagined I would appreciate so much, and it all had come from cycling across a dozen countries on a journey that had changed my life. Yes, I was content to remain in Yerevan for now, but there were still so many places left unvisited. How much more there must still be to explore and learn!

And what better way to experience more of those life-changing lessons than alongside someone who, although completely new to the idea, was ready to give the traveller's lifestyle her very best shot?

Andy had already built and tested it by the time I arrived at his little apartment in Tbilisi with its high ceilings and vine-strangled veranda and grand wooden doors so typical of the city's vintage townhouses. With a blue and white paint job, the sturdy little machine sitting in the basement looked absolutely perfect for what was likely to be a very long and challenging task. I was also due to renew my Armenian visa, which simply involved crossing the border into Georgia and returning the following day. So the fourteen-hour overnight train trip served three purposes: to appease the bureaucrats, to visit my old best mate in his new surrounds, and to collect the bicycle that would depart Armenia beside me – with Tenny at the handlebars.

She was so excited when I returned to Yerevan with her brand new bike! Seeing the world had been a dream for her for as long as she could remember, although I suspected that she hadn't expected the opportunity to arrive in this form (or with that much facial hair). With a couple of months to go until completing a five-year design scholarship at Yerevan's Institute of Fine Art, it had not been difficult to see that continuing the journey as a couple really might be a feasible option. Propelled by the headiness of our early romance, we began making rash, exciting plans to wander the world together.

'How would you feel about going to Africa?'

'Oh, I really want to go to Africa! I want to see the people, the colours . . . very natural, everything. And, er, small children – er – nigger? Nigger? Am I right?'

'Erm. You can't say that in England.'

'Black people . . . ?'

'Mmm-hmm . . .'

'Black people children. Oh, they're lovely!'

'But you really can't say "nigger" in England.'

'OK.'

'It's very . . . politically incorrect.'

'Yes, OK. Ha-ha! Oh my god – sorry – I would like to have black child! I don't know – they are lovely. They are all the same!'

'Oh dear . . .'

There were one and a half million black people in Britain. In Armenia, there were two. One had married an Armenian woman, and now played for the national football team. The other owned a cocktail bar.

'Yeah – every time they are naked, and they are running – oh! It's good . . . yes. And . . . what?'

'Oh – er – nothing.'

Unfortunately, Tenny was one of the eighty million people unfortunate enough to hold an Iranian passport. As I looked through the practicalities of the overland routes we might take, I discovered that there was a list of fewer than ten countries in the world that she could visit as a tourist without a lot of protracted, expensive, restrictive and by-no-means-guaranteed visa applications in Tehran, which hardly sounded compatible with the open-ended odyssey I had in mind. Suddenly I was confronted by a horrible truth: the reason I never met travellers from anywhere other than Europe and North America was not because of a lack of desire to travel on the part of the rest of the world. It was simply because they were not allowed. Sticking a pin in a map would never work for them. Dreams alone hadn't taken twenty-nine-year-old Tenny any further afield than Armenia, one of the few nations still open to her. And this wasn't just true for Iranians. It was true for pretty much everyone.

I realised what an enormous privilege it was to be able to travel with the freedom I'd taken for granted until now. My countrymen and I had instant access to a hundred and seventy-one nations; the ability to pop over to almost any spot on the planet whenever we damn well felt like it, thank you very much. The same was true for almost every Western national, who together made up a tiny proportion of the planet's population, and it was sickening how many took that privilege for granted and instead sat at home in front of their televisions absorbing other people's twisted opinions about the world. The thought made me furious.

What the hell was everybody doing, lapping up that complete and utter crap every day? Didn't they know how lucky they were to be able to see the world for themselves?

I felt helpless in the face of this obstacle; one that all the cycle-touring experience in the world would never help us to circumvent. The least bureaucratically treacherous route I could find turned out to involve forgetting Africa – again – and instead heading for India, via Pakistan and Tenny's homeland of Iran. Though there would still be paperwork required, it would in theory be possible, and I reassured Tenny, as my mother would say, that 'where there's a will there's a way' – even though I had barely the faintest belief in the old saying at that moment.

My mum – bless her. She had inherited a stockpile of those phrases from her Lincolnshire family, and would always pull one out half-jokingly during a pause in a delicate discussion. It always managed to bring a bit of perspective, reminding us that mankind's collective wisdom had already immortalised our conundrum in a clever little package of words.

I hadn't expected to see her and my dad again so soon.

It was quite a brave move, I thought, for two semi-retired schoolteachers from rural England to jet off to an overlooked corner of the former Soviet Union that most Brits couldn't even point out on a map. As they emerged through the arrivals gate at Zvartnots airport on the edge of the city, looking tired and pulling suitcases stuffed full with new cycle-touring equipment for Tenny, I wondered what this place would look like to someone who had woken up that morning in Middleton. A child grew from conception to birth in the time it took me to get here. My parents had done so before the sun completed a single traverse of the sky. How did that feel? What did they see, as we exited this smoky concrete monolith and began to haggle with smelly Lada-driving cabbies over the five-dollar fare for the twelve-mile ride home, past the seedy neon casino strip beside the city limits and through the dark tree-lined boulevards of pink stone and black BMWs and orange streetlamps? I couldn't imagine. It seemed so unnatural to skip continents like that. Yet it was the default mode of international transport for almost everyone alive. People didn't travel for a slow release of small rewards along the way. They travelled to escape. To work. To do something specific. To visit a premeditated destination, for a premeditated amount of time. Yerevan, for a fortnight. The journey there existed for functional purposes and should be as quick and forgettable as possible – in precise opposition to my own journey: slow and memorable, the destination no more important than the colour of my T-shirt.

We exited the taxi near the entrance to my decrepit apartment building. There were no streetlights here. The pavement was torn up through years of use and neglect. A metal service door hung from its hinges, slightly open, and a couple of stray cats darted out and disappeared into the night as we felt our way past with the suitcases. The stink of rubbish drifted through the half-open doorway from the basement room where great heaps of refuse lay uncollected at the bottom of the garbage chute, waiting for a sporadic visit from a collection truck as they had done ever since the Soviet government collapsed almost twenty years ago and the elaborate support systems of communism were left to rot and rust.

Passing the bare tin-roofed gazebo where old men played

chess and backgammon all day, we climbed a small flight of external stairs to the building's main entrance. Gingerly my mother and father stepped over the steel threshold of the dark rectangular opening and past the remains of the mechanical security code keypad, the door itself and the stairway's railings long since plundered for scrap, the keypad now nothing but a few slivers of welded metal surrounding a row of circles punched from the steel. Passing the row of disused mailboxes that still drooped from the wall as they did in apartment blocks spanning the ten thousand kilometres from Kaliningrad to the Bering Straits, we clambered up another flight of pre-fabricated concrete stairs, polished smooth by decades of use, turned left at the first landing and jabbed at the dim red spot beside the elevator. Some distant machine sprang into life and a clattering and a clanking heralded the arrival of the lift. The double doors slammed back with a squeal of tortured metal to reveal the dark brown interior, barely illuminated by a greenish pallor from above and with half-peeled stickers and hastily pasted adverts for taxi services and computer repairs adorning the walls, and I wondered when it would next break down and the neighbours come knocking for a contribution to hire a repairman. Being too small and weak for three people and luggage, I left my parents in the lift and climbed three more flights of stairs in the darkness, praying that the shambolic contraption would deliver its payload safely rather than plummet into the pitch-black depths of the shaft in a tragic explosion of splintered chipboard and human limbs, as the mysterious noises and daily outages suggested it would one day surely do.

But it was my home, and I was strangely happy here. Inside

the flat, Tenny heard the great double-bladed brass key turning twice in the lock and leapt from the sofa, forgetting to turn off the television in a rush of nervous apprehension. And thus did the first meeting between my parents and my Iranian-Armenian girlfriend occur, in an edifice carved from the bleakest period of Soviet history and amid the bloodcurdling shrieks of Armenia's very own version of *X-Factor*.

My mum and dad took to Tenny immediately. It would take a little more work for Tenny's parents to follow suit with me.

First of all was the fact that I was English. *English*. Weren't there enough perfectly good Armenians to choose from? And second, that I'd just rolled up on my bike, unannounced, and that almost immediately said bike was on their eldest daughter's balcony and my clothes were in her wardrobe. I might as well have landed from Mars! An English tramp, with a bicycle instead of a job, looking like he'd been dragged through a hedge backwards and speaking not a word of their language, had snatched away their precious first daughter from her close-knit Iranian-Armenian surroundings and showed every sign of lingering like a bad smell. This simply wouldn't do at all.

I first met Tenny's father in her flat over a delicious meal of saffron chicken and rice, cooked into a mysteriously sumptuous plate of food that only an Iranian would ever be able to pull off. At the time, I was camped out in a friend's flat, Tenny being far too afraid to let me stay at hers while her father was visiting. And I made the almighty error of bringing my digital camera along, foolishly hoping to win him over with a selection of heroic photos of my travels. Instead, he picked up the camera after the meal and began flicking through the pictures himself. This would have been perfectly fine had he not quickly come across the pictures I'd taken of his daughter one morning as she fooled around in her nightie and lay down next to me in her bed. A moment of silent horror came over me as I realised what he was seeing. He turned off the camera without a word while Tenny and I pretended that nothing unusual whatsoever had happened. And the very next day I received instructions to remove my bike from her balcony and to take all of my belongings away.

I was not put off. I cared too much for Tenny to let that happen. But that night put an end to the fairy-tale romance. I rented my own flat, and a difficult period of secret meetings began that would last for several weeks. As time went by and Tenny remained persistent in my defence, it must have become obvious that I was not going anywhere and that our relationship was a choice that we, two adults with enough maturity to know what we were doing, had made. And gradually Tenny's parents must have realised that their daughter's happiness would not be complete until they accepted her very own hairy English biker.

The acceptance did not come without reservation, however, and it was upon an otherwise unremarkable summer's morning that the idea of travelling together by bicycle was first mentioned to Tenny's mother.

Mentioned, and instantly shut down.

'The situation is . . . the situation is that I am not allowed to go travelling.'

Tenny was slumped in a chair in Serineh's living-room, gazing at the floor, fiddling absently with her mobile phone.

'The situation is that . . . I'm useless. I'm not thinking serious. I'm not acting like other girls my age . . . I'm still not independent . . .'

Serineh and I sat quietly, listening.

'Yeah. The situation is . . . not nice.'

'What . . . what do you think we should do?'

'I don't know. But I don't want my mother go back to Iran and tell my father, "I think you should go to Yerevan, because we are not sure what Tenny is going to do."'

In Britain, parents' legal responsibility for their children ends on their eighteenth birthday. Most adolescents' *de facto* independence begins much earlier than that. That aside, I was in lucky possession of a family who had always supported me rather than trying to restrict me, even when they thought that I was making a mistake. My own sense of independence was maybe why, at the age of twenty-three, I'd had few reservations about leaving them behind on a journey that I'd anticipated might take upwards of three or four years to make.

But Tenny's parents still considered their twenty-nine-year-old unmarried daughter entirely *their* responsibility. She was studying in Armenia at their permission, and with their financial support. I also realised another thing that ran much deeper. I realised that I didn't have a leg to stand on in any disagreement about this. Because my side of the argument would only apply to the context in which I'd been raised. My assumptions about my generation's independence, about how we should be free to fly the nest and experiment in between coming of age and settling down, were just that –

assumptions. Now it was my cultural particulars that ran against the grain: I was a foreign interloper in someone else's world, my deeply held principles now quite alien, and it was absolutely outside my remit to meddle too much. Tenny's parents were simply exercising their right to prevent their daughter committing what they saw as a dangerous and irresponsible violation of her role in society, and I was learning the meaning of 'cultural relativism' the hard way.

Of course, Tenny could simply go against their wishes. Andy had had to deal with a lot of needling when he'd decided to go ahead with Ride Earth, but ultimately he couldn't be prevented from pursuing his own path. The difference was that Andy already considered himself a free agent – quite rightly, in the context of twenty-first-century British society. The same did not apply to Tenny, born into the closed and conservative Armenian minority of Iran, and to go against her parents' edict would be to wrong them deeply.

The case was closed, as far as they were concerned. Life continued as before, and I got on well with all of Tenny's family, as long as we never mentioned living or travelling together – not before *marriage*, at least, which was of course the next logical step in our relationship, and after which Tenny was *my* responsibility and we could do as we pleased.

Andy contacted me about a website project he'd been contracted to work on in Georgia, and I agreed to take on half the job as his development partner, borrowing Tenny's computer and working over an excruciatingly unreliable dial-up Internet connection from my flat in Yerevan. The two-month job was relatively well paid, and if I was careful with my expenses I hoped to pass the first anniversary of my departure from England with the same amount of cash in the bank as I'd had when I began.

It was also a welcome distraction from the fact that – whether I liked it or not – the odds were slowly stacking up against the dream I now shared with Tenny. And I began to wonder whether I might have made a big mistake. Perhaps it had been too rash and idealistic to think that it would be that simple. Maria and Magalie had so effortlessly slipped in alongside us the previous year in Hungary, dropping everything with barely twenty-four hours' notice. But I was beginning to learn that differences between my world and this stretched further than concerns of freedom and wealth.

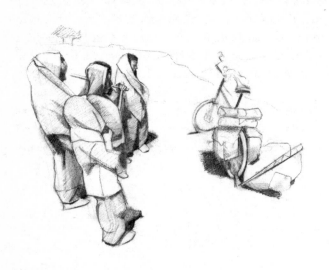

CHAPTER 16

An explosion of dust. A convoy of vehicles barges past at breakneck speed. I make out the dim initials of the United Nations, angular navy-blue lettering stencilled across the brilliant white paintwork, tinted windows and sunglasses streaking past at sixty miles an hour. This has become a familiar sight in Africa.

The clouds of dust kicked up in the village of Gob Gob by the aid workers and diplomats will not settle for another half hour. I pull my headband down to cover my mouth and squint in search of the little blue sign I'd spotted on the roadside – a sign that I guess will indicate accommodation of some description. A tall young man emerges from a low doorway and strolls up to where I have stopped. We exchange greetings – *'Sallam-no!'* – and Melech confirms in fluent if slightly archaic English that it is indeed possible to stay the night here. I wheel my bike through a packed room-cum-restaurant and into the back yard, where there is a familiar-looking little row of mud and timber rooms for rent. Opposite the rooms, a wooden roundhouse topped with a plume of smoke betrays the kitchen. Between the thin timbers and straw matting of the walls I can see red onions being chopped furiously. The household's children rush out to greet me, shake my hand and stand smiling nervously as I test the waters of language, without much success. But they are a kind and gentle crew and I feel immediately welcome and at home here, so I chance to bring out my video camera. The kids fall about laughing at the sight of themselves reproduced in real time on the tiny screen, help me wedge my luggage and bike into the cramped room, and don't once ask me for money.

Melech, worried that I'll be offended by the aroma of damp earth, lights an incense stick in my room and promises to take me to see 'a beautiful place' – but first, dinner: *shiro* and bread. A thick stew of chickpea flour and a spice melange, *shiro* has become a staple meal, packed with protein and energy. It's always too spicy, but the sensation is somehow addictive.

After dinner, we venture out into the town. It is approaching summer and there is plenty of daylight here, one border-crossing north of the Equator. We cross the road and slip between the buildings into the yards beyond. Thanks to the complete absence of privately owned cars, all is quiet up here on the plateaus, thousands of metres in altitude. A large pair of metal gates lies open and rusting, and we enter the 'beautiful place'.

We wander through a labyrinthine garden, Melech in happy silence, I in wonder and bemusement as a large complex of vegetable gardens is revealed on the fringes of the village, with fields divided amongst tree seedlings, beehives, carrots, potatoes, onions and cabbages, all separated and sheltered by hedgerows planted in a bizarrely English-looking fashion. Beautiful indeed; also overly ordered, silent and mysterious, it exudes a sense of displacement in space and time, tended by ghosts and shadows. And, as my host tells the story of Gob Gob, pieces of the jigsaw begin to slot into place.

'This is a plant . . . plantation,' he explains, 'for construct house, for furniture production. For wood. There's a pipe down the middle – do you see?'

Hundreds of tiny plastic plant pots fill the rectangular space like a regiment on parade, inspected by a network of hoses and troughs. It's all the more impressive, and all the more bizarre, for being hidden away behind someone's back garden in the rural Ethiopian highlands.

We continue through the labyrinth.

'These are bees . . . do you know bee? Honey bee?' says Melech as we approach a large wooden box on stilts. 'This is an ordinary system of honey-bee production. It is not modernised. There are about ten thousand bees.'

'In this nest? Ten thousand?'

'Yes. There is the mother bee – the queen. Then there are worker bees. Drones. They are living in connection . . . they are . . . what is it called . . . a "group animal".'

I ask Melech how this place came to exist, and why it now carries this feeling of being frozen in time. Years ago, he says, there was a foreign organisation here. The *ferenjis* had been responsible for running this place. And one day they'd vanished.

After running a productive local enterprise for almost twenty years, continues Melech, feeding the local populace and at the same time giving employment to two hundred people, the volunteers had decided to extend the remit of their project, embarking upon a spate of religious missioning amongst the Orthodox Christian community. The elders of Gob Gob, he says, were incensed by the uninvited meddling. The *ferenjis* had come to sow seeds, not religious disunity! The hapless volunteers were rounded up and kicked out of Gob Gob, and the Ethiopian government followed suit and booted them thenceforth from Ethiopia. The state had then taken responsibility for the project. Within five years, the local workforce had dropped to fewer than twenty people.

We wander amongst the overgrown fields in the evening light, all but a couple given over to nature, furrows still visible through the undergrowth. One has been kept trim as a sort of 'village green' for weddings and other events. The remains of a huge wooden gazebo lie where they fell to earth during a storm, splintered uprights still pointing crookedly at the heavens. Once, not so long ago, this was the place where two hundred workers would convene for lunch every day.

'If you come to work,' says Melech, addressing aid workers across the world, 'simply work with the work – work in development, don't interfere to religious. This region, country, believes Orthodox toward. So, you interfere? Get out!'

The two hundred workers had produced far more food than the village needed. When the aid money was withdrawn from the region, there was no local demand for the surplus produce. And so twenty years of energy and passion in what must have been the toughest of conditions went to waste, because no thought had been given to the cradle in which the project rested – this small Ethiopian community, which needed self-sufficiency and autonomy, not a forty-hour working week and maximum economic turnover. A handful of onions, potatoes and bees in a beautiful, forgotten place is the only legacy.

Gob Gob doesn't have a signboard. Many villages have them still; white paint cracked and peeling, still featuring the hand-painted logos of agencies and organisations from far corners of the world who sent idealistic volunteers and television-appeal money to Ethiopia. Symptoms of problems had been tackled, rather than the root causes. In the aftermath of the awful famine, it must have been so much easier. People are hungry – give them food. People are poor – give them money.

The signboards are not the only memorial of this time.

'Give me four hundred birr,' comes a high voice to my right.

A small girl in a navy-blue frock is marching atop the roadside bank, matching my uphill crawl with ease. She must be seven or eight at the most, with a head of wispy dreadlocks. The unexpected precision of this demand, delivered in clear English, elicits a sudden fit of giggles! Heck, why not five hundred, or a thousand? Why on earth *four hundred?*

I'd recently met some newly qualified teachers from Addis Ababa, the Ethiopian capital, sent to work in provincial schools. They had invited me to stay the evening in their dormitory, for which they each paid a monthly rent of £2.50.

'Don't give the kids anything,' they'd said. 'They don't need money. They have enough of everything. But their parents teach them to ask anyway. We're sorry you have to experience that.'

I'd asked them why most children's grasp of English began and ended with 'you'. They'd had no idea. So I was forced to formulate my own theory. I imagined some guilt-driven do-gooder plonked in the middle of a village with a box of clothes.

'One for you . . . one for you . . . and one for you . . . you . . . you . . . you . . .'

'YOUYOUYOUYOUYOU!!!'

One small boy doesn't bother opening his mouth at all. You, nameless child, you you you you you, are going to bring all that I have endured to critical mass.

He watches me approach, and I watch him, a moody little loner, standing motionless on the rocky earth a few dozen yards from the road, neither moving nor speaking. I ride on – his is just another staring face. I've seen thousands now. But he knows something that I do not. He knows that my route will take me to the far side of the hill on which he's herding his goats. Something in this boy's brain clicks. And he starts towards a vantage point at the top of the rise. He now knows what he is going to do.

Meanwhile I continue grinding up the latest in I don't know how many unyielding inclines, slowly inching round the bend in the road, when a stone the size of a golf ball smacks into the dust a few feet ahead of me and bounces into the meadow beyond.

The world stops turning; I imagine the impact, the ringing in my ears, the blood, the dent in my skull, and all is red: I slam on the brakes and leap off my bike, not caring whether anything breaks as it topples over. The little silhouette has already turned tail and is running pell-mell away from the scene of the crime, limbs flailing, but I grab the nearest pebble and launch it with all my might and anger in the direction of my pint-sized tormentor. It doesn't even reach halfway. In fact, as throws go, it's utterly pathetic. The six-year-old can lob a stone twice as far as I can. He does it for a living.

'Come on then, you little shit!!!' I roar into the thin air. The sky is a perfect blue; these lost, traffic-free highlands are tranquil, but my blood is boiling and I'm locked in battle with a small boy. He stops, turns, sees me standing in the road, arms outstretched. 'Come on!!! I'm all yours!!!'

He hesitates for a moment, then takes the bait, picks up a rock, judges the weight, distance, and lets fly with a rapid swing and a follow-through stagger. The stone sails high into the air; a speck of black against the harsh brightness of the high-altitude summer sky. It's way off to the left, and I smirk. Then it begins to drift back on course – suddenly it's metres away and I realise the skill of the spin he'd applied; I flinch as it drives into the road two metres to my left with a sharp crack. At the same time as I see the moment of impact and the huff of white dust, I notice a group of women walking slowly up the track a few hundred yards away, minding their own business but probably wondering what exactly all the hollering is about.

I snap back to reality and realise it's time to defuse all of this. So I stoop for another rock; the kid knows – and I know he knows – exactly what the action means. I pause, not even bothering to pick up the rock. And he scarpers frantically over the brow of the hill. *Interesting.*

I get on my bike and ride on, passing the group of suspicious-looking women with a fake smile and a wave. I cannot believe what has just happened, and I shake my head: I'm Tom Allen, and I throw rocks at children.

Two Liverpudlian cyclists I'd met in Jordan had told me of the story of a French couple's ride in Ethiopia. They'd been tormented to the hilt by one gang of children and had sought the help of the village's adults; the adults had responded by stabbing the Frenchman in the arm, and he and his wife had fled. The Liverpudlians, on hearing this story, had sworn that they would never set foot on Ethiopian soil.

I don't want to be stabbed, or knocked out by a flying lump of rock. But I do want to have an opinion based on experience and evidence, rather than anecdotes and stories. I ride on and am mercifully left to my own devices for several hours – a record stretch – and slowly I realise that my little incident of man-on-man warfare with the six-year-old goatherd has taught me quite a few things. Firstly, and most importantly, that my treatment is a generalisation. My white skin elicits demands. Tough shit. It's not a function of my personality, or any inflated sense of whether or not I deserve it. I, Tom Allen, do not exist, to those who stop me for handouts or chases or target practice. Only *ferenjis* exist, and they appear and disappear every now and then with no particular purpose. I am one of them.

Having accepted that, I can carry out the remainder of my journey more easily, because I can treat conflicts with all of the practical techniques that I've learnt will be effective. By far the best is to ignore them altogether. It's nothing personal, remember? So I can safely ignore the demands. If I sense a barrage of projectiles, I can easily scatter a group of mini attackers by slamming on my brakes and jumping off my bike. This has the immediate effect of sending all and sundry dashing for cover. And if any particularly cocky ones decide to hang about, my stooping and reaching intently downwards is usually enough to make them scarper.

It works. I cannot deny this simple fact. Ethiopian adults discipline kids by throwing rocks at them. I see this happen every day. And I have learnt to execute these routines on the spot, without guilt. And each time, as soon as it's over,

I remember that it jars with every instinct towards diplomacy I've ever been taught. I abhor the fact that there is no common ground to be had. Michelle, my host in Gondar, spoke fluent Amharic and had told me that even with command of the language, the assumption that *ferenjis* were there for nothing more than handouts was unshakeable. On a moral level, I despise myself for even pretending to throw stones at the marauding kids.

But it works.

But it's despicable.

But it works.

I see more teams of road-builders; Ethiopians laying foundations, Chinese engineers watching through the windows of Land Cruisers and earthmovers. China is paving not just Ethiopia but whole swathes of Africa. By keeping its own currency undervalued, China can offer expertise and infrastructure at the lowest cost on the planet, and assemble a raft of political allies at the same time.

One evening I fail to find my usual refuge of a dollar 'hotel'. Wild camping is now a long-distant memory, Amhara's people being dispersed so thoroughly. A young man tells me that there is a Chinese road-building camp up ahead. This is confirmed to me by the local children.

'China!'

'China!'

'Highland!'

'You! Youyouyouyouyou!!!'

'China!'

I'm not from here. So I must be from . . .

China!

The kids follow me across the dry grass and tyre tracks to the gates of a fenced compound, full of low pre-fab buildings and shipping containers. The Ethiopian soldiers on guard outside won't budge, but soon a grubby Land Cruiser appears, returning from a day surveying the works. An ageing Chinaman and a young woman are sitting in the back, and I put on my friendliest smile and my most evocative performance of pleading yet. The camp's doctor is surprised to see the strange European outside the camp's gates; even more surprised to watch me putting up a tent on the concrete basketball court inside. He disappears, and returns with a large bowl of spicy pork ribs and noodles! Then he restocks my tiny first-aid kit and throws in a few sachets of a herbal remedy that I should mix with boiling water if I get a cold or fever.

I spend the evening with some of the younger staff members – engineers, computer technicians, administrators – hanging out in the camp's conference room with laptops and broadband Internet and the complete Backstreet Boys back-catalogue. They all speak perfect English and seem to represent the young middle class of China: they want to visit Europe, move up in the world, live comfortable and interesting and fulfilling lives. But the European visas are too difficult to get. And, fresh out of university, they've been sent to build roads in Ethiopia for the Chinese state construction monolith. Some of them will be here for the full half-decade it'll take to complete this fifty-mile stretch of road through the highest regions of Amhara – nearly two miles above sea level – with one return trip to China each year to see friends and family. And all the while, the opportunity to travel and be young and free-spirited will be passing them by. Ethiopia seems to have locked itself out of development, whereas China seems to have locked itself into it. Somehow I'm the only one in the room who has managed to tear himself free.

'Why have you come to Ethiopia? I can't understand it,' says Adam. Everyone seems to use an adopted Western name.

'I think your idea of travelling is very different to ours,' says a young guy with a quiff. 'You want to go to the developing world. We want to visit the Western world!'

'It's not that different,' I reply. 'We both just want to see something new.'

I leave early in the morning with a belly full of breakfast and daydreams of cycling across the gargantuan expanse of China. If I ride hard, that might just happen before the year is out. I could stop over in Iran, arrange to meet up with Tenny – my heart leaps guiltily at the prospect – retrieve my winter boots and the minus twenty-five sleeping-bag, and continue pedalling east. I keep hearing that China is exploding into modernity at an unimaginable rate. But somehow I can't rid myself of ridiculous images of conical-hat-wearing rice farmers and pagodas and kung-fu and people who are somehow able to eat soup with chopsticks.

I know, of course, that when I arrive in China this image will fade as another vast and complex portrait of a nation is unveiled. And I also know that I'll probably meet more twentysomething Backstreet Boys fans in China than conical-hat-wearing rice farmers. For all that promises to be fresh and new in the Far East – or anywhere else on the road ahead, for that matter – there will be increasingly more that does not seem so unfamiliar any more.

The road disappears up another stupendous incline. I'm sweating beneath the high-altitude sun, knowing it'll still be cold in the patches of shade. But this hill isn't quite so long, and as I edge my way over the saddle of the ridge, I realise that I'm about to put the Ethiopian highlands behind me.

Two vertical miles of descent is spread at my feet. I release the brakes. And it's just endless. Mind-boggling. My eyes are screwed up in defence against the roaring wind, patches of tarmac dipping violently in and out of existence, and I think back to a time when I considered a 'big hill' to be one that took more than fifteen minutes to climb. Now I'm measuring hills in terms of *days* needed to cycle up them, and *hours* needed to freewheel back down! I overtake a pootling truck, and then a bus, its passengers staring in disbelief as I pull alongside and past the trundling vehicle. A man on the roadside glares at me as I blast past him:

'MONEY!!!'

But I'm a receding dust cloud before I even hear the word! *Ha-ha! Suck on that!*

I stop for food long before I run out of gravity, finding that I've switched planets since I last put pressure on my pedals. Gone are the bald fields and skinny herds, replaced by steep-sided valleys of terraced green, of tall sugar cane and lush mango and avocado trees. The humidity is rising. The road is littered with splintered foliage and barrows and signs of intensive agriculture. At a roadside eatery I dig into a big bowl of *shiro* and bread and have a pleasant conversation with a young man who's also stopped for a meal. After shouting at the waitress for trying to rip me off, he insists on paying for my food, ignoring my protests with a chuckle. This last half-hour, I realise, sums up my time in Ethiopia perfectly: the exhausting mystery of whether the next roadside figure is going to ask me for money . . . or ask me to lunch.

From the town of Weldiya I continue my freewheeling marathon. The landscape switches back to brown, becoming hot, dry and barren, the air hazy with dust. These are the fringes of the Afar desert, also known as the Danakil Depression, or the East African Rift.

This is a place where no aid agencies go. It's a place where, each time I mention it, I'm told I'll surely be kidnapped or shot by the savage tribes who roam the volcanic savannahs. I'm about to invalidate my travel insurance, too, by striking out across this lost triangle of Earth to which the British government has specifically advised its citizens not to go. One young man had made me promise to take a detour by bus to avoid the region. *Of course, of course!* I'd lied.

But I expect no kidnappings or shootings. I'm putting what faith I have in humanity's more sociable tendencies, figuring I'll be exceptionally unlucky to be taken captive by the marginalised Afar tribespeople and used as a political bargaining chip. I hope I'm right. Because I haven't told anyone the truth about what I'm about to do. Not the Foreign Office. Not my parents. And definitely not Tenny.

This area of Ethiopia holds the world record for the hottest place on Earth. And it is mightily hot, even at this early hour. It's already approaching Sudanese temperatures, and apparently it's only going to get hotter as I head across the desert.

They've managed to make me paranoid that I'm going to get shot on this road. Because, apparently, the Afar people are 'very bad', while the local people here are 'very good'. And they all carry AK-47s. And regularly shoot passing drivers.

But, to be honest, I figure that there's no such thing as 'bad people'. If you see what I mean. There are groups of people with grudges against each other. And there are groups of people who pronounce other groups of people as intrinsically 'bad'. But in the end, everybody's just human.

And so for that reason I'm not going to shy away from trying to cross the region. Because I just refuse to believe that there can be a whole society of people, all of whom are intrinsically 'bad'. I just don't believe it. And so I'm going to go and find out for myself.

CHAPTER 17

I opened my eyes. The pale orange of a streetlamp filtered through the thin curtains of the flat, but the sky was still dark. Then I remembered what I had to do, and the worry flooded in, drowning any hope that I would be able to go back to sleep. I lay nervously on my side, reluctant to stir. This was it. This was the day that I had been awaiting for what seemed like forever.

I didn't want to disturb Tenny – she needed the rest far more than I did – so I padded into the kitchen in my boxers and mumbled a few thoughts into the video camera, my face bleached beneath the light of the head-torch strapped to the unit. Though still half asleep and in no mood to dwell on my many concerns, I knew that this moment would be an important one to capture. It was always those moments when I'd rather do anything than talk to the camera that seemed to tell my story best.

It's about five-thirty in the morning, and, um . . . it's the day that we're going to leave Yerevan. I can't sleep . . . we were meant to get up at six o'clock, and leave at seven as it started to get light . . . but I've been awake for about an hour already. I've got too much . . . too many things going around in my head, so . . . I've had maybe three hours' sleep. I had three hours' sleep the night before I left England, as well, and I'm sure those three hours were of far worse quality, so . . . anyway.

So this is it. We're going. It's been eight months since I first arrived here in Yerevan. It's the middle of summer now, and it's definitely time to go. Because the last few weeks I've just been finding it really difficult, this city life. I don't know . . . the routine, the lack of variety . . . I don't know. There's something about it that doesn't fulfil me.

But I'm glad that I've waited this long to leave, because it means that I'm going to be leaving with Tenny, who is someone . . . very special to me. I'm sure it's going to be completely different to how it was when I left England, but I don't know how she's going to cope with it at all. I really don't.

I wrote on my website that I'm 'cautiously hopeful' that things are going to be OK. I've tried to plan things so that we take it slowly – the first thing we're going to do today is cycle to Lake Sevan, which is quite an idyllic place. It's a very large lake that occupies quite a large portion of Armenia. And we're going to camp there tonight, hopefully, and spend two or three days just skirting around the edge, and camping, and . . . hopefully just enjoying the experience away from the city, without having to do too many long days of riding.

And after that, we'll head south, which is where it's going to start getting pretty mountainous. And I'm not going to understate how mountainous it's going to be – the first pass we'll have to climb is just under two and a half thousand metres above sea level, which makes it the highest altitude road I'll have ridden on this trip. So . . . for Tenny to tackle that in her first few days of riding is an enormous challenge, which I never had to face – and she's going to have to do it with no experience at all.

I finished up the video-diary and put a frying-pan on the stove to cook some sausages and eggs. I had no appetite, but

I would force myself to make my last meal in this flat a decent one. The two bikes leaned up against the sofa, trailers and panniers heavily laden, the machines seeming to have grown during their months indoors.

Our preparations had been under way ever since I'd first met Tenny on that fateful night in the Irish pub. The dream of travel had been a driving force in our relationship from the beginning, and it had helped me stay motivated to remain in Armenia until her graduation that summer. After her final exams and degree presentation, we had pressed forward with our plans in earnest. The bike I'd had delivered to Andy in Georgia to avoid a repeat of the sleeping-bag incident had proved ideal, and by July we were fully kitted out and ready to go, with a brand new website developed and launched to tell the story of my new journey with Tenny. The last remaining hurdle was to find the courage to do what we had planned to do. Against our better judgement, Tenny and I had decided that we would make our journey under cover of secrecy.

Her parents hadn't budged an inch, dismissing our travel plans and putting their foot down hard when Tenny's sister, visiting Armenia and in on the secret, had accidentally let slip that we were still planning our bicycle trip. We'd hurriedly covered the mistake, saying that we just wanted to travel around Armenia by bus for a few weeks. We had a roaming contract organised for Tenny's mobile phone in order to appear to be calling from an Armenian phone number – when in fact we would be cycling through Iran itself, drawing ever closer to Tehran as the lie festered. And one day we would surprise her parents by knocking on the door of their flat. They would see how determined she was, that she was capable of doing what she'd decided to do. And they would allow us to continue.

I thought Tenny was remarkably brave to consider doing such a thing against her family's wishes. In fact, I thought she was incredibly courageous to be attempting this at all – a city girl of five foot one who hadn't ridden a bike since childhood. She hadn't slept in a tent since her days in the Scouts. She knew nothing of life on the road whatsoever, save for impressions she'd taken from my own stories and photographs. And she was about to leave behind her home of five years, her closest friends, tear herself away from all that tied her to Armenia, and dive headfirst into a life of complete uncertainty that she hadn't known existed until I'd pushed open the door of Shamrock. Riding the yawning mountain ranges of Armenia to Iran would be difficult even for me, and I was supposed to be the 'big strong man', a fearless adventurer with thousands of miles of riding behind me. I had no idea how she would cope, nor whether she would enjoy it. She was making a sacrifice far greater than I had made; taking a risk that dwarfed those I had taken, and was following her heart into the wilderness so that we could be together. And for that, whatever the outcome, she had my deepest admiration and respect. It was why I loved her.

Just after nine o'clock in the morning, we crossed the city limits and began to edge between the sleazy-looking casinos that lined the highway. This highway would climb three thousand feet up the Hrazdan River valley to the basin of Lake Sevan, a huge freshwater lake that sat amongst the mountains of central Armenia. Dogs leapt barking from their resting spots amongst the scatter of blacked-out SUVs outside the casinos, and chased us up the hill, yapping at our trailers. Clapped-out Ford Transit vans and their Soviet-era imitations spluttered past, belching fumes and road chippings in protest at being forced into service long after retirement age, suspension sagging with the combined weight of a couple of dozen passengers. These faces glared at us from behind filthy windows: *outsiders*, riding *bicycles* – of all things. There were many things about life as a foreigner in Armenia that I wouldn't miss. These suspicious stares were chief amongst them.

The minor detour of Lake Sevan, I thought, would surely beat the dreary flatlands that I'd crossed after leaving Yerevan on the direct route to Iran during my first attempt to leave Armenia by bicycle, which now seemed so long ago. And Tenny and I pedalled in first gear up the long and gradual incline which linked the capital city with the popular summertime destination of Lake Sevan, as well as its wintertime counterpart Tsaghkadzor, the alpine 'Valley of Flowers'. Familiar to both of us, Lake Sevan would be a natural milestone, a place of quiet, natural beauty. The holiday season had recently finished and the beaches and campgrounds would now be empty. Then, a couple of days of easy riding to the south end of the lake would be ample warm-up for the far greater challenges that would await us when we rejoined the mountain road to Iran. But there would be plenty of climbs on the road to Lake Sevan, too.

The first real hills I'd encountered on a fully loaded bike had been in eastern France, riding south towards Lake Geneva and the Alps, the ridges of the Jura emerging high above the farmlands of Alsace-Lorraine. Taking steep back-roads through the increasingly alpine landscape, I'd attacked those hills head on, pumping at the pedals in a rhythmic frenzy, sweat drenching my face and torso, my gasping and panting drowned out by the heavy soundtrack in my headphones. An onlooker would have observed a spectacularly pointless waste of energy by an angry and slightly masochistic young man. And such an assessment would have been accurate.

I'd since learnt that hills were the reason that *gears* were invented. The main function of gears on a bike is to keep the rider's level of exertion more or less continuous on a route encompassing a variety of gradients. There had been no reason to push myself until my vision swam and I felt physically sick – except to appease my bloody-mindedness and my testosterone-fuelled need to prove my own strength. I could have pottered up those hills with ease if I'd wished, though it'd have taken a little longer. I had obviously learnt some patience since those days, since I now found myself ambling along at a couple of miles per hour. And a good thing too, or Tenny would have found herself alone within the first few minutes of the climb.

It refused to end, that climb, each bend revealing another, each hint of a summit proving false, time after time after time. Traffic flew blindly past, drivers fixated on the asphalt runway before them, their vehicles screaming, gobbling the trail of chippings set in hard black tar. We stopped after an hour of unbearably slow progress up the incline, collapsing beneath gaudily painted metal parasols on the roadside. Yerevan still lay beneath us, wrapped in her cloak of smog, still so frustratingly near. It seemed that we hadn't even made a dent in the distance. And now would come more switchbacks, more endless bends that hugged the hillsides, landslide barriers erected to prevent nature from retaking the earth that had been blasted away to make way for this purgatorial road.

Tenny pedalled on, pulling in front of me with what I thought was impressive determination. I resumed my routine of empty-headed spinning, my thoughts straying far from the gruelling task at hand. I had little concept of how long we'd been pedalling for when Tenny suddenly stopped, and I pulled over to the barrier where she'd dismounted. The shoulder was strewn with litter, blown-out tyres, discarded snack-food packaging and loose gravel and glass, with the midday sun beating down through a hazy sky and the dark surface seeming to radiate the same heat back up from beneath my feet. Tin boxes on wheels continued to belt past us towards a place I could now barely envisage.

Leaning my bike against the barrier, I walked over to Tenny, who was struggling to rest her bike upright. The front wheel kept swinging sideways, wheeling itself back into the road under force of gravity. A small basket of apples sat on an upturned plastic crate, with a scrawl of Armenian script on a torn-off cardboard box flap sticking up behind the little pile of fruit. Down the bank from the highway was a small orchard, where an old man had spotted her. Now he invited us to climb the barrier and sit in the shade under his apple trees. Yes – a break right now would be just the ticket.

We sat down on a gentle slope under a tree, feeling the welcoming softness of the thick grass and the delightful respite from the sun's rays in this shady spot, hidden from view below the road's edge. The man and his wife brought us two little cups of strong black coffee as the muffled din of passing trucks continued. Then Tenny buried her face in her hands and softly began to cry.

And I saw before me a girl completely out of her depth, trapped between a fading romantic hallucination and the awful realisation that this life would be *nothing* like she'd imagined. I saw a girl who had been waiting half a year for an experience that had so far turned out to be utter hell from the word go, and showed no sign of becoming anything else. And I saw myself in her; the force of my idealistic dreams changing the course of her life to match mine, and I realised my idiocy with a horrible clarity: I would never truly share my dream with anyone. I would always be alone – alone in this desire to wander in pursuit of something I still didn't understand.

And I reached over to Tenny, to the girl who had walked out of her front door, handed back the keys, and dragged her own body-weight in machinery and luggage up the most revolting highway I'd ever ridden because I'd blithely told her it would be the adventure of a lifetime, without a moment's thought for the realities of life on the road. I touched her on the shoulder. Put the palm of my hand on her back, against her pretty blue and white checked shirt. Felt the heat of her tired body, the weak shudder of uncontained tears.

There was no response. I withdrew my hand. And I sat back on the grass, helpless, looking up at the edge of the endless road.

Tenny had to dig deep in order to continue that day. But continue she did.

'It was the hardest day of my life,' she told me later. 'I was so angry at myself for wanting to quit on the first day of cycling. And at the same time, I was so angry at you! You kept telling me that it was just a little further. It wouldn't continue like this. And of course you were trying to help, but I only wanted shout and cry and argue, because it meant that I should still continue up that hill, which was the last thing I wanted to do.

'And I had this horrible pain in the base of my stomach. It was like period pain. I didn't realise that it might not be normal. But I just carried on because I didn't know any better.

'I never felt such a pain before. And I've never felt it since.'

Much later I learnt that there was a morning train from Yerevan up to Lake Sevan. It would have cost the princely sum of 80p for the one-way trip, for us and our bicycles. But on that day I remained ignorant as to the more sensible option for a beginner cyclist. I also remained ignorant of the quiet and gradual alternative route along the river gorge, and for that matter to every other possibility for what we might have done instead. I had seen only one option – to continue riding from where I'd left off, in the same direction I'd always planned. And if Tenny wanted to join me, she would have to go through the same trials that I'd long ago had to bear. How else would she come to appreciate this new way of life, which would surely be a straightforward continuation of the one I'd been living before?

The sun began to droop towards the eastern horizon, where Aragats, Armenia's highest peak, dominated the skyline. The gradient began to subside and the plateau spread out ahead of us. It had taken an entire day to complete the climb, but we had conquered the worst of Armenia's roads. If we'd overcome that, I thought, then we could hardly fail to tackle whatever lay ahead.

We slept in my two-man tent on a disused patch of ground below the highway. And the following afternoon the horizon began to glitter: we had reached Lake Sevan. We set up camp on a small peninsula in a wooded lakeside compound that a few weeks previously would have been inhabited by families on their summer holidays, barbecuing great skewers of meat and pumping the most god-awful blend of Armenian pop music across the calm waters of the lake. But all was peaceful now, save for a couple of loitering blokes attached to the compound, and a white-haired old lady, tall, stick-thin yet with the most radiant smile, who swept the area clear of leaves and trash and went to great lengths to help us find firewood and settle in.

One night turned to two, then three, then four. Tenny was in no hurry to ride onward, so I kept my mouth shut and tried to stifle my worries about the encroaching autumn and the £4 daily charge I was paying for the pitch, which was an extravagance I hadn't foreseen. So we swam, lay in the sun, hitched to and from the nearby town for supplies, and began to unwind after all the stress and furtiveness of readying to leave, which had been taking its toll for too long.

When we finally set off south, a full week had passed since our departure from Yerevan. We were now headed for parts of the country that neither of us knew. We would roughly trace the lake shore before burrowing into the mountain ranges that had made the South Caucasus so impenetrable in times gone by; mountains that had historically preserved the Armenians as they were driven by occupying powers from lands that they'd inhabited for centuries. I knew that this road would be difficult for Tenny. It would be difficult for me, too. I hoped that a few days of riding, especially the challenging climbs of the first two days, would be preparation for the high passes ahead, among fierce snow-capped ranges rising more than two miles into the sky.

Sevan – the mountain-fringed lake lived up to its reputation, the water crystal clear, the air refreshingly cool after a stuffy midsummer in Yerevan breathing traffic fumes by day and second-hand smoke by night. Yet, as we inched our way south, there were no sails to be seen flitting across the surface of this lake. Water sports had not yet found their way to Armenia, and there was not a yacht, windsurfer, kayak or even swimmer to be seen.

I wondered when the quiet route I'd hoped for would materialise. It didn't. Traffic bundled past incessantly, clapped-out cars, countless dumptrucks, each carrying a single enormous boulder from some quarry in the hills. I followed Tenny closely as she edged along the thin shoulder of the road, and we broke up the journey with visits to a series of roadside kiosks which provided cheap ice cream and a respite from the nerve-wracking traffic. These 'service stations' were not quite the air-conditioned clones I'd found in Europe or neighbouring Turkey. Even though I'd been living amongst the remains of Soviet communism for half a year, I still felt faintly appalled by the conditions in which people were seemingly happy to operate. Little stores were carved from metal shipping containers propped up on breeze blocks, years of botched repairs and modifications making them almost unrecognisable but no less unwelcoming.

Toilets were plank-covered pits with a foot-wide hole cut from the wood, corrugated metal walls imparting some rudimentary sense of privacy, and a strict bring-your-own-toilet-paper policy. The legacy of the socialist republics was the triumph of function over form, and so today the preservation of function was all that mattered, with form now all but forgotten. Entire generations of people had never been permitted to display independence and initiative in public. Their jobs had always been to keep things running just-so for the good of the communist state, only changing the pattern on receipt of instructions from above – instructions that had abruptly ceased to arrive.

After the grim desperation of the '90s, today was supposed to be a time of brightness and hope and optimism for the future. Yet almost half of Armenia's adult population had no means of earning a living. It was a country where demonstrations over alleged election-rigging were met by soldiers firing live ammunition into crowds; where journalists at ballot stations reported having their cameras smashed on the ground by hired thugs; where it was alleged that hundreds of millions of dollars in development funds mysteriously 'disappeared' on a regular basis; where high-ranking officials from the Ministry of Nature Protection were accused of spontaneously declassifying parts of protected areas in order to build luxury lakefront properties, with no functioning judicial system to stop them. Several people I knew in Yerevan lived in apartments that were missing floorboards, because much of the nation had been without gas and electricity during the winters following the Soviet collapse, and the residents had had to rip up the planks beneath their feet for firewood to avoid literally freezing to death.

It was time to leave Armenia. Part of me would always remain here, hoping that the country's corrupt core would one day be hollowed out. I followed Tenny between freshly harvested fields of wheat as the south shore of the lake appeared on the horizon, and soon we came upon a track leading down to the water's edge. At the bottom of the track we found another little resort hidden amongst the trees, which consisted of a handful of shipping containers converted into lodgings, a couple of benches and tables nearby, and a beach that was covered with tiny little frogs. It looked like an ideal place to stop for the night. Then I learnt something new about Tenny, which was that she was terrified of frogs. Especially tiny little ones.

'They jump so fast! And they're slippery. And I hate their tongues,' she said, shivering with disgust, and told me the story of the time she'd been sunbathing elsewhere by Lake Sevan, lying on her stomach with her bikini top untied to avoid unsightly tan lines. She'd felt something moving just below her armpit, looked down, seen the all the tiny little frogs that had come to pay a visit, and leapt a mile, squeaking and hopping about the beach, limbs and bits of bikini flailing all over the place, which had resulted in general hilarity for everyone in the vicinity (and no doubt a lot of guilty-looking little frogs).

The caretaker was a veteran of communism who had seen better times and was content to dedicate his remaining days to a single task, even one as drab as looking after an empty lakeside camp for nine months of the year. Armenia was littered with these characters – old men now, each proudly fulfilling the same repetitive task that they had been practising since time immemorial, whether or not it still came with the same salary or greater purpose that the socialist dream had once provided. They maintained the old city parks that the state had abandoned. They prevented the disused instruments of former rulers from falling into ruin. They repaired the tools and machinery and vehicles built by industries whose factories had long since closed down, whose visionaries and engineers had died or been deported or passed out of memory. They tended to the old tree-lined boulevards, kept the ancient railways trundling, operated the flea markets and the dingy canteens that served them, and performed a thousand other invisible duties for little or no tangible reward. And in doing so, they single-handedly preserved the last remnants of a system that once promised life's essentials to all the societies of the world – shelter, food, family, purpose and unity – as long as they never spoke out.

Communism was a loaded word now, stinking of death and deportation, cast as the antagonist in the good-versus-evil narrative of twentieth century history. But communism had provided hundreds of millions of people with everything they needed. It was its disappearance, not its presence, that had pulled the rug mercilessly from beneath those people, leaving them barely capable of functioning, all of the things they'd taken for granted suddenly missing. Elderly people remembered the peak of the Soviet era with happy nostalgia – a time when everyone had a job and a car and central heating and vouchers for the finest holiday resorts the Union had to offer. Of course, they were the ones who were still talking, not having been trotted off to Siberia. Still, was it was worse to watch industrial society disappear in front of your eyes, or to never have seen it in the first place?

Armenia was still in the throes of that torturous

readjustment. There had been fourteen other nations in the Union before its dissolution, putting three hundred million people in the same boat as the three million Armenians here — three hundred million people who'd had their life-support systems suddenly unplugged in what must have been an unimaginably desperate and tragic moment in history, which had occurred silently and invisibly while I'd been happily traipsing the half-mile between school and home in Middleton, Northamptonshire, aged eight, building go-carts out of pram wheels and planks.

Darkness fell, the friendly family who had been finishing their barbecue departed, and a new trickle of crinkly old men began to arrive in a series of standard-issue white Ladas. They were friends of the caretaker, and when they came over to the tent with an enthusiastic invitation to join them, I realised that we were a long way from an undisturbed night's sleep. For the antidote to these modern-day ills was about to be administered, with the help of a decoratively carved shot glass; the antidote to the knowledge that the happy times had passed, that the dream of communism had come to an end. It was the antidote that blotted out the memory that the greatest social experiment in human history had failed. It was vodka.

'Come and drink with us!' blurted an invisible voice by my ear as I struggled out of my sweaty Lycra and tried to slip into something more comfortable. Someone outside was fumbling with the tent's zip. Tenny barked diplomatically at the disembodied voice as we wrestled with bags and clothes and inflatable mattresses in the cramped tent that I'd never expected to find myself sharing. I didn't understand Armenian, but the sound of receding footfalls and diminishing voices was clear enough. Then someone switched on a car stereo and turned the volume up to eleven.

Tenny sighed in the darkness. 'I just don't have the energy for this,' she said. 'I know what this is going to be like. I know this kind of people. I'm sorry – I'm just not very interested in drinking with old men.'

She was exhausted. It had been another long day.

'Well, we've got to go and say hello, at least,' I said.

'Why? No! Can't we just stay here?'

'They'll just come back! At least if we go over and have a couple of shots they might get drunk and forget us.'

So we put on false smiles and warm fleeces, as the September evenings in the mountains had taken on a chill, and made our way gingerly over to the metal table around which the caretaker and his friends were seated. The table was laden with the usual bread and herbs and salty cheese and tasteless pink salami, and a big steaming pot of mutton swimming in oily broth formed a most unappetising centrepiece for the spread. We shook hands and rambled pleasantries, and the sour spirit was poured and poured again, 'to take the dust off the glasses', as we sat amid the smells and splutterings of communist relics while long-winded toasts were cast off into the night.

But for Tenny, who had already lived for five years in Armenia, it was an experience she'd had too many times for it to be worth enduring again. While I could use this night's events as a mental landmark in our journey to Iran, and even extract some novelty value from it, there were few places she wouldn't have rather been.

It had been light for some time when I gently called her

name the next morning, but Tenny didn't stir from the depths of her sleeping bag, nestling mouse-like within the puffy feather-stuffed folds, showing no sign of wanting to face the day. She hadn't slept at all well – not only because of the shouting and music and car headlights that had persisted until the early hours, but also because of having had to navigate a minefield of tiny little frogs in the middle of the night. At least she'd been warm enough in the big winter sleeping bag, which was a relief as she felt the cold keenly. I was glad that the bloody thing had finally come in useful.

Tenny remained quiet as I followed a few metres behind her, edging slightly out into the road to force passing vehicles to give us a wide berth. That evening, camped wild amongst the tall trees of Lake Sevan's nature reserve at the south end of the lake, I decided that the time had come for the frankest kind of discussion. Because I was becoming worried that we disagreed fundamentally on what would be worthwhile about this new life together on the road. And that would have profound implications for the future of our relationship, because there would be no motivation to overcome the inevitable challenges unless we could both see the point of doing so.

Tenny had obviously spent the day thinking along similar lines, because she unhesitatingly identified her vulnerabilities and the things that she was finding the most difficult. She wore her heart on her sleeve and had a sharp mind for the ebb and flow of the human condition. The next morning, over a cup of instant coffee, I asked her to speak frankly for the video camera.

'I'm getting very depressed,' she told me. 'Even very small

things make me . . . yeah, just give up and go home.' Then she laughed, as if at how embarrassing it was to lose control of her mood over such insignificances. And that gave me hope, because it meant that she understood what was happening to her, acknowledging that mood swings were inevitable, and that they would pass, given enough time. Putting the camera down, I told her again of the first weeks of my journey, when I'd often acted towards my two best friends like the rattiest son-of-a-bitch they could ever have been unlucky enough to meet, let alone travel with. I'd been used to living within a small world that I knew well and could just about mould to my liking. Travelling had spun that notion right around, and I'd had to broker a hurried peace deal with uncertainty.

I knew what I *didn't* want, and that was for Tenny to follow me around simply because I was too stubborn to give up travelling and settle down to a stable, 'normal' life with her. The pressure would ruin our relationship and destroy whatever there was to gain from travel. Likewise, I couldn't just quit this life on the road for good, because I'd invested too much in it; there were so many reasons I needed it, and giving it up would be ruinous. Finally, I felt it was critical that she get past this break-in period, because I knew that the rewards of this kind of travel did not come quickly and easily. Tenny understood this. But the decision was ultimately hers. And if she didn't want to continue travelling, well – well, I didn't know what we'd do then.

As we talked about the process, I felt a palpable sense of how much I must have matured. Tenny's growing pains reminded me vividly of myself in the not-too-distant past. Except that it didn't seem to be me. Instead, it was like watching someone else through a window from outside in the dark. I wasn't used to thinking back through my own history and finding a different person inhabiting my memories. But that was exactly how it seemed.

CHAPTER 18

Lake Sevan vanished behind us as we began to climb up into hilly land, the valley sides green but bare, carved with patterns like tree roots where rivulets of water had for centuries delved. The air grew dry, the sun ever more fierce as we gained altitude. We were far from any major route through the country, and people and settlements were few. This road would weave through the highlands, summit a final high pass and then descend into the far valley where we would join the through-route to the Iranian border, two hundred miles distant.

We met a shepherd on the roadside. His flock was scattered like rice in the meadow far below. He produced a bundle of cloth containing bread, cheese and herbs, offered us lunch, and asked about our journey. Tenny told him we were heading for Iran, and that I'd cycled from England. That's great, he said, and cast his attention back to his flock. A friendly exchange; unremarkable. Yet rarely could I have left our flat in Yerevan with my beard and shorts and sandals without the feeling that I was being eyed or mocked, insidiously if not overtly, simply for looking different. After half a year of it, this easy encounter with a quiet outdoorsman was exactly what I needed – a return to a life of simple things.

The empty mountain road emerged at the edge of a wide,

silent plateau. A low ridge in the distance separated this high-altitude meadow from the indigo sky. A half-mile away, I could make out wild horses nibbling near the meandering outline of a river. Close to the road, the plain was studded with tiny houses built of stone, short and stout and with dark holes for windows. Their doorways were partly dug into the ground, and grass sprouting from their uneven roofs gave them the appearance of having been summoned from the earth by some arcane magical force. Free from power lines and telegraph cables, the place felt weirdly ancient, as if we'd accidentally stumbled into a Tolkien-esque fantasy.

Curious, we stopped and called to a figure by the closest of the houses. The woman trudged up the bank to the road and spoke to Tenny in a thick accent.

'We use it as our summer pasture,' she said. 'Nobody lives up here in the winter – the weather's too harsh. The roads get blocked by snow, and facilities are too far away.

'Sometimes we see a few tourists up here, though,' she continued. 'They come for some historical thing. A *caravanserai*.' Of course: the Silk Road, longtime magnet for the romantic traveller; an irresistible hook on which to hang a journey through Central Asia. I'd met plenty of backpackers who'd bragged that they were 'doing the Silk Road'. Indeed, entire guidebooks existed on the topic of how to 'do the Silk Road', complete with detailed rundowns of which cities contained the most important sites, directions, opening times and entrance fees, plus all the easiest ways to travel between them – and of course which places to avoid because they had nothing to do with 'doing the Silk Road'.

Then I stopped, catching myself looking down upon the Silk Roaders, and gave my cynical old self a mighty wallop.

Because I understood perfectly well why people embarked on these fantasy journeys. I'd been there. I too had planned idealistic routes across foreign lands, dreaming of riding off-road, forgetting that it would actually mean climbing a thousand fences whilst bypassing all human contact. I'd bought the brass rabbit snares too, and packed my copy of the *SAS Survival Guide* – for a *road* trip. And I'd drawn a forty-thousand mile line round the planet because a circumnavigation was the only way my insufferable ego could make sense of its yearning to wander. I'd been so sure that I was right; that my way was the best way. And sure – some travellers on the well-worn Silk Road might have a genuine and lifelong fascination with Afro-Eurasian trade routes of antiquity. But most were just trying to make sense of their desire to travel in a vast and complex world by making things simple and easy to follow. Things might become more nuanced with time, as they had for me. It was a natural and necessary process. And what was wrong with that?

At the southern end of the plateau a steep climb loomed ahead of us – surely the final hurdle before an epic downhill into the next valley. This would be a huge victory for us, as it would represent the pay-off of having climbed into the mountains and summited the first of the five huge passes between us and Iran. What a prize for Tenny to enjoy that exhilarating descent!

She stopped at the top of the pass and dismounted to enjoy the view. I pulled up beside her.

'I'm scared.'

'Scared? Of what?'

'This hill. I don't like going downhill very fast.'

Below us, the asphalt spiralled and seesawed into a gigantic abyss.

'Right . . . can't you go down slowly?'

'I don't want to. I feel I can't control myself properly – my speed.'

I hesitated. And then we flagged down a passing farmer, bundled our bikes into the back of his hay truck and hitched a ride to the bottom of the most incredible downhill that I would never ride.

And the next day, pedalling along the lush valley bottom to Yeghegnadzor and seeing the beginnings of an equally gigantic climb ahead, Tenny thumbed another ride for us – this time with an Azeri trucker. He was piloting his empty lorry back to Iran and was quite happy to have some company. And four breathtaking mountain passes came and went like scenes from a vaguely interesting slide-show. Before I knew what had happened we'd been deposited twenty miles shy of the border. We would reach Iran the next morning.

I'd compromised. And that had actually come as quite a surprise. It was another sign that things were moving on from the hard-headed days of plugging away at the road for no reason other than to get the distance done. There was a new priority now, and it was to find a position from which I could help Tenny learn what already came naturally to me. Surely that was my duty, as the person beside her, committed to occupying that role in her life? I should embrace that responsibility, and accept that the journey was no longer all about me. The challenges would not be found in climbing high passes, but in trying to understand how the world looked from her point of view, in overcoming my own stubbornness and learning patience and diplomacy, and in remaining one step ahead, removing barriers before they appeared in front of her. Andy, by contrast, had been perfectly capable of looking after himself. Travelling with Tenny was unexplored territory, and that made it exciting and fresh and new. It made it worth doing.

Dragons' teeth of golden stone rose from the Iranian side of the River Arax, reaching high into the blue. Walls of jagged rock overhung the road that we followed along the gorge towards Jolfa, a small town in the Turkic province that formed the north-west corner of Iran, just a stone's throw from Armenia's own forbidden frontier with Turkey.

'That was the exact opposite of what I was expecting!' said Tenny, excitedly, as we wheeled our bicycles away from the border post and into the Islamic Republic. 'It was the Armenians who were very serious, asking a lot of questions . . . but on the Iranian side, that very serious security officer just smiled to us! Oh, that was great!'

Tour buses pulled slowly up to the barriers, their occupants dragging suitcases and laundry bags full of goodness-knows-what from the luggage holds and into the building that housed the security apparatus of Iran's solitary land-border with Armenia.

'It was really good to be arriving in the Iranian part,' continued Tenny, 'because I knew the toilet was going to be much better than the Armenian one. Water and everything! So I spent maybe more than half an hour there.'

'I know,' I replied. 'I thought you'd gone back to Armenia!'

We had only been on the road for a couple of hours when, without warning, the heavens opened. The two of us had been riding quite happily along, unsuspecting; within sixty seconds we were cowering under my poncho behind a pile of rocks as a freak storm blew through the gorge, drenching everything in its path. I heard a crash of metal, and then another. Lifting the lip of the poncho I saw that the wind had blown the two heavily loaded bicycles and their trailers over and into the road, shattering my rear-view mirror. I dashed out to rescue the bikes before they were flattened by an oncoming truck, and returned to the dripping wet poncho beneath which my girlfriend was shivering.

'What will happen to us?' she cried. 'We can not even stay in a hotel! If I don't have marriage certificate, they don't even let me to stay in separate room. I'm not allowed to stay in a hotel . . .'

She peered out into the storm, wretched beyond tears, shrouding her face in the flapping camouflage-patterned fabric.

'What . . . where . . . where is . . . where is here? . . . I wanna go . . . go home!'

Two miles along the road lay the village of Siyahrood; a tiny farming settlement that also happened to lie on the main road route between the neighbouring capitals of Yerevan and Tehran. Travellers were well catered for in Siyahrood, and we quickly discovered that one of the cafes had a room upstairs available to rent. Tenny had been shaken by the suddenness and intensity of the storm. And I knew well that feeling of helplessness in the face of the elements; the knowledge that there was nowhere to hide, just you and the weather facing off against each other. A memory snapped into focus: a roadside verge in Northamptonshire, Andy tweaking the angle of his saddle, Mark cracking jokes, the

familiar limestone villages, and rain beginning to spit from
the grey sky – just a few big drops, but enough to remind
me that I would now be living a life outdoors, through all
that the world could throw at me. And the world, of course,
would always dominate. There was no real protection, no
doorway to retreat to, no looking out from behind a window; only a kind of acceptance of being permanently on the
outside of all those doors and windows. A steep learning
curve indeed, and now Tenny was climbing it too.

'It's strange,' she said, once we'd got warm and dry and
settled into the little room for the evening, 'because I lived
in Iran for twenty-four years but . . . I still don't quite feel
safe here. Especially that I'm the one who is communicating
with people, asking things of men especially, who are
looking at me in a strange way . . . because me, and what
I'm doing, is really . . . something new for them.'

We sat on a rug on the floor. A neat stack of bedding and
mattresses inhabited one corner of the room; a gas heater
was the only other furniture. The village mosque began its
sunset call to prayer, the soaring minarets lit with fluorescent
green light, the piercing song of the *mo'azzen* distorted as if
through a loudhailer.

'I'm really looking forward to . . . be in a place where I can
have my privacy,' Tenny continued. 'I don't know, maybe
I'm a little bit fussy, but . . . I really miss living in a stable
place, and knowing that it's my home. Sometimes it's nice
to be outside, but sometimes . . . I'm really scared to think
that I have no idea what's going to happen the next day.'

'It definitely takes a bit of getting used to,' I said. 'It took
me months to really settle into a routine.'

'I understand that,' she said, 'but in Iran, it's a little . . .

mmm . . . I know that you cannot feel or understand what I feel, and it's not your fault. You're here from a completely different country with different culture, everything different, and you're in a place that I'm sure is very different for you. But . . . I – I don't feel safe. I don't feel safe here. I lived alone for five years in Armenia. But I cannot live in Iran for five years alone. Or for one week. Even in my family home, I cannot.'

'What do you mean, exactly?'

'I don't know how to explain. But I want you to know that I am just being honest. I hope we will get to my home soon, and I hope that it will make my parents happy – I mean, I hope they will smile to us, not get angry that we did this without telling them.'

The following day our route was quiet and remote, and we had ridden thirty miles on the evening we reached Jolfa, which was the furthest Tenny had cycled in a day. She was adapting; working out her own way of tackling the daily duresses of riding, rather than simply reacting to them. I could see it in the subtleties of her actions. She responded to the sound of an oncoming car depending on how closely it was about to pass her. She shifted into optimal gear a split second in advance of a change in gradient. She dismounted with nary a wobble of the forty-kilogramme bike, using her hips to edge it against a wall in a position where it would stand without falling over. She corrected her steering when looking behind her, and instinctively knew when and how much water to drink during the course of a day. These were just some of the subtle marks of her graduation from novicehood, clearly visible through the lens of my own experience.

Tenny pulled out her mobile and called a number we'd been given earlier in the day. The driver of the passing car had spotted our bikes leant up on the roadside while Tenny had been crouching behind a nearby rock, and had reversed back up the road to talk to us. Mr Sabri was somewhere in his mid fifties, a kindly face resting between a neat moustache and a receding hairline, smart shirt and trousers suggesting a professional caught between meetings. He'd been so overjoyed to meet travellers that he didn't question what Tenny had been doing as she clambered back up to the road. She spoke to him again on the phone in the musical airs and graces of polite Persian, hung up, smiled, and said that he was on his way.

We sat in the shade on the edge of a wall on the town's high street. Traders operated out of little square retail units – a bakery, a mobile phone shop, a confectioner's. Customers came and went, going about their day. After Armenia, this seemed somehow novel. I remembered that it was once normal for people to seem busy and purposeful. How great it must be to live in a country where one's efforts actually contributed to society, instead of disappearing into the void; where making a living was as simple as going out and doing it!

A young man came over, dropped a couple of delicately wrapped chocolates into our hands, and asked us if we were looking for booze, because he could get us some if we wanted. 'No, thanks!' we smiled. Ramadan had been under way for two weeks.

Then Mr Sabri sailed past in a white Peugeot 405, spotted us, pulled a U-turn and parked up beside us. He quickly realised that the boot of his family saloon would not fit a pair of three-wheeled touring bikes and their luggage. So he told us not to worry, brought forth a mobile phone, and magically summoned a man in a pick-up truck. And we all departed for his house, which turned out not to be in Jolfa at all but some miles away in the mountains near the town of Hadishahr, and was less of a house and more of a palace.

In Armenia, such a home would usually turn out to belong to a medium-ranking mafia family member. The Sabri family, on the other hand, received us with utmost warmth and humility. The man of the house was a successful and well-respected local vet, specialising in the artificial insemination of cattle, living with his wife and daughter in a spacious, air-conditioned home. Their son, he said, was studying in the city of Tabriz a couple of hours' drive away on the other side of the mountains. But the place was not without its curiosities. The sofas appeared to be permanently shrink-wrapped, as did the remote control for the television, a fuzzy circle of worn plastic shrouding the red power button. The wife and daughter prepared the evening meal in the fully featured kitchen, sitting on the floor to chop vegetables, encircled by towering, unused worktops. And in the back garden, Mr Sabri proudly gave us a tour of the ornate swimming pool, which lay invitingly in the sun, surrounded by fruit trees and grapevines, completely empty of water.

I'd heard so much of the hospitality in Iran. Tales of lore spread by hippie pioneers in the '60s and '70s had built her reputation, and the foundations of these tales lay in the insistent invitations that these travellers would receive on a daily basis – invitations which would completely scupper the idea of actually getting anywhere. This was, of course, the polar opposite of the media stereotype I'd grown up with. So there seemed to be a poetry in the fact that you could call the country by two very different names – uppity Iran on one hand, dreamy Persia on the other – and still be talking about the same place.

I shouldn't have been surprised when, having been detained after breakfast for a tour of the local area's historical and natural wonders, including a spectacular underground lake and a fortified Armenian church, we were told that we should *obviously* remain a second night at the family's pleasure. And, whilst Tenny and I were being held hostage at the hands of Persian (or perhaps Iranian) hospitality, Andy cycled past Hadishahr, alone.

It was some time later that we worked out precisely when he must have overtaken. But on that day he passed right by us, unbeknownst to all. I'd known that he was preparing to leave Tbilisi around the time that we planned to leave Yerevan. In yet another coincidental turn of events, Andy, too, had been planning a route across Iran to Pakistan and India – one of the early route options we'd looked at for Ride Earth. Indeed, the way in which his story had mirrored mine was almost poetic.

The obvious difference, of course, was that he'd left his girlfriend behind, while I had brought mine along for the ride.

CHAPTER 19

Leaving Hadishahr with our hosts' well-wishes ringing in our ears, Tenny and I trundled back towards the main road for Tabriz, where we found several lanes of traffic encased by metal barriers. Mountains rose again in our path, solemn and unflinching. Three or four days of this was hardly a pleasant prospect, and the climbs would be long and monotonous. But there was little for it but to begin.

We set off up the hard shoulder in a low gear. It was wide enough to ride double file, so we did, chatting about this and that while the landscapes drifted past; bare spurs of rock in pastel yellows and browns, streaks of vigorous green where small rivers delved between them. When we ran out of things to talk about, Tenny asked to borrow my music player. She didn't share my taste in music – in fact, like everyone else, she actively disliked it, something that even a fairy-tale romance was unable to cure – but she wanted something to listen to. In that way, lunchtime arrived rather more quickly than usual, and along with it the town of Marand, where we realised that we had nothing to eat at midday in the middle of Ramadan.

'Let's go down some side-streets,' I suggested as we followed the main road towards the town centre. 'Maybe we'll find a shop or two, or a bakery, or something.' I wasn't convinced.

Traffic increased, making it difficult to communicate over the din of cars and trucks and the mopeds and motorbikes that buzzed around every town, laden with all manner of unlikely and precariously balanced goods. Then one of the motorbikes pulled a U-turn and stopped ahead of us, two teenage boys enthusiastically flagging us down. Quick as a flash, the pillion hopped off, pulled two polystyrene takeaway containers from beneath the cargo straps of the bike, deposited them in our bewildered hands with a blessing, hopped back on and lurched back into the traffic. I looked at Tenny, laughing. Inside the containers were two freshly grilled skewers of saffron chicken, balanced upon great steaming heaps of buttery rice.

'What the hell?!'

Tenny had recently been picking up a few of my favourite exclamations.

'Well . . . that's pretty good, isn't it?'

'But where are we going to eat it . . . ?'

Tenny had a point. Even though Ramadan didn't seem as rigid as my schoolteachers had led me to believe, there was still the issue of potentially offending people (and breaking the law) by eating the delicious-smelling kebabs in the street. Reluctantly we got back on our bikes.

'Tenny!' I called after her as she rode away. 'We might as well get food for dinner and breakfast while we're here – do you want to ask if there's a shop?'

A couple of enquiries brought us to a typical little convenience store, shelves stacked high with all manner of unidentifiable tins and packets, as alien to me as a Chinatown grocery. Tenny, however, knew exactly what she was looking at.

'Mahan – this is a good brand. And Yek-O-Yek. No – I want to get Mahan. We can get a tin of *ghormeh sabzi* and eat with some of that rice . . .'

I already knew what *ghormeh sabzi* was, since Tenny and her friends, while retaining their Armenian language, had very much integrated Persian cuisine into their culture. This particular dish was a fragrant stew of diced veal, red kidney beans and prodigious quantities of minced herbs, the smell of which had a habit of seeping from one's pores the morning after consumption. Utterly delicious, it would beat any camping food I was likely to come up with. I nodded enthusiastically.

Picking up some apples from a fruit bazaar on our way out of the far side of Marand, we also inherited a teenage boy on a bicycle. He quickly became attached to us, finding it hilarious and bizarre that an Iranian woman could be travelling in this way with her 'husband'. As teenage boys are wont to do, he fell back on the tried and tested pastime of showing off, blasting past us one second, pulling a skittery wheelie the next, and on several occasions narrowly missing out on what would likely be an unhappy fusion of human and lorry. Cars slowed alongside us, their occupants winding down windows in order to take pictures of this unlikely entourage on their mobile phones, doubtless later posting them on Facebook via ever-evolving circumventions of government censorship.

As we left the city behind us and pedalled back up the highway towards the mountains, Tenny attempted to be diplomatic with the young lad, who showed no sign of getting bored.

'Don't you have anywhere else to be right now?'

'Nope!'

'Won't your mum be worried?'

'Nope!'

It was late in the afternoon before the hapless youth turned tail and began wobbling his way back to Marand on the wrong side of the road. We'd been pedalling for long enough without eating and decided to stop early, find a camping spot in the valley and have the feast of chicken kebab, *ghormeh sabzi* and rice that we'd been fantasising about all afternoon. Fields of diminutive tomato plants basked in the sun around us, which meant that farmers couldn't be far away, and farmers were always a good bet when it came to finding places to sleep. Soon we were set up in a small triangle of pasture set aside for the farm's donkey, who stood belligerently in the middle distance, attempting to stare us into submission while we dished up our *ghormeh sabzi*. Then Tenny's mobile phone rang from inside her handlebar-bag. It was none other than Mr Sabri.

'Hello . . . ?'

'Hello!!! Where are you?'

Mr Sabri arrived a short time later, leaving his car on the hard shoulder, jumping the barrier and joining us on our tarpaulin for a nice cup of tea in the evening sun, while the donkey gazed on with silent but palpable displeasure. Our guardian angel had a quick chat with the farmer, checked again that there was nothing we needed, gave us his son's phone number in Tabriz, and drove away as darkness descended upon rural Iran. And as we drew closer to the city over the next couple of days, he turned up several more times, just to make sure that we were alright, to have a quick chat, or to give us sweets and fruit.

It was never quite clear whether he was passing through for work, or whether he'd simply taken on the responsibility of making sure that we, a pair of complete strangers, arrived safely in a city a hundred miles from his home.

By the time we arrived in Tabriz, I had noticed a change in Tenny. She had really started to adjust to this strange routine. Days of riding passed without incident, without tears or arguments, and I was filled with renewed hope for the future of our journey together.

And what a fascinating journey it was turning out to be! It was so refreshing to be travelling with someone not only fluent in the local language, but also fully versed in the way things *really* worked here; things which would otherwise remain obscure to me. Through Tenny I learnt about the lives of those we met, their political views, their interests, their take on the local gossip. I could ask her to translate any road sign or menu or scrawl of graffiti into words that I could understand. No longer would I stand confused at some social nicety whose meaning had gone over my head, because Tenny would be there to negotiate the appropriate etiquette.

It would be exactly the same, of course, if I took Tenny to England and acted as her guide. I would explain to her why people apologised when she held the door open for them. I would help her understand why it was proper to refuse an offer of biscuits with your tea, even if you actually wanted them, but fine to accept on the second attempt. I would be there to remind her to cycle on the wrong side of the road, to tell her what was meant by 'a fiver' or 'a fortnight', and to explain that 'in a jiffy' was not in fact a reference to a popular brand of padded envelope. I'd show her the rectangular holes in people's front doors through which, once a day, a man in a blue shirt would insert a bundle of material exclusively produced for the topping-up of recycling bins. I would intervene when she got confused because people said the opposite of what they actually meant, and that this quaint form of local humour was known as 'sarcasm'. None of this would be particularly interesting to me, because I knew it all so well. And that probably explained why travelling in Iran was not particularly exciting for Tenny.

'I know this country,' she told me over an amber glass of tea in the common room of the Hotel Mashhad, where our cheap silver 'wedding rings' and an innocent smile had secured us a room together. Backpackers wandered in and out, discussing the contents of their guidebooks, making plans to visit the ancient wonders of this mythical, modern city.

'There is not much surprising and new things for me here. Maybe if I be in a new country, completely new, where I can feel myself as a tourist – because I'm not tourist in Armenia, and I'm not tourist in Iran; I know about these places very well – maybe when I go to new country, which will be completely new for me, like Europe, or England . . . I would enjoy cycling much more.'

I could see her point, of course. But at the same time I found it slightly sad – not that she felt that way, but because her home country had not yet had the chance to surprise her. I had felt the same about England, seeing my ride to Harwich as a necessary evil. Instead, I'd been invited to finish off someone's strawberry pavlova, had bacon sandwiches brought to my tent one morning and been invited to camp in an animal sanctuary the same evening, been handed homemade jam and freshly picked strawberries on the roadside, and given a free cabin on a ferry to Europe. Her home country could only treat Tenny thus if she allowed it to, and it would surely surprise her if we continued south and east, where Iran was by all accounts a very different place indeed. And after we crossed into Pakistan and journeyed further into India and beyond, an entirely new world would open up for this girl who'd never ventured beyond the borders of Iran and Armenia.

She was ready, I decided. Tenny had made it through the stressful adjustment to life on the road. No longer would she be cowed by the routine of finding food and places to sleep, or of cycling all those miles. No, she was ready for the next step: to leave what she knew behind, and to begin exploring anew in unknown lands.

True, it was still unclear for how long she would want to live such a life. But – at the very least – we were ready to give it a try.

Tenny dismounted, leaned her bike up against the metal garage door beneath the overhanging balconies of the small block of flats, and took off her helmet. She was laughing. I suppose it was, in a strange way, quite funny that we were about to do the very thing we'd planned for so long – the moment we'd lived in fear of for so many months, concealing every possible clue to the truth, to the extent of hiding Tenny's bike in a friend's basement when her parents were visiting, and fabricating a pedestrian-sounding itinerary of monastery visits and bus rides in safe, homely Armenia as a cover story for being on the road. But an ill-concealed nervousness floated through Tenny's laughter.

She tapped the intercom button twice in quick succession. It was just the way her father did it, she said. His car wasn't there, meaning he was out, so her mother would be expecting the buzzer to ring like that on his return. The outside door would be released without anyone asking who it was, and the second-floor flat's front door left ajar to save having to answer a second time.

Tenny crossed herself.

'That's not going to help,' I said, rather abruptly. I was in no mood for anything but the most rapid possible acceptance of whatever fate awaited us. God, I reasoned, probably had better things to do.

The latch clicked. Tenny pushed back the door and went inside without waiting for me. I hesitated, unsure what to do. Of all the inappropriate situations in which to arrive, unannounced, wielding a video camera, this surely ranked as a new personal best. And suddenly the moment of truth was about to occur while I was fumbling around with my bike!

My heart felt ready to burst through my ribcage as I dashed upstairs after Tenny, fiddling furiously with the focus ring of the stupid camera while trying to come to terms with the possibility that I might be about to film the demise of everything I lived for. But as I approached the second floor, I heard more laughter – the laughter of another voice.

'Hello! Hello!' came the voice of Tenny's mother, who couldn't quite figure out what she was looking at, laughing in a faintly confused way, waving us inside.

She had been on the phone to a friend when her daughter had walked into her home, out of breath and dressed for the outdoors, with her foreign boyfriend in tow, still wearing his cycling gloves.

The next morning, Tenny and I rose early, ate breakfast in the kitchen, and left the house quietly. We walked together through the streets of central Tehran as the city roused into life, and soon the roads were filled with honking cars, the pavements crowded with people going about their business – and, of course, swarms of buzzing little motorbikes, whose riders didn't seem to find it necessary to distinguish between the road and the pavement at all.

We were headed for somewhere far quieter than the streets of downtown, however, because we had something important to do. And to get there we would use Tehran's underground metro system, which far outshone London's cramped and grubby Tube. Shiny, spacious platforms awaited the arrival of modern, well-lit locomotives which glided to a halt amid science-fiction sound-effects, and before long we were back above ground and queuing up for admittance to the visa section of the Embassy of India. We would lodge our Indian visa applications here before heading back downtown to the British Embassy to collect a 'letter of recommendation', where I would pay £65 for a letter of haughty prose to the effect that the British Embassy didn't issue 'letters of recommendation', which the Embassy of Pakistan would then accept as a letter of recommendation and give me a visa for Pakistan. Our chores in Tehran would be done. And it would give the bureaucrats something to do.

There was another reason we'd come to the Indian Embassy so early. Taller than anyone else in the crowded waiting room by a head's height, Andy's unruly bush of curly hair, unkempt beard and incongruously smart 'off-bike' shirt meant we could pick him out instantly.

'Wahey!!!' beamed my old mate in a trademark greeting, and we gave each other an awkward man-hug in the crowded waiting room. Then he hugged Tenny – equally awkwardly, as it meant almost folding himself in half to make up their difference in height.

We left the Embassy and used the long walk as an opportunity to catch up and exchange anecdotes. The usual tales of hi-jinx involving random invitations, bizarre sleeping spots and run-ins with bored policemen were banded about. But behind all of this, Andy seemed driven by some invisible momentum. His stories were entertaining but they told of a man on a mission, making decisions in order to cover distance. He was filled with purpose and direction: staying still was not part of the programme. It was a curious opposite to the downshift in pace that I'd felt in myself over these few weeks of travel with Tenny. I couldn't quite fathom out whether Andy's impetus came from behind or ahead; whether he was driven more by the need to put distance between himself and his life in Georgia or by the desire to explore the lands that still lay beyond the horizon. I guessed it was probably a mixture of the two. Travelling alone for the first time would surely involve riding out a challenging period of adaptation. In any case, he seemed at ease with whatever came his way, and I felt happy for him – and a tiny bit envious too.

Dealings with the stiff officials in the enormous British Embassy compound were completed with typical efficiency, and we invited Andy round to Tenny's flat for tea. It was shortly after he departed, all set to continue his journey towards distant Pakistan, that all hell broke loose in the Adamian family home.

Looking back, it seems quite amusing that we'd continued to act on our plans, spending a whole day getting our visas arranged, as if having the stickers in our passports would make the slightest bit of difference. What was Tenny going to do – wave them madly around the living room: 'But look, we've got *permission*!!!'

It was like I imagined a really bad comedown might feel; an awful moment where you find yourself glued to an armchair, looking around at a room full of people and feeling your insides shrivel up in horror as you realise that you have *no idea who these people are*. You can't remember what was happening ten seconds ago, and you want to *run away*. But you can't. Some force glues you, mute, to your chair. You have no choice but to watch the melodrama raging in front of your eyes, not understanding a single word. You contemplate how purgatory might feel. And something within you dies.

Well . . . here I am, on the roof of Tenny's flat.

Don't know where to start, really . . .

Well.

I dunno . . .

Ugh – I can't do these video diaries any more, it's just . . .

Let me try again.

We arrived in Tehran, at Tenny's flat, as, we knew, we hadn't . . . er . . .

No, it's just crap, isn't it? It's just complete and utter bollocks.

OK. I'll make it as simple as possible.

Before we got here, we knew that one of two things was going to happen. Number One: Tenny's parents would see that we'd cycled here. They'd see the photos and videos, hear our stories, and understand that we'd done it anyway, and that it wasn't actually all that dangerous, and it was actually quite good fun, and it led to a lot of good experiences. Which it did.

Well, that didn't happen. Instead, what happened was Number Two.

On the second night we were here, we came home, Tenny and I, and . . . we had an evening of shouting, crying, and . . . being told in no uncertain terms that there was no way on this planet we were going to continue.

So. Either we disregard Tenny's parents' wishes entirely and continue travelling by bike. Or, we basically do what they want. Which is pretty much as follows:

Forget about travelling.

Forget about living together.

Forget about having any kind of freedom to make choices together.

Until the day we get married.

I'm not trying to make out that Tenny's parents are bad people. They come from an extremely conservative culture, and it's not going to suddenly drop away overnight. And who am I to say it should?!

And I spent – predictably – I spent one entire sleepless night with all of this kind of stuff churning around in my head, and . . . an incredibly heavy weight on my shoulders, because everything we'd hoped for when we arrived here had just been blown away, erm . . . mercilessly, basically.

(There appears to be a man playing an accordion in the street below this building. Maybe you can hear him.)

I don't really want to spend my life on the wrong side of my wife's family. And I don't want to drag Tenny with me because I'm too stubborn to let go of my travelling plans.

(By the way, these musicians don't go away until you've given them money, which is a bit annoying as I don't have any money. And it's getting dark. Well – I'm going to continue regardless, because I have no choice, apart from to wait until tomorrow, or until his lungs burst.)

And I know that this might sound a bit . . . like a bit of a shitter, but I . . . if I didn't carry on travelling by bike, then . . . I would spend the – I know that I would spend the rest of my life wondering what would have happened if I had. So I really can't just forget about it.

Tenny and I both know that I still have these stupid, ridiculous, selfish dreams for learning about the world and travelling. At the same time, I've found the girl I want to spend the rest of my life with! That's . . . seriously epic, and awesome. It really is!

But before that . . . there's something I've got to do. I don't know what it is, but I think if I just . . . go . . . maybe one day I'll realise that I've 'done it', or that I never actually needed to 'do it', or something like that.

It's a very confusing bit of life, right now.

And maybe I'll look back at this and think, 'What an idiot I was back then – what a complete fool.'

Because I'm going get on my bike, and leave Tenny here, with her family. And I'm going to disappear.

Basically.

Yeah. I'm going to go. I'm going to throw away everything that I can't live without – I'm going to get rid of absolutely everything, every scrap of stuff that's not necessary.

And I'm going to head south, towards Africa, on my own.

And I've no idea what's going to happen . . . where I'm going to go . . . how long it's going to take . . .

And it's like – I dunno . . . I've no idea if it's the right thing to do or not.

I just feel like I haven't found what I'm looking for yet.

CHAPTER 20

I look out across the dusty plain from my vantage point. Beside me is a rickety watchtower in which a soldier is slumped, dozing, wrapped in a blanket. He and the rest of his squad have been posted here to look after yet another crew of road-builders – all native Amharans this time. They're surveying the area, hoping to lay another streak of asphalt across a landscape which looks like an artist's rendering of some prehistoric savannah. The sun has not yet risen, and the air is a hazy grey. The headlights of a pick-up truck nose slowly through the maze of wiry trees towards the camp. I half expect a group of raptors to leap from nowhere and drag its screaming occupants into the bush.

As I roll onto the faint tyre tracks, I know that I am venturing into another stereotype. While the raw spirit that exists in Ethiopia is real, it doesn't mean that suffering is non-existent, nor that the most basic human needs are always fulfilled, nor that some aren't still struggling vainly towards distant future hopes. That's the trouble with generalisations. Likewise, it's easy to see all indigenous, tribal communities through a romantic filter of face-paint, topless women, bows and arrows and blow-darts, and to talk as if 'Africa' denotes a single country of chanting warriors and wildlife, or at least a group of fifty-odd nations so uniform that there's little point distinguishing between them. I have seen not one of those ever-so-African creatures, and I have seen no landscape that resembles the continent of my childish imagination. Until today.

The thick layer of dust flows and parts like water beneath my tyres. Wrestling with the handlebars, I try to pick the best route amongst the submerged rocks. There's no sign of human life. Camels wander in a clearing, contemplating the prospect of nibbling at the dry scrub. A dozen large, plump birds waddle out of my path and disappear into the undergrowth. One of them reappears in my mind's eye, steaming gently on a platter next to a jug of home-made gravy and some roast potatoes. But this is not the time for admiring wildlife, nor drifting into daydreams: I have the toughest task yet in front of me, a limited supply of water, and a couple of hundred miles of burning wastes through which to pick a path. There'll be time for reminiscing when I arrive in Djibouti.

Alert for a glimpse of the Afar tribespeople, I peer between the leafless trees that line the track and spread out across the plain in all directions, obscuring whatever life there is. But I can see only more of the same scrawny trunks. Above the screen of vegetation, a solitary volcano rises on the horizon to the north-east, low sloping sides topped by a rounded peak, the area's sole landmark. The active volcano Erta Ale lies out of sight to the north, but it would be too far and remote to reach by bicycle without some guarantee of support.

A pair of legs appears between the low branches – and then the unmistakable shape of an AK-47 slung across the chest. I stop, flinching as the disc brakes sing. The legs have gone. Nothing moves.

I keep pedalling, unsure of whether or not I've been seen, and equally unsure of what might happen if I am. But several hours of cycling pass uneventfully, with only the sound of rattling baggage and loose rocks giving way beneath the tyres to break the silence.

Then, out of nowhere, I hear a low growl.

I turn.

It's a lion!!!

No.

A pick-up truck is bouncing across the earth a hundred yards away. It's slowing down. My body stiffens.

'Hey!' shouts the driver, as the truck stops. There's a soldier in the passenger seat, flaunting his rifle. 'Remember me?'

'Erm!' I reply, trying to bring back his name. 'Yes, I met you . . . at the . . .'

'It's Muraf! From the road-building camp! Yes! How are you?'

Off the hook again! It is long ago that I gave up hope of remembering everyone I met, let alone where and how I met them. Muraf is oblivious, and I tell him I'm fine, thanks, if a little on the warm side out here. He'd passed me the previous day, told me to come and find him at the camp, and when I'd arrived he'd invited me for a cup of coffee – locally grown and just this minute roasted, he'd said, handing me a tiny bowl of the strongest and most delicious coffee I had ever tasted. I'd ended up staying the night. He briefs me once again on how to act if I encounter a 'native'.

'You must be very strong. Very strong! You should speak strong. Loud. Tell him to go away.' I am instructed to treat the tribesman like the animal he is. 'If he doesn't go – pretend to talk on your telephone. Say: "Police! Police!" Say this and he will go!'

'OK – thank you,' I smile, forgetting to inform him that I don't have a telephone. He wishes me well, gives me a bottle of ice-cold water, and lurches off east in the direction of another road camp. They'll take me in for the night if I insist. There are Chinese road-builders there.

I uncap the bottle immediately and drain the unspeakably cold contents, savouring the precious seconds of pleasure. Left out, it would reach the temperature of a nice hot bath within minutes.

I continue tentatively eastwards along the faint route that has been beaten through the badlands, and the dense scrub begins to slacken off, the terrain rising and falling just enough for me to get a glimpse across a wider expanse of land. I already know that it's widely thought that this is the precise region of Africa from which hominids emerged – the pre-human beings from whom we are all ultimately descended.

And I try to grasp the enormity of the fact; that if I were to go back through my family history, back beyond my great-grandfather who made shoes for a co-operative in Leicester, past his grandfather who was a framework knitter at the beginning of the Industrial Revolution; if I traced – with some magical omniscience – whoever it was that first migrated to the British Isles with my genetic material, and even further back to whoever it was that journeyed little by little along some unknown route through the same landmasses that I'd now crossed on a bicycle . . . that if I did all that, then I would finish the journey right here, where I stand now, looking at my own blood ancestor as he existed five million years ago.

But I can't. I can't grasp it. I simply see hardy treetops and skyline – barely a hint of green in an otherwise colourless expanse of overgrown, dusty, rocky wasteland, the Amharan highlands fading away behind me and lands entirely wild and unknown in every other direction. A few hundred yards away to my right, a stray twister of spinning dust and foliage glides across the middle distance of the silent birthplace of humanity.

Minutes later I stop again, because a herd of goats has begun to trickle, single file, across my path. Curious, I whip out the video camera and grab a couple of shots. Then I notice a man, walking alongside the animals. He looks at me; stops dead in his tracks. The goatherd! Is this a real Afar nomad?

He hesitates for a second. Then, as I watch, he turns – and runs directly towards me.

Muraf's advice is ringing in my ears as I flick through the contents of my bar-bag, searching for something that might pass as a mobile phone. I look up again, an electric shiver passing through me. But he is closer now, and it looks like his run is really more of a trot; he moves casually, as one might jog across the road to greet a friend. He slows to a stroll as he approaches, and stops on the edge of the road a few yards away, resting a goat-whacking stick on his shoulder, and assumes a posture of casual observation. He sports a whopping black hairdo that would put the Jackson Five to shame, and is otherwise naked, except for a loincloth, and a very big knife.

There is a moment's pause. And then a huge grin spreads across his face.

I can't help but grin back. How utterly bizarre we must appear to each other! For the first time I feel like an utter novelty, a thing entirely without precedent that has appeared in someone else's territory. This must be wrong; I can hardly be the first foreign traveller to the Danakil Depression. There are plenty of 'adventure tours' to the volcanoes and salt mines further north, although my attempts to find records of independent journeys by bicycle or otherwise produced absolutely nothing. But the look on this man's face is incredulous, as if I had turned up and performed some kind of close-up magic trick. He makes no further approach or attempt at communication.

After a long stalemate, I decide it's time to break the silence. I can't think of anything to say other than the name of the village at which I'm hoping to rejoin an established road. I point vaguely ahead.

'Millie!'

'Millie?'

'Yes!' I reply triumphantly. 'I'm going to Millie!'

Ridiculous. I might as well recite Shakespeare.

We keep grinning at each other until I feel sufficiently uncomfortable to wave goodbye and resume riding. I look back after a few pedal strokes; the young man is jogging back in the direction of his goats, and I continue wrestling my bike across the blazing rocky plain, neither kidnapped nor massacred, but tickled by the little episode of mutual slack-jawed curiosity. The off-road riding is still painstakingly tricky to negotiate, and I amuse myself by wondering how the conversation will go when my interlocutor returns home this evening.

'You know what I saw today?'

'What?'

'Well, I was taking the goats for a walk as usual, minding

my own business, when this white guy came past on a bicycle!'

'Say what?!?'

'I went over to see what he was doing, and he just kind of stood there and stared. It went on for ages. You should have seen him – filthy shirt, ripped trousers, and this big sunhat with "I Love Egypt" written across it. He looked ridiculous!'

'Ha-ha! Did you speak to him?'

'Not really. He said something I didn't understand – something about Millie. Then he looked uncomfortable and went off again on his bike.'

'Weird, aren't they, these foreign types? I mean – perfectly good asphalt road to the south, us up here with our guns and goats and crazy hair, and he still feels the need to cycle off-road across this bloody desert! Must be mad . . .'

Later I spot another group of figures in the distance: a dozen adults walking towards me along the track. Judging by the hairstyles on display they're not road-building engineers, and since they've had plenty of time to see me coming, I put on my harmless passer-by act, smile nonchalantly at them as I approach, and call: 'Hello!' just as I pass, which gives me enough time to clear the group and recede down the track before anyone can decide whether they have anything further to contribute. I immediately curse myself for being a coward and not stopping to try having a proper chat. Whatever gripe might exist between the Afars and the Amharans, as I predicted, does not appear to extend to me. I'm a curiosity, to be investigated or ignored, just as I have been for the last two years. A solitary figure pedalling a bicycle is not a threatening image, does not carry an invasive agenda. Nevertheless, this place is so alien that it's got my nerves up, and I've ridden straight past the group, intimidated by my own irrational fears.

I arrive at the promised road-workers' camp in the early evening. Under normal circumstances I would jump at the chance to wild camp for a change, but I've been spooked; tales abound of lions and hyenas, people having their faces bitten off in the night. And, of course, I might well be invading someone's tribal territory. People get jumpy when it's dark, and I am occasionally unable to contain my snoring. Do I really want myself and my tent to be the unwitting provocateurs of a paranoid night-time ambush by people with AK-47s and very big knives?

These excuses are a convenient way to hide one simple fact: I am too afraid to sleep outside. So I trundle up to the camp gates to try my luck. My calls are answered by a man with an AK-47. He invites me to sit in the shade, alongside a group of Afars with very big knives.

I guess that the men are vaguely attached to the road-building project as a kind of multi-party delegation. It's interesting to see that they're a mixture of Amharans and Afars – the latter conspicuous by an absence of clothing and footwear and the presence of a true 1980s hit parade of haircuts. Nowhere else have I seen so many spectacularly coiffed Afros and mullets in one place outside a vintage *Top Of The Pops* re-run. They're all affable and interested in the contents of my panniers, and I avoid bringing out any expensive camera equipment – not because I'm worried it'll be stolen, but because it'll help me avoid the all-too-common question of how much everything costs. I'm not convinced of my ability to decide on a plausible-but-inoffensive figure here. In any case, the camera seems unnecessary: I'm unlikely to forget this experience in a hurry.

The Chinese engineers – just three of them – are fortunate enough to have their own private compound, but they have not yet returned from surveying. Once they do, I'm told, they'll ask if I am allowed to stay the night.

'They're different,' says one Amharan. 'They eat *peeg*! You know peeg?'

I probably do; I just need to figure it out. Peeg . . . *pig*. Pork!

The man makes a face of disgust. Travelling through the Islamic world, I haven't eaten pork for almost half a year. I realise that I am salivating like a dog.

A small water-tanker roars into the little camp in a cloud of dust, and I spring up for a much-needed refill. I've drunk eight litres today, yet I feel drained and dehydrated. The Chinese arrive shortly after, driving their four-by-fours straight into the fenced-off compound, and there is an agonising wait while the leader of the ragtag bunch of soldiers implores the Chinese to accept a traveller for the night. While sleeping in the Ethiopians' quarters would be perfectly comfortable, my mind has already drifted hopefully back to that Chinese doctor, those big bowls of spicy noodles, and the mind-blowing prospect of peeg.

The leader returns: the answer is yes! Overjoyed, I jog into the compound and thank the Chinese heartily; they regard me as perhaps one might a cat being sick. Nonplussed, I set about arranging my new bedroom, hanging the mosquito net above the slab of plywood on which I will sleep, writing my diary, and taking a few experimental photographs to pass the time before I am invited for dinner. This, of course, happens, and – though it would be unlikely to win any awards – turns out to be as delicious as I could possibly have dreamed, prominently featuring peeg amongst the fried and steamed meats, noodles and vegetables. The Chinese find it hilarious that I can just about handle a pair of chopsticks, despite having never been anywhere near China, and I explain at length about the popularity of Chinese food in Britain as they gaze blankly at me. I try to imagine the converse – how bizarre it would be to discover that on practically every street corner in China there were an English takeaway, selling fish n' chips, pork pies and Cornish pasties.

The next day I meet a teenage girl on the side of the trail.

'Hello!' I call. No answer.

'How are you?' I try. Nothing. The girl, hair carefully braided, skin of pure black, stands grinning at me. Grinning, of all things!

Then I notice that she is in fact topless, and that my African stereotype has finally been fulfilled.

'Do you speak English?'

My conversational skills are deteriorating today. And I rattle onward, having gleaned no further insight into this mysterious, staring, grinning tribe of award-winning hairdressers and goatherds from this one teenage girl with her breasts out. Then, through the wiry bushes, I notice a man-made shape. I roll forward until I can make it out better. It's some kind of tent; a small curved dome five or six feet high, a frame covered with panels of canvas. It looks like a sweltering place to be, but at least it's shelter from the fierce elements. It's a home, that's for sure. And, like my own little green and yellow tent, it's a home for someone on the move.

As I watch, a figure appears from the side door. The figure

is tiny; the head grossly out of proportion. Of course. It's a child. A little boy. No more than two or three years old. He totters out and stands in the sun, looking about. He hasn't seen me. But then someone or something summons him from within the tent, and he looks back and turns before wandering purposefully back into the structure. I watch for a little longer, but he doesn't reappear.

The scrubby desert gives way to rising crags of sharp, multicoloured rock. And the heat seems to engulf not just my body but all my other senses too, indescribable in its oppression, as crushing as a sack of bricks. I run my tongue around the inside of my mouth. It feels cool in comparison. The rims of my eyelids burn, and I can almost hear the ground sizzling. Some point of sensitivity deep within each nostril stings sharply, as if I am inhaling flames; all moisture dragged from the creases and crevices of my face and into the ferocious void. Memories of wilting in Sudan are reduced to mere pleasant days in the sunshine. And maybe I have begun to understand what it means to live in the hottest place on Earth.

The image of the tiny child by his front door stays with me, and it takes a little time to realise why. It's because I have travelled to what by any standard measure is one of the most remote, uncivilised, impoverished and undeveloped regions on the planet – and what have I found? A worried mother calling her toddler indoors. Communities of people living together. Tradesmen and professionals eking out a living. I will find exactly the same scenes played out in all manner of varied ways in every society on Earth. Nothing separates me from these nomads – or from anybody else alive – but for the lottery of birth.

As an asphalt road shimmers into view up ahead, I realise that I have taken more than just a shortcut across the desert. I have inadvertently made a journey to the end of the Earth, via the birthplace of man. And, somewhere between Weldiya and Millie, the romantic idea of some mysterious and fundamental stratification amongst the people of the world has been destroyed.

Given that, how much longer can I continue to roam in childish wonder?

Just a thought, really. Just a very very quick thought, that's all.

It's technically incorrect to describe that girl as having 'had her breasts out', when, in all likelihood, she never 'had her breasts in' in the first place. So, I guess I should just say, 'that teenage tribesgirl, with her breasts'. Maybe.

My point is that it's a matter of perspective, isn't it?

Anyway, I'm going to shut up now. Night.

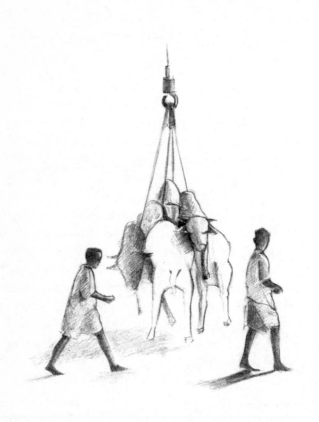

CHAPTER 21

Djibouti City is a bizarre place indeed. On first impressions, it seems to exist for two reasons – firstly because every country needs a capital and a seat of government, so this might as well be it; secondly because the landlocked nations of East Africa need a seaport for trade. Under different circumstances this might have been the recipe for a thriving city of zeal and commerce. But, as I nose my way through the dusty sprawl, this is not what the place appears to be.

It reminds me of Khartoum; a low, whitewashed colony of fenced compounds and street-sellers and a few half-hearted attempts at 'modern' infrastructure and superficial gloss. What's different is the number of people in the city's streets. It feels populated, but by the aimless and wayward. As I draw closer to the port the impression intensifies. Young men, all dressed in grubby fluorescent safety vests, wander the pavements and roads of the docklands in small groups; waifs slowly drifting, like the distant ships in the placid waters beyond them. I later find out that they're waiting for a container ship to arrive, hoping to score a few hours of casual labour in exchange for a few francs. This might not happen for many days. At night they will simply sleep on the ground, inert bodies lining the sidewalks along the roads around the immense port gates, possessing nothing but the clothes they wear and the company of those around them.

They will not be allowed inside the port without a permit which identifies them as a genuine labourer with proof of employment. Security is hard-line; any man who tries to sneak into the port is ejected gently but firmly by the plentiful security guards, and I watch this happen a dozen times in my first afternoon, unaware that this will be my life for the next five days. I, too, have no permit. I wonder how the hell I'm supposed to find a boat without one.

The atmosphere is languid, hopeless and utterly depressing, and I feel guilty and uncomfortable, however bedraggled my appearance, because simply by being here I am flaunting the fact that I've done so out of choice, in the face of the massed crowds of young men who have no choice at all. I start reproaching those who stare too hard, as I've grown used to doing in self-defence, but find myself being met by offended looks. I realise that I'm not in Ethiopia any more. These are Somalis – Muslims – and, with a distinctly genteel aura pervading even these quietly desperate streets, any rowdiness is totally out of place. I must drop my prickly defences and dig out a bit of compassion and sensitivity once again, seeing suddenly how thick-skinned and detached I'd had to become in order to traverse Ethiopia with my sanity intact.

Maybe it's the *qat* that keeps the peace around here. It seems ubiquitous enough. Bunches of these shiny, plump, lime-green leaves appear around midday from flimsy plastic bags and soon take up residence in the cheek pouches of the populace, unemployed or otherwise. Despite the lack of work, there still seems to be enough money around to bargain for an awful lot of *qat*. I think back to the Ethiopian border town where I'd met Mike, the schoolteacher on his way to Sudan. What had he said?

'It makes everything in the world look OK . . . when really, it's not!!!'

I can see him now, glassy eyes empty but with a slightly crazed twinkle to them, slumped in the shade with his back against the wall of the hotel block, mouth mechanically chewing, flecks of green and spittle, his teeth churning like a concrete mixer. His image is duplicated a thousand times on the streets of Djibouti. Spread across the concrete all over the port's surrounding yards and inspection bays and quaysides, in little patches of shade, are the bulging cheeks and sprawled limbs of those who've decided that they want everything in the world to look OK (when really, it's not). Whether it actually does look OK I don't know, because I still take myself too seriously to accept one of the many offers to pack my own cheek with *qat* and see the world differently for an afternoon.

If only everyone in the region spent their days as pacified as this. I'm well aware that the stretch of water I want to cross is the most pirated on the planet. Somalia, with its two thousand miles of coastline directly to the east and south, is what politicians call a 'failed state'. Its people apparently haven't had an effective central government for nearly two decades; the cause – or, maybe, the effect – of it being statistically one of the poorest and most violent nations on Earth, the real-life implications of which I don't wish to try to imagine.

I try to put preconceptions of Somalia to one side. Such thoughts have never yielded fruit, and I've no reason to believe that this time should be any different. But it's been only one week since an empty oil tanker was captured by Somali pirates just ten miles offshore from the Yemeni port of Aden, which is precisely where I aim to go. Sixty-one pirate attacks were recorded in the Gulf of Aden in the first three months of this year; ten times more than last year.

On the other hand, I notice that business still seems to be running fairly normally in this languid yet bustling port. I sit and watch from my spot of concrete outside the port security office by the main gate, just opposite an enormous mosque which serves thousands of workers and thousands more destitute hopefuls. Despite a life which would, back home, be described by stern-faced TV presenters as 'appalling' and 'desperate', there is relief on hand for the soul, and not only in the form of mild narcotics. Intellectual, scientific, rational atheism is of little value to those whose earthly lives offer no respite from hopelessness, no relevant answers to existential conundrums. What use is there in telling the hungry men sleeping on the concrete outside the port of Djibouti that there is no reason for living other than to propagate their genetic material, or that they should forget their indoctrinated superstition in favour of the wonders of scientific empiricism, or that their five daily pilgrimages to the prayer hall are futile, worthless and insulting to human intelligence? Even the most militant atheist, shouting from his Western soapbox, could not stand in this dusty square, take in all he sees around him, and then harangue these men for whom hope and meaning comes from family and faith alone. Though holding no religious beliefs myself, I am faintly embarrassed to have once counted myself amongst those very vocal militants, so scathing of the priorities that still hold for the majority of people in the world. And I give thanks (to nobody in particular) that I've grown a little wiser since then.

Troops of burly and disinterested sailors march from the port and disappear in SUVs, arriving back hours later. They look so ridiculous, with their starched, spotless uniforms, sunglasses and purposeful swaggers, glancing stupidly about at us.

Their white skin looks so abnormal.

Ferenj.

I meet Hassan, a young, unemployed Djiboutian, over a roadside lunch of the spaghetti Bolognese which appears to be the city's staple meal. Fingers prove an interesting choice of eating utensil, but it somehow seems to work. Hassan's English is about as bad as my French, but it's enough to get chatting, and we quickly click. He's interested in what drove me to undertake this journey, and I try my best to explain that in all honesty I'd simply wanted to throw myself at something massive, unknown and terrifying, just to see what happened, and that cycling alone through the Middle East and Africa without a map, guidebook, mobile phone, laptop, GPS or any real research was the most massive, unknown and terrifying thing I could think of to do at the time. And while I'm talking, I begin to laugh, because it seems so absurd now; the scale so pitifully small, the unknowns so benign, and the imagined terrors so illusory.

But Hassan seems to see where I'm coming from. I'm used to being gazed at like the whimsical, self-indulgent rich guy I undoubtedly am, so his curiosity and non-judgemental attitude are refreshing. He is younger than me and was obviously a keen school student, but his education and zeal have been undercut by an absence of opportunity to put them to use. I imagine that he's far from alone. I offer him a sum which I think will help him without being insulting or propagating an image of rich white guys, and he agrees to help me find a ship. I don't really believe that the odds are against me. What's the worst that could happen?

OK – being taken prisoner by a gang of swashbuckling Somalis would suck. And the lack of any discernible system to the chaos between here and the quaysides is going to be a tricky one to negotiate. But hell – I've got to give it a try.

Hassan tells me he's found a ship leaving today, but I'm aware that it's as likely to vanish into thin air as to depart on time. He says he needs another ten dollars' worth of francs to put down a deposit with the captain for my passage. Goodness knows how he's found this information, or how he's got inside the port to talk to anyone. But he takes my money and disappears into the throng.

Waiting listlessly for Hassan's return, I make friends with an Ethiopian shipping clerk who stopped to talk to me on his way into one of the nice air-conditioned offices hidden amongst the concrete shells of disused buildings outside the port gates, and we spend a few hours chatting; his English is excellent. But there's no sign of Hassan by the end of the day. I sigh and decide to give him the benefit of the doubt, but it's time I found another place to sleep. My new friend Salim says he'll think of something and to come with him. So we walk the streets after another dead-end day, tired out – me by the endless string of false leads and non-existent boat-rides, him by the constant power-cuts and Internet disconnections that leave him unable to work for hours on end every day.

'What you have to realise,' says Salim as we walk the darkening pavements towards the city, 'is that nothing works. And this is "the African way".'

It's a long walk and almost completely dark before I find out where he's taking me: one of the big, whitewashed compounds turns out to contain a church and community centre to serve the tiny minority of Protestants in Muslim Djibouti. Fair enough, I think; in Muslim countries where I'm perceived as a Christian, I've often been handed over to the local Christian communities, regardless of their creed. I think back to Egypt, where I ended up sleeping in Coptic churches for three nights in a row. Well, I think, there's no harm in trying. After all, I'm just looking for a six-by-two-foot patch of ground to lie on for a few hours.

The doorkeeper is unconvinced that we're worth disturbing the pastor for, but eventually tells us to head round the back of the generous compound to the other entrance. He lets us in and we walk down a footpath between nicely tended gardens in the fading light of the evening, past the church itself and towards a concrete two-storey complex which I guess is the community centre. A wide flight of stairs sweeps up to a terrace, and a row of candles burns piously in an upstairs window.

'He is from Germany,' whispers the church watchman, while the doorkeeper ventures up to the penthouse to fetch the pastor, and I'm wondering whether I should compose my standard explanation of myself in German, French or English when the door opens with a loud muttering and the doorkeeper appears with another figure. The pastor stops silhouetted at the top of the steps, fifty yards from where I'm standing with my friend, folds his arms, and looks down upon us. My eyesight is too bad to make out the man's face in the darkness. I make to introduce myself. But the pastor speaks first.

'This is not a hotel,' begins the decree. A mocking lilt, a slight exasperation underlies the words, and the pastor – a practiced speaker, no doubt – continues. 'It is not a campsite. It is a church. Now, clear off. Go!'

The last word is accompanied by a flick of the arm, the sort you might use to dismiss a low-ranking servant. Without waiting for a response, he spins on his heels, slamming the door behind him. Through a small window, a silhouette resumes its candle-lit supplications.

The three of us turn and walk back through the well-ordered gardens, stopping outside the church. I look at the dignified, sharply dressed shipping clerk, feeling embarrassed even to have come from the same continent as the man we've just encountered. Salim just gazes at the ground in confusion.

'Why . . . why is this man so rude?!?'

He's genuinely confused. I just shake my head. The priest hadn't even given us a chance to explain ourselves; he'd just shooed us away.

'You can sleep in the church,' chips in the church warden, breaking the silence. 'Don't listen to what he says. He is not a good man.'

He wrinkles his nose in the direction of the building down the yard.

'If I say you can sleep here, you can sleep here. He will never know. Just – you must leave early.'

I was wrong about Hassan. On first impressions, I thought that he was just a particularly friendly vagrant who'd hopefully refrain from pinching my stuff. But I realise I've underestimated him when he reappears the following day and offers me a place to stay.

Yesterday's promised boat ride didn't exist, and nor will there be a sailing today, so I'll clearly need somewhere to spend another night, and I am more than welcome to come with him to his home. But out of the blue comes a distant memory – of Sebes, of the dreary post-communist decay and rain and mud, and of Simon, his moustache and leather jacket, his underhand attempt at extorting cash in return for a night spent sleeping on his floor, and I'm frustrated that this image has reared its head, because it means that suspicion and fear still linger, despite all of the goodness that has done so much to dissolve them, and I suddenly feel less strongly about the pastor's unpleasantness the previous night, reminding myself that we are all capable of gross errors of judgement. In a kind of self-punishment I decide to take Hassan's every word at face value from that moment forth. So I take hold of my bike and follow him on foot down the dusty tarmac, away from the port gates. We reach a gap in a high wall and I hear the buzz and chatter of a horde of people from its far side. Rounding the corner and passing between a pair of gateposts in the wall, I am confronted with a thousand stares from another universe.

The scene is so bewilderingly chaotic that I almost instantly lose track of where I am or where Hassan is taking me, and I try to make sense of what appears to be a vast, clattering community of working men and their legions of unemployed cohorts, crammed into a walled compound a couple of hundred yards square and left to build whatever they like there. It's the most contrived slum scene that Hollywood has ever come up with, presented in three-dimensional smell-taste-touch-o-vision, and at the same time nothing like it, because it's real and right there in front of me with a depth and richness that fiction could never replicate. Bare light bulbs hang from knotted cables; windows of pink sunset emerge between tin sheets and walls of tarpaulin and string. Hassan brings me along a meandering walkway which seems to have spontaneously evolved out of the disordered piles of wonky tables and stools and makeshift walls that divide up the colonies of dimly lit kiosks. Below, chefs toss great wokfuls of spaghetti Bolognese into the air above roaring gas-stove cylinders. Literally hundreds of Djiboutians pause mid-mouthful, wherever they are sitting or standing, to watch my white face cross through this den. They look like survivors from some science-fiction apocalypse, closed off from the rest of the world, lost in time.

I'm expending all my energies trying to pretend that there is nothing unusual about my presence and that I am entirely unfazed by the spectacle, when Hassan stops in front of one of the little shoulder-width kiosks, shakes a few hands in the shadows and introduces me to his uncle.

'My uncle will look after your bike for the night,' he announces. And the shadows wait expectantly for my compliance.

My entire worldly possessions handed over to a complete stranger in a compound full of unemployed African men? While I follow another man, who I hardly know and who barely speaks my language, across this vast, poverty-stricken city on the promise of a bed for the night?

Alright then. Face value, remember?

'See you tomorrow!' I say in French to Hassan's uncle. '*À demain!*'

I grab my bar-bag with my diary, passport and wallet inside

it, Hassan and I leave the compound, and ten thousand permanently jobless dudes know that the white guy has left his million-dollar bike and its blatantly cash-packed panniers lying around somewhere on their sovereign territory. It's almost dark as we wait to hop onto a minibus decked out with fluorescent trims and decals and pumping bass – the gaudiest thing I've yet seen in this stark, sun-baked peninsular. I look out the window and try to figure out where we're going and distract myself from the overpowering smell of too many sweaty humans crammed into a tin box on wheels. And within minutes I am completely lost.

'Get off here!' Hassan shouts at me, barking something else in Somali or Arabic to the driver. Djibouti's stew of languages is brain-melting – officially French and Arabic, as can be seen from the road signs and shop-fronts and newspapers, but Somali is what's spoken on the ground. And there's a fair bit of Afar here too, I've heard, though I've seen precious few Afars since I left their lands in Ethiopia.

We disembark and I suddenly realise that this is somewhere I've seen before: a central open-air bazaar strung with trails of energy-saving light bulbs and mountains of fruit piled high into the night sky. But we're not here to shop; we're changing buses. Hassan clambers aboard a bigger vehicle which looks like an antique hand-me-down from some rich European nation, pays again for the two of us, and we lurch off in another direction. It is a long time later that we climb down and onto the street, by which point I've long since lost my bearings. It's much quieter here, more open, slightly hilly; I can see nothing except dim outlines of a road and walls and telegraph poles. It appears that there's no electricity supply right now.

I follow Hassan through the pitch-black silence, the ground faintly illuminated by a full moon, and we turn down an unpaved side street. *Where exactly are we going?* The mystery and unpredictability, I realise, are thrilling. This is the very essence of adventure; nothing mighty or medal-winning, simply embracing the unknown, abandoning fear and hoping for some degree of joy or intrigue. And if I've found both in a dark alley in a Djibouti backwater, so be it.

After a few hellos to passing shadows in the street, we arrive at the large, metal gate of a compound. My companion calls softly to its occupants and the big gate creaks on its hinges, revealing several pair of eyes in the darkness: Hassan's family.

We venture inside and I struggle to make out the figures, but it's clear that a fair few people live here. There's a single-storey building to the right with a few doors, a good-sized yard within the compound's fence, dotted with white mosquito nets draped over mattresses, and a little wooden shack raised up on stilts in the far left corner, which I assume must be the toilet. I'm greeted in whispers by a middle-aged couple and one much older man, and then smaller children and teenagers erupt silently from the shadows and press around me. Everyone speaks with hushed voices, and it's bizarrely serene for what I guess newsreaders and geography textbooks back home would describe as a developing-world slum. Not a vehicle, generator, dog, chicken or voice can be heard: the sounds that make up my normal daily life are all absent this evening, the world sitting quietly under the full moon.

A smiling face accompanies the arrival of a bucket of water and shadowy hands gesture me to follow them to the toilet block where I discover a second area for showering, and I wash myself in the darkness with the cold water. Then I'm guided to where another mattress has been laid out beneath a mosquito net in the yard and made up with fresh sheets: this will be my bed. Pleasantries exchanged and goodnights bidden, I lie down in the cool night air beneath the stars in this silent East African shanty town, my mind a world away from the endless hustle to find a ship across the Gulf of Aden.

Hassan wakes me up quietly. It's still completely dark and silent. I throw off the mosquito net, pull on my disintegrating linen trousers and grab my bar-bag, and we leave through the big metal gate, walking back up the dirt road towards the asphalt where we'll catch another pair of buses to take us back to the port. Hassan makes this journey every day, and it's clear that it's not for himself but for his whole family that he does this. He can't afford not to – one day off and he might miss the only earning opportunity for weeks.

We stop on the corner and sit under an awning on a couple of old chairs. A man brings us two cleaned-out tin cans full of tea. There's a dash of condensed milk in the tea, and as we drink and the purple dawn creeps over the horizon, I'm aware of how centred I feel, sitting here, drinking tea with milk, even though I've spent the night in a home I couldn't see, in the company of a family I met only as spectres. I still find it incredible that I can make almost anywhere feel like home for a night, simply by accepting it for what it is, rather than dwelling on what it isn't.

But the bus grinds up and all too soon I'm back in the roasting hubbub of the port. We walk quickly to the medieval circus where I left my bike. And, running the gauntlet of the wide-eyed stares once more, I pick out the kiosk, head quickly round to the far side of it – and all of my suspicions are confirmed.

My bike, my video camera and all of my luggage is precisely where I left it. It is completely undisturbed.

CHAPTER 22

Mokha isn't my ideal destination, but it ends up being the first available boat ride. The port once gave its name to a variety of coffee bean which was exported from its harbours before more profitable crops like *qat* took prominence in Yemen. Five crewmen, a handful of passengers and six hundred cows watch the twinkling lights of this port float towards us through the darkness, and suddenly – as if to welcome our humble vessel – a firework display bursts into life above the faraway string of streetlights. I'm transfixed by the pink and green airbursts, the rockets and screamers, the pair of high-velocity missiles that blast diagonally across the sky . . .

What the hell did I just see?!?

I look at the young Somali man next to me who is also watching the display, and he stares pointedly at me, shaking his head almost imperceptibly:

'Don't ask any questions. You didn't see what you just saw.'

Which means I *didn't* see two sudden streaks of flame across the night from within the little pyrotechnic display, disappearing out of sight and into orbit within a split second. Which means the fireworks *weren't* there to distract any onlookers in Mokha from a covert missile launch!

The sensation of being in a Hollywood spy movie

intensifies as I watch everyone else lug huge bags and chests towards the gangways in preparation for arrival, as if nothing has happened. If I'd found myself the sole witness I would be more inclined to put it down to a sleep-deprived half-dream or hallucination. But the Somali is still gazing into the distance, perplexed. And then we're coming into the port and suddenly it's a race to unload six hundred cows before everything gets covered in poo. I dutifully forget what I've seen, and never mention it again.

By the time I've made it past the little customs house, emptied and repacked my bags, and had my passport stamped in for a three-month visit, the rest of the passengers have long since bundled into taxis or pick-ups and scarpered. Entirely alone in a new country – continent, in fact – all over again, and exhausted from almost two days on the trot without sleep, I pedal down the nearest dark road and drag my bike through the soft sand behind a few crescent dunes. I somehow muster the energy to ramble into the video camera for a few seconds and then fall asleep as soon as the inner tent is up, too tired even to peg out the corners, let alone find my mattress or sleeping-bag, reduced to a snoring pile of sweaty limbs on a nylon groundsheet – neither knowing nor caring what my first day in Yemen will bring.

I'm in . . . I'm in Yemen.

And I'm in my tent about one kilometre from the security gates at the port.

It's completely dark, apart from the moon . . .

I have no idea what this country's going to be like at all. I have no idea, really, how things work. But basically I've just hidden beside some trees on the side of . . . in the sand on the side of the road. And hopefully here is safe enough, and hidden enough, to be able to rest for the rest of the night.

It's been a very, very exhausting week. Tomorrow I'm going to get my bearings and work out what my route is going to be, and just see how things work, I guess. Because I don't have any prior knowledge of Yemen. I don't have a map, or a guidebook, as usual, so I'm just going to go off and see what happens.

Well – I have a small idea of what it's going to be like, because it's another Arab nation. And the hospitality here is very welcome for a traveller, especially if you're travelling alone, because you're never far away from a helpful smiling face. Even if it is – one hundred percent of the time – a male face!

The landscape is pretty dramatic, too. The most similar place I can remember was the Sinai Peninsula of Egypt, or parts of Jordan and Syria. How long ago was that . . . ?

Syria didn't really look like I'd pictured it. But then nowhere ever quite did.

I had left Tenny and Iran behind in the most difficult parting of my life. I was now on the lip of the Arab world, at the beginning of an entirely new journey – a profound diversion from anything I'd previously imagined. Within a few short weeks I would be riding on African soil; the continent where I had once sworn never to go. Now I was using that fear as a punishment: I had left the girl to whom I'd promised my lifelong companionship in favour of some selfish urge to explore the world anew and to challenge myself again. And the only way I could justify that awful decision was to set a course for the place I feared the most

– Africa – and to throw myself at its feet, alone and exposed, until I could no longer remember the person I'd been when I started out. I'd had no idea where I would fetch up, nor how long the process might take. But I'd been left with little choice but to go and find out.

Only one self-imposed rule remained: at no point would I leave the surface of the Earth. And travelling overland to Africa would mean using the Middle East as a through-route. I had been on the road for long enough to have heard the travellers' lore of the absurd displays of kindness and generosity that they encountered there, thanks to the region's deep-set culture of hospitality. And I was now riding south into the heart of the region. Turkey, Armenia and Iran lay at my back.

I hadn't expected grim skies and torrential rain, roaring trucks and road spray on the hard shoulder of Syria's main highway. But I was desperate to put distance between myself and the events that I had left behind, still raw and disorienting. Understanding now why Andy had seemed so driven when I'd met him in Tehran, I pedalled hard through the rain and cold of a dismal Mediterranean January, my bike lighter and nimbler than ever before, my body drenched, feverish, but set once again to its task. I never stopped for sightseeing, whittled my daily routine to the sharpest of points, and slept wherever I was offered: in a roadside prayer-room, in the kiosk of a petrol station, behind a bakery, in a caretaker's cabin beside an archaeological dig. The roads were ruled by Toyota pick-up trucks and swarms of Honda motorbikes, all piled high with goods and families and livestock. Curiously, instead of the standard monotone bleep, some factory worker had decided to make the reverse-gear warning sounds for the

Honda bikes a little more spicy, and thus the back-streets of Syria echoed with crazed electronic renditions of the 'Lambada'.

Let me just try and kind of summarise Syria.

It's been pretty tough riding. It's rained every day, and I've had a headwind most of the time. Camping last night, I was shivering and sweating into my sleeping-bag, and it's now quite wet, which means it won't be very warm tonight. But today I took the decision to turn off the highway and head inland, because I heard that it was – er – desert. And I thought there'd be less rain in the desert.

Well, I was wrong about that. It's only just stopped raining! But I have indeed found the desert. And it's a big . . . empty . . . bit of . . . orange . . . sand. Ha-ha!

I'm sorry I'm a bit incoherent. To be honest, I've only just started to feel better after having this cold and fever for the last few days. I'm probably going to get rained on again tonight. The only saving grace is that I've got some pasta and stock cubes to cook, which I will be doing very shortly.

Yesterday was . . . well, it was the pits, basically. It was the worst day I could have imagined. I cycled all day into the rain; into a headwind. I had a cold, and a fever, and a high temperature. And I slept – like crap – about five metres from the highway, in my tent. And it rained. And I just felt revolting. Absolutely disgusting.

Not only that, but I found myself missing Tenny an awful lot. Because my little green and yellow tent reminded me of us camping together while we were cycling through Armenia and Iran. Those times I hold very dear in my heart. Because they were . . . well, they were just very special. Just the two of us, out in the unknown, together. That's the thing I miss the most at the moment. Now that I'm doing it alone, I can feel how good it was to have been doing it with her.

Striking out into drier climes, I found myself covering longer and longer distances each day, driven by a need to reach some place from which I could no longer feel the pull of the world I'd left behind, fuelled by falafel sandwiches and the staccato fury of my beloved electronic music. With no landscape features with which to track my progress, time began to flow weirdly in the desert, as if all the punctuation marks had been removed from the paragraph of the day; just one endless goods train of thoughts carrying a few scattered images: a shepherd boy who ducked and dived in front of my camera lens as if it were a pistol; a camel tied to a roadside post, patches of leathery skin torn away from its knees; crescent clouds edging across the sky like fish scales; a signpost in the emptiness offering a choice of destination between Damascus and Baghdad.

Single-mindedly I bypassed the great Levantine cities of Beirut, Amman and Jerusalem altogether; traversed the cavernous wadis and giddying peaks of Jordan; camped hidden in the hills above the Red Sea port of Aqaba. I rolled down the ferry's ramp and onto Egyptian soil, and soon I was travelling into the mountainous desert of Egypt's Sinai peninsula, clutching the tailgate of a flat-bed truck with an outstretched arm, trying to decide whether this was more or less painful than climbing the hill under my own steam.

At the top, I waved goodbye to the truck and its friendly driver, shook my agonised arm back into life, and dropped down once again into the grovelling-over-my-handlebars posture I'd adopted in the face of the insufferable wind, which seemed to adjust its direction with uncanny precision to oppose my own. Only wind, I was beginning to discover, had the power to make a mockery of my best efforts. Since leaving Turkey for Syria, I had been pedalling stoically into it, the fluorescent yellow flag of my trailer bent over backwards by its relentless force. Days of perfect flatness had passed, with me spinning the pedals in first gear, inching forward at five excruciating miles per hour. In desperation I'd tied a thick woollen sock around the end of each handlebar, creating two crooks in which I could rest my elbows and drop my head like a racer in an attempt to make myself more aerodynamic. It had, at least, taken my eyes off the never-approaching horizon.

Setting off into the wind once more, I stared again at the bag mounted in front of my handlebars, which contained my camera, a wallet of small-denomination banknotes and my weathered passport. And hidden between layers of material, I knew, was a pendant of St. Christopher – the patron saint of travel – which my mother had tearfully given me twenty months previously, making me promise to carry it with me. When I would next see my family, I did not know.

Attached to the top of the bag was a transparent plastic folder containing a print-out of the Arabic alphabet and its equivalent pronunciation in English. Long days in this hunched-up position provided ample time for study, and with a little concentration I was now able to decipher the road signs and shop-fronts. This was enormously useful, as I had brought no maps of the region. Instead, I was navigating by memorising towns along my route and employing common sense and intuition in order to travel between them, and I could feel this method working on me. Parts of my brain that had lain dormant – rendered redundant by the Information Age – were being dusted off and brought back into action. Mental models of new places evolved ever more quickly; I could read the shape of landscapes now, and guess with precision where road-builders would have chosen to lay their stones. And I grew a subconscious affinity with the subtle way in which, over time, villages had become towns and then clustered into cities, motivated by commerce and transport and resources and waterways, their individual roads conglomerating with predictable logic, which meant that I was happily sailing through even the largest of settlements with no concern about losing my way. Soon I'd ditched the traditional idea of being lost or found altogether, rather I felt like I was percolating gradually through these ancient and awesome nations. And I'd never felt so alive.

This was the very reason I'd come on this journey. If only once, I desperately needed to experiment with life, entirely on my own terms; nobody watching, judging or setting expectations of route or distance or motive but myself.

Sunset. The world rolled to a halt. I dismounted and stood looking about in the grey dusk. The horizon's rocky fringe still glowed in the west, beyond where lay Cairo and the mouth of the Nile, still a couple of hundred miles away. My trouser legs flapped in the breeze. All else was quiet on this road, a detour that spanned the peninsula's uninhabited interior, away from the goods traffic that made its way to and from the capital further north.

I pulled from my head the sleeve of cotton that had been protecting me from the elements – a useful freebie from some sponsor, long ago. With the sun growing stronger as I drew south, and the desert wind and dust tormenting my skin, I would soon need to find a proper sunhat. I was sure that I'd be able to find one for a dollar or two in some Egyptian souvenir shop.

A faint set of tyre marks plunged off the road and into the sand to the north, disappearing behind hills of crumbled rock in the middle distance. I wondered whether or not to follow them. At best, they might lead to some huddle of workers or other – a quarry, perhaps, or a mine – and the men (they would of course be men) would welcome me to stay the night; another memorable punctuation mark in my new routine as a solo bicycle traveller. At worst, the trail would lead to a concealed patch of desert in which I could camp undisturbed; just another hidden spot that I would make home for the night. There must be thousands of those scenes playing out this very instant, unseen by the rest of the world – solitary figures setting up canvas and poles in the twilight, the orange glow of petrol stoves coming to life, peace returning as the fires fade away into darkness, and then the deep sleep of physical exhaustion. The same figures would be up before dawn, boiling water for tea as the tent was packed away, and then the wind in their tangled hair and tarmac crackling beneath their tyres as they hit the road to do it all over again.

I glanced back along the fading road; looked again at the tyre marks, shrugging off that familiar but subsiding twinge of fear. Well – given the choice between two options, I reminded myself, I might as well take the more interesting one.

I followed the trail towards the rocky hills, the road a receding line across the sand in the distance. The tracks skirted behind the shadowed eastern side of the hills, and as the road disappeared from view behind me, I saw – as predicted – a tiny cluster of low, makeshift buildings. A single earthmoving machine was parked beside the biggest hut, and next to it a trailer-tank. I leaned my bike against the tank and gingerly knocked on the door of the hut. But all was eerie and quiet.

Then I heard a faint cry. Looking round, I saw a solitary figure trudging through the sand towards me. The man was dressed in a desert robe of faded grey, a neat bundle of white wrapped tightly around his head above his ears. As he came closer, I began to make out his features in the failing light – creased eyes, kind but serious; a broad nose; a black moustache streaked through with white; some days' stubble framing his mouth. Unhurried and quiet, he shook my hand, took a brief look at my bicycle, and wordlessly beckoned me into the hut.

I sat quietly on a heap of folded blankets in the corner, while the man sat on the single mattress opposite, pulling a bag of bread from its hiding place, unscrewing the cap of a large plastic bottle and decanting some of its contents into a china bowl. He gestured at me to eat. I tore at the bread, shaping it between my fingers, and then the smell of the dark syrup in the bowl hit me: molasses, the by-product of Egypt's vast sugar-cane industry. The usual game of interrogative charades was never attempted, and we ate in silence in this little corner of light in the darkness – not exactly basking in the pleasure of each other's company, but at least agreeable, on some wordless level, to the idea of seeing the evening out together.

After we'd eaten our fill of the bread and treacle, the man switched on a dusty old radio, so established in its place that it seemed until that moment to have almost melted into the wall of the room. Strains of music floated into the air, a crackling, wailing ode to some person or sentiment long since passed. Then he brought forth a small water-pipe and sat tinkering with its tubes and valves, and the room was soon rendered vague and dim with smoke.

I sat back on the blankets, watching this old Egyptian man. Somewhere in these hills, or perhaps in a town or village, this man had a family – a wife, maybe two or three; and children, or perhaps they'd now be adults too. In any case, here he was; a man displaced from these things, doing what he could to find some solace in his solitude. And maybe that was the thing that lay behind the strange bond I felt with this man: the knowledge that whatever was said or done, it would be said or done in loneliness. His was the loneliness of having been dragged away from those he held most dear to serve time in this hut. Mine, on the other hand, was self-imposed: the loneliness of the dream-bound traveller, questing in solitude towards some imaginary goal. No matter how enlightening or meaningful or humbling this quest might turn out to be, I would do well to remember that – for as long as it may continue – I would still sleep alone.

CHAPTER 23

Aden is a nice place, I think, as we race along the cliff-hugging roads in and around the crater of the extinct volcano that houses the city. This upwelling of rock off the south coast of Yemen is connected to the mainland by a narrow strip of land. Without this isthmus, Aden would just be a curious-looking island poking out of the sea. But the remarkable configuration of land and water once made it one of the old Empire's main shipping stop-offs between Britain and India, poised halfway between the Suez Canal and Bombay. We drive through the old town, embedded within the natural fortress of the crater, then up and through a short tunnel in the rock to the crater's exterior where the vast Indian Ocean vanishes behind the curvature of the planet, then down again and onto a long, modern strip in the vibrant Mu'alla district, all electronics shops and swanky restaurants and Internet cafes full of small boys playing extremely violent computer games. These gaudy establishments are built into the ground floors of huge, terraced, colonial townhouses – indistinguishable from their siblings in central London, now reassigned to look hopeful and glamorous in a nation still troubled by disunity, like so many former colonies of European imperial powers.

Khalid is in the driver's seat; he's a university student, Aden native, and friend of Romain, the young and laid-back French teacher with whom I'm staying in Aden. Khalid, a dark, naturally good-looking twenty-year-old with designer stubble and a stylish head of carefully gelled hair, regales us with tales of the shenanigans of the young and liberal in Aden.

'Everyone's getting it on with each other here,' he boasts. 'That's why the Saudis come here on holiday. Me? Different girl every week. Beautiful girls. Really beautiful.' He laughs. 'Of course it's all behind closed doors . . . these girls, students, want to have fun, but nobody can find out. The families can never know. We have to be really careful to avoid being seen. But it's all a game, you know?'

I haven't seen many obvious pick-up opportunities – strictly speaking, associations between unrelated men and women are forbidden here. But I'm about to find out how the youth of Aden get over that hurdle.

'Let's go to the mall. I'll show you.'

Off we drive to Aden Mall, the pinnacle of the small moneyed class's material aspirations, where every shiny lifestyle toy can be bought at a premium price within a premium setting. Dubai doesn't just export goods and satellite television – it exports the very idea of itself across the Arab world.

'We don't come here to buy anything,' says Khalid. Romain is content to come along for the ride; he's been here more than a year and has been recently trying to make headway with the gorgeous girl behind the counter at the public phone-booth centre, but is unsure how to ask for her number.

'I know her,' says Khalid, putting his arm round Romain's shoulder as we walk. 'Don't worry, my friend! We'll get you with her. She's into you. I know it!'

In the mall, all space and polish and glass and meticulous lighting, we head for a juice bar. Fresh juices have become my ambrosia in this region. A blender full of mango, whole lime and lemon, orange or – my personal favourite – ginger, is never far away, the contents waiting to be whizzed up with ice and poured through a sieve and handed over.

'Now look around,' instructs Khalid. The place is pretty quiet, with only a few families, merchants and the occasional pair of slim black shrouds gliding quietly across the marble floors. 'OK, we're early. The best time to come is after university has finished – especially on Thursdays.' (Friday is the weekend.) 'Girls will come here to pick up guys. Right now, this is the place. When you see a girl looking right at you from across the mall, that's a pretty good sign. You need to wait and see if she looks again. And if she does – then you know she's interested.'

Right . . . and what next?

'Well, are you interested? If so, we have some special words. Innocent words. For example, you go up to the girl and ask: "Excuse me, what's the time?"'

Not a line I've heard before. And then?

'If she tells you the time and it's correct . . . well, bad luck, my friend. But if she tells you the time and it's ten minutes out – *then* . . .' And he laughs. 'Or, another one is: "Excuse me, can you tell me the way to Pizza Hut?" And a wrong answer means "Meet me outside in five." Obviously it's easier when it's dark . . .'

Yemeni food is turning out to be the surprise highlight of the country, so we head down to the fish market where small motor-boats are still arriving with their catches. After selecting a suitably enormous specimen and giving it to the chef of the restaurant next door to bake and serve with a pile of steaming flat-bread and spicy sauce, the conversation continues.

'I know I'll want to settle down, find a good wife, marry, have children,' says Khalid. 'I wouldn't marry any of these girls I'm seeing, though – I know what they do, how they behave. I wouldn't trust them.'

'But that's double standards,' replies Romain, ever the Frenchman, not shy of a good argument over dinner. 'You want the young, beautiful ones now, but when you marry . . . you want them to be pure – virgin!'

'Yes. Every guy wants his wife to be a virgin. Of course!' Khalid shrugs.

'So what will these girls do?' I ask.

'Oh, it's easy enough for them,' he says. 'They'll have . . . operations, to restore . . . you know. There are plenty of doctors here doing this. Then they can get married, and their new husbands will never know!'

'So how can you be sure?' continues Romain. 'How can you be sure that your new wife won't have had that operation?'

'I'll just know,' returns Khalid, although he sounds more hopeful than he does convinced.

The conversation turns to religion. Renan, a traveller from Turkey who's also staying with Romain, is interested to know what kind of reception I've had, being stereotyped as a Christian.

'I'm an atheist,' I tell him, 'and the first few times I was asked about religion – in Turkey – it didn't go down too well. It was difficult for them to comprehend that someone can have no religion at all. It seemed like the idea just didn't exist.'

I remember my evening in a caretaker's hut near some Roman ruins at Ebla in Syria, where I'd met a very sharp and well-educated Syrian man of about my age with whom I'd talked long into the night. But when the topic came up, he'd told me in no uncertain terms that not having a religion was equivalent to not having a heart. Some things, evidently, were still set in stone. From that moment forth I'd decided it would be easier to run with the Christian stereotype, even though that came with some complicated explanations of the subtle nature of Anglicanism.

'Really?' says Renan. 'Because I'm also an atheist. I don't believe in any of that crap. But Turkey isn't as secular as you'd think, unfortunately. Religion is always getting in the way. We have this stupid Islamic government on one side, and the army defending religious freedom on the other. Did you know that the national identity card has an entry for religion? And "atheist" isn't an option. So mine says I'm Muslim!'

Like me, Renan had travelled through the Levant before taking a flight from Cairo to Yemen.

'But I never lied about it,' he continues. 'I'm Turkish, and I speak a bit of Arabic, so I suppose it's easier for me. If anyone asks, I just say that I was brought up in a Muslim family, but when I got old enough to have my own ideas, I realised it wasn't for me, so I'm not committed to anything right now. And that was fine – people could understand that. I don't think you need to pretend.'

The next day I have some chores to do. I must find the police station and get a permit to travel east from Aden, through central Yemen and on towards Oman. The route will pass through the 'dangerous' region of Hadramout, which – aside from being home to loads of normal people living normal lives – is also where four South Korean tourists were blown up a couple of months ago while posing for a photo in front of some ruins. The region also boasts a history of kidnappings by remote communities, branded with the indignity of the 'tribal' label, who, like the Afar, need leverage to get their marginalised needs fulfilled. Build a bridge here – we'll release these foreign hostages. Pave that road there – we'll release these foreign hostages.

I produce my passport and tell the police chief I need a permit to travel on roads east of Aden.

'Yes, that is correct,' he says, with a sigh, reaching for a drawer in the sweltering little room. It's more the humidity than the heat – still, oppressive, lethargy-inducing, bringing a permanent sheen of sweat to the skin. The slightest breeze tickles the body like a wave of purest pleasure, whatever the source – ceiling fans, open car windows, the brisk brushing past of a pedestrian – cruel instants of respite from the maddeningly hot, moist, invisible, salty fog that lies across the land.

'How is the road?' I enquire as he fills out the form. 'Is it safe?'

'Yesterday, safe. Today, safe,' he replies. 'Tomorrow . . . ?'

And he shrugs. The message is clear: Nobody knows, so keep your fingers crossed. Things can and do change overnight here. But he's giving me the permit, so the risk can't be all that great – can it?

I cycle east out of Aden, savouring every breath of breeze that the act of cycling generates. Thick air lies across the coast like a blanket, and I ride as if pushing through hot, invisible mist. My clothes are soon soaked. Stopping for a break, I find that it is possible to wring pools of water out of the sleeves of my shirt.

I'd discarded the ragged remains of my trousers in Aden and bought instead a *futa*, a traditional wraparound garment, tucked into itself and fastened with a belt, rather like a long kilt, albeit with the distinctive patterning of the Orient. It is clear why Yemeni men still wear this: in this climate, only the kind of full and easy access allowed by such loose folds of fabric can keep one's nethers adequately ventilated. I soon learn the knack of arranging my *futa* to take full advantage of the oncoming breeze, yet at the same time avoiding undue alarm when encountering passers-by.

Arriving at a checkpoint a few hours' ride along the coastal road, I brandish my permit with a confident smile. This, I have heard, is as far as travellers in Yemen have been allowed in recent years. The province of Hadramout lies ahead, Yemen's tribal heartland, and too many politically motivated kidnappings have taken place in Hadramout for the security forces to risk allowing another vulnerable foreigner alone upon its roads. I brace myself for the order to turn around; for my ride towards Dubai and Iran to be stalled. And I am taken by surprise when the guards wave me casually through. I cannot quite believe it: they are allowing me to continue!

And so I ride on, into the empty coastal dunes of Yemen. I had not quite been prepared for this, and I realise that my supplies for the road ahead have been ill thought out. I'm not even sure how far I'll have to ride before the next town! It shouldn't matter – there's a steady stream of traffic, should I run out of the essentials. But I can't help wondering why I hadn't taken provisioning as seriously as I usually would.

A few miles later I spot a pick-up truck on the side of the road in the distance. As the shape grows more distinct, I notice something mounted to its roof. By the time I have realised that the 'something' is an enormous machine-gun, half a dozen men in camouflaged overalls have sprung from the truck and are marching towards me. They are all carrying the world's most popular firearm: the AK-47.

I roll to a halt a couple of dozen yards away, quickly dismounting. Then I wheel my bike towards the oncoming men. They are already reaching for my bicycle. And I already know what is going to happen.

'Mister Allen?'

'Yes?'

'Come with us, please.'

My bicycle is being taken away from me. Clumsy, careless hands are dragging it onto the back of the truck. The pedals are clanging against the tailgate; the chain falling off, sagging; a pannier crushed mercilessly as the bike is wedged between the men who are now resuming their positions on the benches; I am already checking off its contents in my head, noting what is likely to be damaged; then I am ushered round to the passenger door of the pick-up and offered the seat between the driver and his buddy. I ask to be allowed to take my handlebar bag inside, with my passport and wallet and video camera, and the hidden pendant of St Christopher that my mum gave me. And the soldiers of the Yemeni military – my personal bodyguards for the road through Hadramout – are happy to oblige.

As we speed through the empty wasteland, windows down and engine roaring, sand and rock and scrub flying past on either side, hazy mountains on the northern horizon and the flickering blue of the Indian Ocean on the south, I begin to see what was *really* sabotaging my single-minded pedalling routine. I had not paid due attention to the prospect of cycling the full length of Yemen for one simple reason: *I didn't truly want to*. A protest had been playing out in my head as I'd realised that the security forces were about to snatch me from the road, but the bigger part of me had felt relief, not annoyance, that my ride was going to be shortened by several hundred miles. Something is dragging me towards the prospect of seeing Tenny, now, and in this tug-of-war that I sense happening within myself, the opposing pull of my much-dreamed-of life on the road is beginning to lose the fight. There are greater forces at work here, and I am being dragged faster than I am able to ride.

By the time the day draws to a close we have journeyed half the length of the nation's coastline to a soundtrack of crooning Arabic pop. Each soldier has had his turn at manning the machine-gun, and at wearing my sunglasses whilst doing so, and there hasn't been cause to employ the weapon; indeed the driver seems to know personally the men who raise the barriers for us on the way into and out of each small town along this road. I suppose that security here relies on friendships and allegiances, rather than on some prim and proper notion of law and order, and I guess that there is in fact some merit in having these soldiers along: it is the calming influence of the known and trusted, rather than the brash threat of a firefight, that is keeping me safe.

The villagers of Bir Ali suggest that we camp for the night upon a nearby beach. Arriving at sunset, there is nobody to be seen, just a scattering of ramshackle huts and a few sun-bleached wooden deck chairs that look to have been thrown together in a hurry and forgotten. There is an air of abandonment here, as if this was once a popular local tourist destination, before the economy began to collapse and the region fell again into unrest. And I realise that this place has all the makings of a paradise on Earth. The sun is sinking behind the inland hilltops in a cloudless sky. Turquoise shallows extend out into a sheltered lagoon, warm and clear and calm. The sand is as pale and smooth as the fairest skin. It is every bit the archetypal beach towards which Alex Garland had Richard and his fellow backpackers questing. And, just as in that story, it seems that such surroundings are soon overshadowed by more human concerns.

Some of the more attentive amongst you may have noticed that I have a new shirt. And yes. I bought a new shirt. I shelled out a whopping four dollars here in Yemen to replace the tattered rags that were previously adorning my upper torso.

What I should talk about – and I know I've rambled a lot here – but the main thing that's coming out of all this is that I'm . . . mentally, I'm struggling to appreciate being here. The reason is quite simple. It's because my mind is set on getting back to Tenny.

And so I'm really struggling to focus on the day that I'm experiencing.

I know that it's a long way. I know that it's another two thousand kilometres to cycle back to Tenny. And I know that every single day, I should just think about that day, and not about the two thousand kilometres ahead of me. But . . . if I no longer care about what I'm seeing, and I no longer care about meeting people, then . . .

I've been alone – for a long time, now, I've been doing this.

And you know what?
I think I'm getting tired.

I return from the quiet spot at the far end of the beach with my video camera. It is almost completely dark, and the soldiers have set up camp in one of the huts. Unpacking my sleeping gear on one of the beach loungers some distance away, I notice a figure walking towards me. I'm surprised, and a little confused, when I see a Chinese-looking face emerging from the darkness on this abandoned beach in the middle of Yemen. And I am even more surprised when he greets me in perfect, Canadian-accented English.

'You must be the cyclist I've heard about!'

'Er – yeah. Yeah, that's right!'

'Joe. Nice to meet you.'

'I'm Tom. Erm – what are you doing here, exactly?'

Joe tells me his story as we walk back over to the little open-fronted beach hut in which he's set up for the night. He's been living on this beach, he says, for almost a month. Joe is a Canadian photographer with Chinese origins, about the same age as me, unfortunate (or fortunate) enough to have been studying in Beirut at the moment when Israel's military decided that it was high time for another invasion. Anthropology degree on hold, he'd grabbed an ageing camera, convinced a Western war-photographer to let him tag along, and had snapped a picture that had gone on to win first prize at the biggest photojournalism award ceremony on the planet. That award had launched his career.

'I'll probably go back to Beirut and finish my studies some day,' he says, 'but right now it's pretty cool to be making a living like this – travelling the whole time, and to a lot of

places that outsiders would never usually get to see, like here
– and I get to take photographs, which is something I've
found a real passion for doing . . . and I've got a home base
in New York, as well . . . it's a pretty nice place to be.'

I sit back as the Milky Way emerges and begins to
illuminate a world in which all other light is absent. The
soldiers, along with Joe's government-assigned guide, are
talking quietly in a hut nearby. Looking up at the starscape,
I get the sudden sensation of being stranded on a rock,
hurtling through space, while the ancient stars peer down
at these weird little beings, convinced beyond doubt that
their affairs and concerns are universal in magnitude as they
pop in and out of existence, like sparks, upon the surface of
that hurtling blue rock.

The next day, I badger the crew of sleepy gunmen mercilessly,
and I eventually cycle off, leaving them behind. The sun is
almost up: I need to get some miles behind me while it's still
cool.

They catch up a few minutes later and the Landcruiser
trundles annoyingly along behind me at thirteen miles an
hour, the soldiers no doubt wishing they'd never agreed to
let me back on the road. Before too long I hear a horn being
sounded. The pick-up has pulled to a halt behind me and the
occupants are gesturing that they'll catch up further on. So
much for a personal bodyguard.

I ride undisturbed through the flowing undulations of sand
and rock. Alone again in an empty landscape, I can think of
nothing but the incredible slowness of my progress on this
bicycle. Why had I been so insistent with the soldiers that I
continue to ride? What am I gaining by doing so, except

further confirmation that I am indeed able to force my body to pedal endlessly through the most debilitating of conditions? I know this already. I have confirmed it time and time again.

The truck is nowhere to be seen, and I ride for half an hour before I round a bend and find a large crowd of people walking along the road towards me. Drawing closer, I realise that these are no Yemeni locals. The group of twenty or thirty, some barefoot, a few clutching plastic bags of clothes, but most empty handed, trudge forlornly and quietly through the sand beside the road. Then I realise that these are the people that Joe has been waiting to meet for a month.

I speak to the young man who leads the group.

'What are you doing here?'

I'm not sure what else to ask.

'We have come from Somalia,' he starts, in good English. 'We have just arrived here. We have nothing. We don't know where we are . . .'

He trails off and gazes down the road, the men, women and children behind him silent, staring blankly around them.

'When did you arrive, exactly?'

'Last night. Down there.' He points towards a nondescript piece of coastline. The ocean, flecked with white, extends beyond as far as the eye can see.

'We arrived by boat. From Somalia,' he continues.

The truck has appeared in the distance behind me and is approaching at speed.

'We need help. Anything you can do to help, we would appreciate. A place where we can go – anything.'

'Erm . . .'

The soldiers overtake and park up the road ahead of us. I

can hear them talking on the radio, but none of them get out of the truck. They are waiting for me.

'I'm sorry . . . I'm not from around here.' It's all I can think of to say. How stupid I sound. I am here of my own free will. They risked their lives last night to stand here today. The group may well have been larger when it departed from Somalia, and these people may now be wondering what became of the friends and brothers and sisters and children and parents who were supposed to arrive alongside them on this stretch of coastline. And they *will* arrive, in a few days' time, lying in the sun on Yemen's beautiful empty beaches; bloated corpses which were once alive and determined, having taken that leap of faith to abandon the place they were born in; the place that – until yesterday – they called home, knowing that they may never see land again. And in taking that risk, they will have lost everything to a roll of the dice. Their bodies are what Joe came to Yemen to photograph.

But I have to do *something!*

'OK – about five miles that way,' I say, pointing down the road behind me, 'there's a village. There are already people from Somalia there. A refugee camp. If you go there, they might be able to help you.'

And that's all that this heroic 'adventurer' can offer. The group shuffles off down the roadside, plastic bags rustling in the silence.

I walk to the truck, and soon we are hurtling down the road once more at a hundred miles an hour. Part of me considers asking the soldiers to call Joe to help him with his story. But the very idea seems absurd. Joe's news story isn't a god-damned *story*. It's a group of people; people with histories and families and feelings, who have just stood barefoot on the roadside, stared me in the face and asked for help – any help, anything at all. Joe's story will blend seamlessly into the ocean of bad news that breaks against the strongholds of the wealthy and free, masquerading as exposition of the world's woes, but really achieving little but convincing us of how much awful stuff is happening 'out there', of how lucky we are not to live in such hopeless desperation – and of how fearful of losing that position of privilege we ought to be. He might even win another award for his pictures.

Nevertheless, I find myself envying Joe. He knows precisely what he is doing, here, in Yemen. It doesn't matter what his government-assigned guide thinks, or what opinion a passing bicycle traveller has of his work. He is doing what he thinks is right; he is making a contribution to the world, and he is doing so with determination. Even the refugees, trudging silently along the roadside, have grasped their fate with both hands. They too have determination; they knew precisely what they were doing when they clambered aboard the rickety boat on a Somali beach under cover of darkness, and even if they have not yet lived out a single day under the Arabian sun, they at least know what they had in mind when they arrived here.

The Omani border is drawing close. Oman; home of the fabled Empty Quarter desert. A thousand miles of sand. The scorching heat of June.

It will be the final push – the last big challenge of this journey – all the way to the Gulf. There, I'll find a ship to take me across the water to Iran. And then I'll arrive in Tehran, at the door of Tenny's family home. So much time and so many miles has passed between us; I have no idea whether that rift will heal. Like so much of this journey, it will be a foray into the unknown, driven by hope and curiosity. I will get to know her all over again, and she will get to know me – a man who has delved too far into his own head, by way of half of the African continent and a lap of the Middle East, and is trying to find his way back. I suspect that I will have to get to know myself again as I re-adapt to life within society; of seeing people more than once after waving goodbye, of sleeping in the same bed each night, of holding a conversation with someone other than myself.

The winter boots are waiting in Tehran, as well as that winter sleeping-bag, so that I can continue through Central Asia and Tibet, and eventually to the Far East. For as long as the journey remains relevant, I'd said to myself. But many times recently have I been reminded that my journey is in need of a renewed purpose. I need to acknowledge this; that momentum alone may not be longer enough. I have been stubborn in the past, and that stubbornness has certainly got me where I needed to go. But there is a difference between stubbornness and determination. Determination is inspired by clarity of purpose. Stubbornness exists in spite of it. If I set forth from Tehran for another journey of months or years, leaving Tenny behind once more . . . which of these things will be driving me?

Saying goodbye to my armed escort at Al-Mukalla, I lift myself into the saddle and scan the horizon. Soon I will be in Oman, and then the Emirates. Only a few more days of riding now remain.

Stomach full, I lie back upon the sand. A dune the size of a house watches over me as I look up at the obsidian sky, and I begin to sink into the kind of sleep that only a hundred-mile day of desert cycling can produce.

Funny, now, to think that I'm here because of an idea to cycle round the world. Instead of a day's ride short of Dubai, I'd be somewhere in Australia right now, had I followed the path laid out by Ride Earth, desperately thinking up ways to get to South America without flying, then setting forth for another few thousand miles, reaching Middleton a couple of years later, arriving beneath another banner of white balloons to a pat on the back and a cup of tea.

What an anticlimax that would be – to close the book like that, leaning my bike up in my parents' garage, saying, 'Yes, I have finished.' I would never look at a fully loaded bicycle again! My life during that time would become a neat package, something kept on a shelf and occasionally dusted off to flick through with a sigh whenever someone asked what I'd done with my twenties. I no longer feel the need to start with a capital letter, put a full stop at the end of last line, and keep things in between nice and neat. I don't want to build my time on the road into an achievement so grand that I'll spend the rest of my life trying to get one over on my younger self, trying to frame my future actions to sound bigger and grander than before.

What drove me to leave England, I remind myself, was a desire simply to *learn* – not for any distant end, but for the joy of learning itself; about the world and, I suppose, about myself. Though it will take years to process, I've learnt so much that I could not have learnt any other way. And I could continue, experiencing more of the world's natural beauty and the rainbow of human expression that dwells within it.

But I need time before I do that, because another upheaval is due. I need to bring some things together that until now have been kept distant from each other. I need to remedy the ills that have begun to plague my experience. There is so much about this lifestyle that I truly love. But surely these simple and fascinating journeys might be even more satisfying if balanced with that rooted contentment I felt in Armenia, and the joy I find in reconstructing my experiences in words and sentences – writing a book, perhaps! – and, above all, that sense of sharing a direction in life that I felt next to Tenny? Is it possible, somehow, that I can forge a life that consists of all of these elements combined?

I have no idea. But I feel compelled to find out. And the prospect excites the hell out of me.

The desert falls into darkness, the last few cars audible from the road that runs through this ever-shifting sea of dunes.

In the morning, I get up early, wolf down some breakfast, and pack up my meagre belongings, eager to get some miles behind me before the sun rises to its infernal daytime heights. One more day of riding; one last sea-crossing. I am sure that this ferry journey to Iran will be far less memorable than the time I spent aboard the *Sina*, leaving Egypt behind for Sudan, bypassing the two nations' political squabbles as we glided across the surface of Lake Nasser, watching the monolithic tombs of Abu Simbel drifting past at sunrise, eventually fetching up in Wadi Halfa – where I'd bought a reassuring amount of food and water and then pedalled south into the Nubian desert before could I change my mind.

There's one more task that I must do before I set off, so I

rummage for my video camera. Flipping open the tiny screen so that I can see myself, I grin with surprise. The familiar matted greasy hair has gone, replaced with a freshly trimmed head of hair that might even be described as smart. My beard has disappeared, subtracting a decade from my age. The bridge of my nose is still burnt deep red, of course, and my skin and clothes are still coated in a beige film of dust, sweat and grease, but I look ready for what lies ahead. My face, it seems, could tell my story on its own.

I adjust the camera to produce the best possible picture. The well-practised calibrations happen in an instant. Pressing the red button, I zoom in slightly and my mirror-image fills the frame: some guy, talking to a camera in the middle of a desert. I fold the screen back out of sight, fix my gaze on the dark circle of glass, open my mouth, and begin to speak.

I must continue telling this story.

CHAPTER 24

'What was it Mark said three and-a half years ago?' I joked to Tenny. 'Cycle on the left, cycle on the left, cycle on the left . . . or die!' And with that we rolled off the ferry and onto the British mainland. There was no turning back now: we had escaped the Continent and set foot and rubber on the soil of England, five days short of my parents' driveway in Middleton, Northamptonshire.

The late afternoon autumn air felt chilly and damp as we rode alongside the Victorian terraces of the Dover seafront. Looking for a grocer's, we were befuddled by the town's illogical one-way system and, with daylight failing, we cut our losses and rode up and out of the settlement towards the eastern cliff-tops, shrouded by low cloud. Leaping a stile, we set up camp in a misty paddock opposite an army barracks, and in the morning remembered why we'd needed supplies: there was nothing left to eat for breakfast.

'Don't worry,' I said confidently to Tenny as she gathered up the wet fabric of the tent. 'This is England. There are villages everywhere, and they all have these great little village shops.'

We set off into the freezing fog. Unlike any other type of fog, the English variety seemed able to penetrate every thread of clothing I possessed, and no matter how hard I pedalled, my fingers and toes still throbbed in the damp and insidious cold. South Kent seemed more hilly and remote than I had imagined. After two and a half hours of slogging on empty stomachs through lands devoid of all life, we passed a village churchyard and spotted a figure through the mist. The grey-haired woman was closing the gate behind her. She wore a long coat and dangled an empty watering can from one gloved hand.

"Scuse me,' I called, trying hard to make the question I'd asked a million times in a dozen languages sound casual. 'You don't happen to know if there's a shop around here, do you?'

'There's a village store,' replied the woman, ambling across the road to speak to us, "bout two 'undred yards up the 'ill there, on the left. Right next to the 'all.'

'Er, that's great. Thanks!' I said. How freakish people sounded — in *Kent*! But to hear a fellow Brit speak gave me a tug of deep-seated recognition, like hearing a snatch of a lullaby your mother once sang you, or getting a whiff of something that transports you instantly back to your grandparents' kitchen on Boxing Day.

The woman looked me up and down, glanced with a grin at my panniers packed for two.

"Ere, you're good, in't yer? Luggin' that lot up an' down all these 'ills?!'

I smiled weakly, my body screaming out for sugar. 'Er . . . well. I've had worse.'

It had taken us two months to reach the south coast of England. There'd been a long-winded series of bus journeys and an overnight ferry before Tenny and I had set out on another two-wheeled adventure, the most appropriate we could think up. It was not a journey through the soaring ranges of Central Asia and Tibet. India, too, would have to wait. For instead of Far East, we had travelled Far West, to the place that Tenny had dreamed of going for as long as she'd been capable of dreaming: Europe.

When I'd arrived in Tehran at the end of my journey through the Middle East and Africa – knocking on the door of the Adamian family home, Tenny answering the door, a look of bemusement across her beautiful face, then leaping in shock, warm tears rolling down her cheeks, her head pressed hard against my chest – I knew that this life of journey-making could no longer be all about me. Alone, I had gone as far as I needed to go. Europe was the most exotic-sounding place that Tenny could imagine, a place where everything would be captivating and new, and I would be a poor selfish fool not to give her the opportunity that only I – with my trusty British passport – had the power to grant. And so our adventures would now be led by her. A couple of months' riding through Europe would bring us within striking distance of England. Spending the festive season with my family seemed a natural thing to do. And after the New Year . . . well, I had a few ideas.

The sunny olive groves and espressos of southern Italy were a dwindling memory as we lay in our tent behind what I now realised must be the University of Canterbury's nightclub, listening to the patter of rain on the flysheet and the squeals of drunk students. But a breathtaking sunrise revealed a chilly but pleasant October's day, and soon we were passing county markers of increasing familiarity. Only a couple more days on the road now separated me from the place I had left a lifetime ago. If I was still numbering the days in my diary, I would have known that it was 1,222 days previously that I'd first transferred my weight onto the right-hand pedal, gripped the handlebars, and stepped away from the ground and into motion. But I'd stopped counting long ago.

Pressing north from London, we'd been invited to stay the night with one of the veteran cyclists on whom I'd long ago sought to model myself, whose stories had inspired something I'd once called Ride Earth. Tenny and I rode down a narrow lane to a farmhouse deep in the countryside and leaned our bikes up by the double garage. She welcomed us indoors, introduced us to her husband and their two young daughters, and took great pleasure in force-feeding us an entire roast chicken.

Though the workshop at Royal Geographical Society was now a vague memory, I still felt a strange pang of disappointment to find that the heroes I'd seen up there on the stage didn't really exist. This woman, for all her impressive-sounding adventures, was a human being too. As I considered this over a bottle of Black Sheep ale, I came to realise that it was actually a relief; a welcome reminder that the adventurous life was open to everyone, and that facts and figures were always beside the point. And I knew that my own journey, when I told of it, would be misinterpreted too. It was inevitable. Listeners would reconstruct the meaning of my story to please themselves, whether seeing it as an accomplishment beyond their reach, using the statistics of the journey as a benchmark for their own, or belittling my exploits as tales of weakness. But that was also the reason that I had to tell the story. Because only by making sense of what had happened for a listener would

I make sense of it for myself. And none of this would stop me from continuing to live a life – with Tenny at my side – as close to or distant from the definition of 'normal' as we chose. That could mean living with two children in a cottage in Berkshire. But I suspected that it would turn out to be something a little different.

After dinner, I asked if I might hang our tent up to dry. *Of course*, came the reply. *Just through that door into the back of the garage. You'll find somewhere to put it, I'm sure.*

I retrieved the sodden bundle of fabric from my bike, gave the stuck door a gentle kick. It creaked open. The room was dark except for a line of sunlight that edged beneath the big garage door that occupied the far wall. I ventured in, looking for a hook or a horizontal pole or a line on which to hang the flysheet. As my eyes adjusted to the light, I saw that the garage was strewn with belongings. Backpacks and boots littered the floor. Beneath a workbench along the side wall was a row of open boxes. One was stuffed brimful with cooking pots, stoves and parts. Another contained a patchwork of waterproof bags. On the workbench itself was a neat row of packed-up tents in different sizes, ready to grab and go. And in the far corner I could see – illuminated by the strip of light – the familiar-looking shape of a touring bicycle, tyres firm, chain oiled, resting against the wall, pointed in the direction of the garage door. I could have mounted it there and then, pedalling away into the sunset for another lifetime of adventure.

But the bicycle would still be there to ride tomorrow.

On the final day of our ride through England, something unexpected occurred.

I was the first to clamber free of the tent that morning, emerging into a world encrusted with white. My breath condensed in front of my face; my eyelashes soon sticky with ice crystals. About thirty miles of cycling remained between the frosted field where we'd set up camp and the family home in which I'd once lived, and I expected that we would arrive in the middle of the afternoon while my parents were still at work. There would be no camera crew to record our arrival; no gathering of friends and family to celebrate what they would want to call my 'homecoming'; no banner of balloons hoisted aloft above the main street of the village. In fact, nobody but my parents really knew that we were due in England at all.

'Oh my god!' exclaimed Tenny as she emerged into the pinkish light of dawn. There wasn't a sound to be heard. 'It's f-f-freezing!'

'I know – it's unbelievable!' I said. 'Why don't you do some star jumps while I take the tent down?'

I fumbled with the tent pegs. My hands were numb with cold, and I couldn't grasp hold of anything. I clumsily pulled on my gloves, but this only reduced my dexterity further. So I gritted my teeth and tried to pack up the ice-rimed tent away as quickly as possible with my raw and stinging hands. Neatness didn't matter now; especially as I wouldn't be using the tent again. Not for a couple of months, at least.

Tenny put on every scrap of clothing she could and we set off along the narrow lane. After a few miles of riding, we rounded a bend, and as I saw a junction appear up ahead, I suddenly knew exactly where I was. And I realised that it was the first time in three and a half years that I'd known exactly where I was, and exactly where I was going.

We arrived at the junction, and I automatically turned right.

I soon warmed up as I pedalled, as I was carrying not only my own luggage but Tenny's as well. I'd realised before we'd left Armenia that doing this would balance the pace, me being a head taller than Tenny and quite a bit stronger after a few thousand miles of African dirt road. She would carry her essentials in a handlebar bag, and I would take the strain, like a chivalrous male of old, and our jaunt through Europe would be smoother and more enjoyable. But now, spinning unencumbered beside me, Tenny was finding it hard to get warm. So in the small town of Raunds we decided to stop for a second breakfast in a cafe on the high street and wait for the sun to climb a little higher.

We took two seats at a table by the window, and the bell rang as the door was pushed open again.

'Morning, Paul!' said the proprietress of the cafe. 'Usual, is it?'

'Yes, please,' said Paul, removing a woolly hat and a pair of work gloves. He wore a grubby fluorescent yellow vest over a thick winter jacket. 'Brittle out there!' he said, to nobody in particular.

Two plates arrived: fat-oozing sausages with crusty blackened bits of skin, slices of salty smoky bacon, fried eggs with turgid yolks just waiting to burst forth, mushrooms and beans and tomatoes, and inch-thick slabs of granary toast, slathered with molten butter, sliced from a fresh tin loaf with a dark round top – something impossible to find anywhere else in the world but upon this curious little island in the north Atlantic. And then I looked across at my left hand, and saw that my wedding ring was no longer there.

I blinked. Looked again.

Only a circlet of shiny skin remained.

'Oh.'

I felt cold.

'What?'

'Oh shit.'

'What?!'

'My ring.'

Tenny looked at my hand, gave a sharp intake of breath, and clasped her hands to her mouth. Her own ring, of course, a smaller version of my own, was still present on the ring finger of her left hand. I'd put it there myself, standing in a tiny octagonal chapel in Yerevan, surrounded on all sides by a press of friends and family, my tearful mum and my proud-looking dad, my younger brother Ben, Tenny's parents and brother and sister and aunts and uncles, all craning for a glimpse of us, while Andy, my best mate and my best man, held a heavy crucifix above our heads in yet another impressive display of endurance. I started looking on the floor for that comforting flash of metal, moving my legs, craning my neck, looking over and over again at the same patch of floor in that stupid way you do when you can't yet face the fact that what you're searching for is simply not there.

I looked back up at my wife.

'I don't believe it.'

'When did you last *see* it?!'

'Erm . . . well, I'd have noticed last night if it was missing then. It's got to have been this morning!'

'Have you checked your pockets?'

I checked. They were, as usual, empty of anything useful.

While I dug through the bits of accumulated fluff in the seams in search of a white gold ring, I made a mental trip back out of the cafe, retracing the last hour of riding, noting every spot at which I'd stopped and removed my gloves: the thick grassy verge where I'd taken a pee; the lay-by in which I'd set up the video camera to get a shot of the two of us cycling past; and of course the site of our previous night's wild camp itself, which I had trudged about in for about twenty minutes before we'd set off. But really it could be anywhere along a ten-mile stretch of road – a tiny sliver of precious metal amongst the miles of frozen grass. What chance did we have of finding such a thing?

'Sorry to interrupt,' interrupted Paul from across the room, halfway through a bacon bap, 'but did you say you'd lost a ring?'

'Er . . . yes, it looks like we have,' I said, half-laughing, and looking down again at the floor by my feet.

'Just asking, 'cos I'm picking litter up and down here all morning,' he continued, 'so if you've dropped it anywhere along this road, I'll probably find it. D'you want to give me your mobile number, just in case?'

'Oh . . . yes, that would be great,' I said. 'Very good of you to offer!'

'Well, I'll do what I can,' he said. 'If I'm able to help someone out – then why not? That's how I see it!'

'Well, it's definitely worth a shot – thank you.'

I looked at Tenny again, who was smiling. I knew that Paul would not find the ring in Raunds, but his altruism was heart-warming. England wasn't really such a bad place. I'd once convinced myself that it was, of course, in order to justify leaving. But England now looked quite different.

Tenny sat across the table from me, putting on her fleece gloves and her helmet.

'Well,' she said, 'we can come back and look for the ring – if it's there, in that field, it'll still be there in a few days' time. But right now I'd like to go home.'

We thanked the waitress and Paul and stepped out into the bright sunlight. The frost was melting now, tiny streams of water trickling down the fringes of the road. Tenny pulled her bike away from the wall outside the cafe, I followed, and together we rode on through the quiet back-roads of Northamptonshire. I looked at Tenny, pedalling alongside me. She would continue to be my wife, of course, with or without the ring. The commitment that I had made to her that day was in my heart, not on my finger.

And so, although it was a pleasant shock to find the ring, three days later, nestled between tufts of long grass in precisely the spot where I'd pulled out a tent peg that frosty morning with my raw and stinging hands – it really wouldn't have mattered if we hadn't.

We cycled on.

Later that afternoon we came to the outskirts of village called Middleton, and we zipped down the hill together towards the bend that would lead out onto the main road. As I passed the drinking fountain set in the hillside, from which I'd filled cycling water bottles for as long as I could remember, I flicked through some of the options for what I might say into the lens when I arrived on the far side of the bend. Rolling off the tarmac and up the gravel drive, I came to a halt, uttered a few choice words before the camera's battery ran out, dismounted, and wheeled my bike to the steps that led up to the entrance of the house.

There was nobody at home. But the key had been left under the mat for us. So I unlocked the door, ushered Tenny into the warmth, and went into the kitchen to put the kettle on.

THE END

Read the epilogue and see
images from Tom's journey at:

http://janapar.com/extras/book